Social exclusion
Rhetoric, reality, responses

INTERNATIONAL INSTITUTE FOR LABOUR STUDIES
UNITED NATIONS DEVELOPMENT PROGRAMME

SOCIAL EXCLUSION:
RHETORIC
REALITY
RESPONSES

EDITED BY
GERRY RODGERS
CHARLES GORE
JOSÉ B. FIGUEIREDO

A CONTRIBUTION TO THE WORLD SUMMIT FOR SOCIAL DEVELOPMENT

ISBN 92-9014-537-4

First published 1995

Copies can be ordered directly from: ILO Publications, International Labour Office, CH-1211 Geneva 22 (Switzerland).

Preface

The ILO is dedicated to the quest for social justice in the context of economic and social change. For nearly three-quarters of a century, the Organization has sought to promote policies which reconcile equity with growth in such fields as labour relations, conditions of work, social protection, human resource development, and employment.

The problem of deprivation — both absolute and relative — is central to these concerns. Over the years it has been addressed both through ILO programmes and in collaboration with other international organizations.

In 1993, the International Institute for Labour Studies of the ILO convened a Symposium on poverty in order to assess these efforts; to examine new lines of enquiry; and to stimulate innovative policy prescriptions. The concept of social exclusion suggested itself as a subject for future exploration.

Developments in economic and social organization over the last decade suggest that transformations are taking place in the nature of poverty and deprivation. The deepening of social inequalities, labour market segmentation, and changes in the quantity and quality of jobs, are now occurring in all countries — in the developed economies, as well as in countries undertaking economic reform or undergoing economic transition. These changes are marked by varying degrees of participation or marginalization of different groups and individuals in civil and political society.

The concept of social exclusion suggests an analytical framework to encompass a variety of dimensions which are becoming increasingly relevant for an understanding of the notions of deprivation and poverty. These considerations include the need to:

(a) link poverty with employment and social integration;

(b) link the economic with the political and social dimensions of poverty;

(c) examine the role of social processes and institutional structures in creating deprivation or generating inclusion. This would complement the current emphasis on macro-economic growth, incentives and individual skill development;

(d) explore the implications of globalization for anti-poverty strategies, social cohesion and social justice;

(e) explore the link between rights (civil, political and social) and access to livelihoods and markets.

Supported by the United Nations Development Programme, the Institute launched a research project on social exclusion to contribute to the discussion at the World Summit for Social Development and to explore ways in which the analysis of exclusion could make anti-poverty strategies more effective. This volume summarizes the initial project findings in three areas: conceptual issues; empirical studies, including analyses of social exclusion, policy experiences and implications for policy design; and policy issues. At a subsequent stage, the project will culminate in a Social Policy Forum which will bring academics together with practitioners to assess the final results.

The concept of social exclusion is familiar in Western Europe, as it has recently become central in discussions on the emergence of "new poverty" associated with economic restructuring and long-term unemployment. The original concept owes much to institutionalist thinking and to certain traditions of European political philosophy. The Institute/UNDP research project has sought to "deconstruct" the original term with a view to examining its utility in a variety of country settings. This has entailed conceptual work; the review of existing literatures on poverty, marginality, discrimination and deprivation; and empirical studies to explore the dimensions of exclusion in development paths in different parts of the world, with varied economic and social characteristics.

The intention is to seek a framework which would capture the interrelationships between the material and non-material aspects of deprivation; to provide a better understanding of the way they interact with the processes of economic growth; and to relate them to the concepts of participation and social identity, which are becoming salient at a time of great change. The ultimate goal is to contribute to the design of acceptable and effective policy interventions.

It should be stressed that this project is a pilot venture in several respects. The case studies undertaken thus far have only begun to explore the full analytical potential of the concept of social exclusion. The common guidelines for the country studies were designed to give maximum discretion and scope to local multi-disciplinary teams, and to allow and facilitate the process of evolution of the analytical framework. Questions of macro-economic policy and its intersection with institutional change; the social aspects of globalization; the implications of new technology — all these remain to be further mapped.

The results to date, however, do point to several important areas for future action. They suggest that more attention should be given to the way social institutions, political rights and economic processes interact to generate better livelihoods, social justice and social cohesion. Macro policies, and more particularly their interface with micro programmes, is of critical significance for anti-poverty strategy and greater social inclusion. Above all, the terms "inclusion" or "cohesion", immediately raise the question of the structures or processes with which cohesion is sought, and the manner in which it is to be achieved. These are thorny and delicate issues, but they have to be grasped at the outset of policy formulation and implementation.

This publication is intended to serve as a point of reference for policy-makers, practitioners and academics and to stimulate thinking on the challenges posed by economic transformation for social equity, political stability and democratic citizenship.

Padmanabha Gopinath
Director, International Institute
for Labour Studies
Geneva, January 1995

Acknowledgements

This volume is based on the ILO's International Institute for Labour Studies project "Patterns and causes of social exclusion and the design of policies to promote integration". Funding for this project has been provided by the IILS and by the UNDP. The project was initiated and directed by Gerry Rodgers, in collaboration with José B. de Figueiredo. Charles Gore, a consultant to the project, wrote the introduction, with contributions from the other editors, and had the major responsibility for the substantive editing of the rest of the text. The editors are grateful to their colleagues in the IILS and in particular to Ajit S. Bhalla and Frédéric Lapeyre for their valuable suggestions; to Hazel Cecconi for skilful and speedy copy-editing and proof-reading of the papers; to Françoise Charpentier for production advice; and to Carmen Ruppert for secretarial support during the two workshops which brought project participants together.

Just as the volume went to press, we were sad to learn of the death of Marshall Wolfe, one of the contributors. Marshall brought to the project a long experience of social development issues and a subtle understanding of processes of social change, and his quiet commitment will be much missed.

Most of the papers in the volume are summaries of more fully documented reports which are presently being finalized. In some cases, significant editorial revisions have been made to authors' original texts in order to harmonize the different contributions to the volume. Opinions expressed in this text are not necessarily endorsed by UNDP, by IILS or by ILO.

Gerry Rodgers, Charles Gore and José B. Figueiredo
International Institute for Labour Studies
Geneva, January 1995

Contents

Preface v

Acknowledgements viii

Contributors xi

1. Introduction: Markets, citizenship and social exclusion
Charles Gore, with contributions of José B. Figueiredo and Gerry Rodgers 1

PART I - CONCEPTUAL ISSUES

2. What is special about a social exclusion approach?
Gerry Rodgers 43

3. Reconceptualizing social disadvantage: Three paradigms of social exclusion
Hilary Silver 57

4. Globalization and social exclusion: Some paradoxes
Marshall Wolfe 81

5. Social exclusion and social change: Insights in the African literature
Charles Gore 103

6. Social exclusion and Latin American analyses of poverty and deprivation
Vilmar E. Faria 117

PART II - COUNTRY STUDIES

A. Synoptic country studies of patterns and processes of social exclusion

7. Patterns and processes of social exclusion in Russia
Natalia Tchernina 131

8. Patterns and processes of social exclusion in Thailand
Pasuk Phongpaichit, Sungsidh Piriyarangsanan and Nualnoi Treerat . . . 147

9. Patterns and processes of social exclusion in Tunisia
Mongi Bédoui and Ridha Gouia . . . 161

10. Patterns and processes of social exclusion in the Republic of Yemen
Mouna Hashem . . . 175

11. Patterns and processes of social exclusion in Tanzania
Anna Tibaijuka and Frederick Kaijage . . . 187

B. Issue-oriented country studies

12. Social exclusion and social inequality in Peru
Adolfo Figueroa, Teofilo Altamirano and Denis Sulmont . . . 201

13. Economic restructuring and social exclusion in Mexico
Sara Gordon Rapoport, Rosario Cobo, Lorena Paz Paredes, Carlos Salas and Enrique Dusell . . . 215

14. Ethnic solidarity and social exclusion in Cameroon
Samuel Inack Inack, Joseph Edou Mbida and Paulette Bea . . . 229

15. Social exclusion in respect of basic needs in India
Paul Appasamy, S. Guhan, R. Hema, Manabi Majumdar and A. Vaidyanathan . . . 237

PART III - POLICY ISSUES

16. The design of policy against exclusion
Gerry Rodgers . . . 253

17. Policies to combat social exclusion: A French-British comparison
Hilary Silver and Frank Wilkinson . . . 283

Contributors

Teofilo Altamirano, Centro de Investigaciones Sociológicas, Económicas, Políticas y Antropológicas (CISEPA), Pontificia Universidad Católica del Perú, Lima.

Paul Appasamy, Madras Institute of Development Studies, Madras.

Paulette Bea, Université de Yaoundé I.

Mongi Bédoui, Consultant, Tunis.

Rosario Cobo, Instituto Maya de Investigaciones Agrarias, Universidad Nacional Autónoma de México.

Enrique Dusell, Facultad de Economía, Universidad Nacional Autónoma de México.

Joseph Edou Mbida, Université de Yaoundé II.

Vilmar E. Faria, Centro Brasileiro de Analise e Planejamento, São Paulo.

Adolfo Figueroa, Centro de Investigaciones Sociológicas, Económicas, Políticas y Antropológicas (CISEPA), Pontificia Universidad Católica del Perú, Lima.

José B. Figueiredo, International Institute for Labour Studies, Geneva.

Sara Gordon Rapoport, Instituto de Investigaciones Sociales, Universidad Nacional Autónoma de México.

Charles Gore, Consultant, Brighton.

Ridha Gouia, Consultant, Tunis.

S. Guhan, Madras Institute of Development Studies, Madras.

Mouna Hashem, Consultant, New York.

R. Hema, Madras Institute of Development Studies, Madras.

Samuel Inack Inack, Université de Yaoundé II.

Frederick Kaijage, Department of History, University of Dar-es-Salaam.

Manabi Majumdar, Madras Institute of Development Studies, Madras.

Lorena Paz Paredes, Instituto Maya de Investigaciones Agrarias, Universidad Nacional Autónoma de México.

Pasuk Phongpaichit, Political Economy Centre, Chulalongkorn University, Bangkok.

Sungsidh Piriyarangsan, Political Economy Centre, Chulalongkorn University, Bangkok.

Gerry Rodgers, International Institute for Labour Studies, Geneva.

Carlos Salas, Facultad de Economía, Universidad Nacional Autónoma de México.

Hilary Silver, Department of Sociology and Urban Studies, Brown University, Providence.

Denis Sulmont, Centro de Investigaciones Sociológicas, Económicas, Políticas y Antropológicas (CISEPA), Pontificia Universidad Católica del Perú, Lima.

Natalia Tchernina, Institute of Economics and Industrial Engineering, Novosibirsk.

Anna Tibaijuka, Economic Research Bureau, University of Dar-es-Salaam.

Nualnoi Treerat, Political Economy Centre, Chulalongkorn University, Bangkok.

A. Vaidyanathan, Madras Institute of Development Studies, Madras.

Frank Wilkinson, Department of Applied Economics, University of Cambridge.

Marshall Wolfe†, Consultant, East Arlington.

1 Introduction: Markets, citizenship and social exclusion

Charles Gore
with contributions from
José B. Figueiredo and Gerry Rodgers

I. Conceptual issues

1. The meaning of social exclusion in West European policy discourse[1]

In Western Europe, the term "social exclusion" has recently become a key concept amongst analysts and policy-makers seeking to understand and alleviate some of the negative social effects of economic restructuring. It is an appraisive term, which both describes and expresses an evaluation of a situation and a process and, as such, it has an evident appeal for politicians and policy analysts. But, as a persuasive call for public action, "social exclusion" has acquired various meanings. In Western Europe, those meanings are embedded in the emergence of the term in French political rhetoric and the specific institutional history of the European Union.

The term was originally coined in France in 1974 to refer to various categories of people who were unprotected by social insurance at the time but labelled as "social problems" — "mentally and physically handicapped, suicidal people, aged invalids, abused children, substance abusers, delinquents, single parents, multi-problem households, marginal, asocial persons and other social 'misfits'" (Silver, Ch. 3, p. 63). However, in the 1980s, this stigmatizing and narrowly social view of social exclusion was superseded as the term became central to French debates about the nature of the "new poverty" associated with technological change and economic restructuring. Social exclusion in this context was not equated with

[1] This section is based on Silver (Ch. 3). For a longer version, which includes the deep historical context of recent debates in France, see Silver [1994].

poverty. It rather referred to a process of social disintegration, in the sense of a progressive rupture of the relationship between the individual and society, which was occurring because of increasing long-term unemployment, particularly focused on unskilled workers and immigrants, the inability of young people to enter the labour market for the first time, greater family instability and isolated single-member households, increasing numbers of homeless people, and rising tensions and periodic violence in the low-cost housing settlements on the periphery of cities (*banlieues*). This tearing of the social fabric of society seemed to be occurring as the result of long-term transformations in the structure and organization of economic life. It was regarded particularly seriously in France because social solidarity, in the sense of a "social bond" (*lien social*) between the individual and society which is expressed in the active participation of the citizen in public life, has always been central to French Republican thought.

The concept of citizenship and social integration which underlies the notion of "social exclusion" in this French tradition is difficult to grasp for people working within a liberal individualist tradition. The latter, which permeates Anglo-Saxon thinking, sees citizenship as a social contract based on the possession of equal rights by all individuals, and views social integration in terms of freely-chosen relationships between individuals, rather than a relationship between the individual and society [Silver, 1994, p. 18]. But this sharp conceptual divide has not prevented the wider adoption of the term in Western Europe. The European Commission has taken up the concept as central to the formation of social policy. In so doing, it has linked the notion of social exclusion more closely with the idea that it is the inadequate realization of social rights. This is particularly apparent in the work of the Observatory on National Policies to Combat Social Exclusion, which defined social exclusion "in relation to the social rights of citizens... to a certain basic standard of living and to participation in the major social and occupational opportunities of the society" [Room, 1992, p. 14]. With this shift, social exclusion became more closely equated with poverty, but this was seen in much more multi-dimensional terms than income or expenditure. A central question of the Observatory was to link standards of living with the possession of social rights to employment, housing, health care, etc., and "to study the evidence that where citizens are unable to secure their social rights, they will tend to suffer processes of generalized and persisting disadvantage and their social and occupational participation will be undermined" [ibid., 1992].

The combination of high intuitive appeal together with flexible definition means that the notion of "social exclusion" must be treated with caution. As Silver (Ch. 3, p. 77) points out, "Fighting 'exclusion' means different things to different people". But the notion has more than rhetorical force and the novelty value of a fashionable emerging policy bandwagon.

Interest in social exclusion has grown in Western Europe in relation to rising rates of unemployment, increasing international migration, and the dismantling, or cutting back, of welfare states. The emergence of the term reflects an attempt to reconceptualize social disadvantage in the face of major economic and social transformations.

Such rethinking is required for various reasons. The structural, rather than cyclical, nature of the new poverty, and increasing informalization of labour markets, mean that social benefits attached to employment are available to fewer and fewer people, and the provision of social insurance against risks of temporary difficulties is less relevant. Fiscal crises, coupled with neo-liberal ideologies about how to achieve competitiveness in the face of globalization, have reshaped traditional welfare states away from universal provision to targeting, a process which in itself is stigmatizing and exclusionary. Increasing international migration has posed the problem of the links between citizenship, nationality and rights in increasingly multi-cultural societies.

Given the multiple meanings of the term, the "social exclusion" approach may lead to misunderstanding. But, as a reconceptualization of social disadvantage, it has not been an abstract intellectual exercise. It is providing an important framework for thinking out alternatives to the welfare state. By linking poverty, productive employment and social integration, policy analysts in Western Europe have posited responses to the new situation which emphasize integration and insertion in the labour market rather than welfare insurance, active and personalized participation rather than means-tested benefits, and more multi-cultural concepts of national citizenship. These ideas are now being implemented (see Silver and Wilkinson, Ch. 17).

2. Relevance and value in a global context

Whilst the notion of social exclusion definitely has something more than rhetorical force in Western Europe, its relevance and value in a broader global context, and in particular in developing countries, has not yet been established. In The United States of America, the concept of the "underclass" is used by some, notably William Julius Wilson, to refer to a similar reality to that described by the term social exclusion in Europe. But the term "social exclusion", as currently understood in Europe, has not been widely used in an analytical or operational way in developing countries, even though there is a vast literature on poverty, inequality, entitlements, deprivation, and marginalization. The questions which arise are the following. Does social exclusion offer a framework for analysis and policy which adds anything which cannot be provided by existing approaches? Does the analysis of social exclusion offer a new way to approach the problems of poverty, inequality, employment and social integration in developing countries? Is there any advantage to be gained by applying concepts of social exclusion, and policies to combat it, formulated in rich industrial and post-industrial societies to poorer countries? Is it simply a way of re-labelling old and long-standing problems? (Rodgers, Ch. 2).

A. The findings of literature reviews

Preliminary literature reviews,[2] which focus in particular on existing literature on poverty, deprivation and marginalization in Africa, Asia, Latin America and the Middle East, reinforce natural scepticism about the value of "exporting" concepts from the North to the South, from situations where the great majority are well-off to situations where the great majority are very poor. But the reviews also suggest some reasons why a social exclusion approach might add value to existing debates, and propose some ways that it might be possible to formulate a concept of social exclusion which is not Eurocentric, but rather capable of yielding analytical and policy insights globally.

Scepticism about the value of applying a concept formulated in Western Europe to developing countries is reinforced in two different ways. First, it has been suggested that the emerging social problems of Europe reflect a process of "Latin Americanization", in the sense that European economies and societies are moving closer in their forms of organization to those of Latin America [Yépez, 1994; Touraine, 1992]. As that occurs, the language to describe and analyse the situation in Europe is catching up to one already widely deployed in Latin America, where debates about marginalization were already vigorous in the 1960s and various concepts of the informalization of the labour market have been deployed for a long time. Projecting the European discourse of "social exclusion" on to developing countries, and in particular Latin America, would, in this light, be a grotesque relabelling of long-standing approaches

---

[2] Regional literature reviews were specially commissioned for the IILS/UNDP research project. See Gore [1994], Faria [1994], Yépez [1994], de Haan & Nayak [forthcoming], Bédoui [forthcoming].

to problems, whose only rationale would be the supposed intellectual superiority of European concepts.

Second, it has been suggested, perhaps precisely as a consequence of the longer and deeper engagement with marginality as a problem, that poverty and deprivation are *not* associated with "lack of integration" as the European literature implies. In Latin America, poverty is generally seen as being structurally related to the ways economies and societies function. But the structural processes generating it are grounded in the peripheral integration of Latin American economies into the world capitalist system and the mode of integration of classes, social groups, families, individuals, and regions into the prevailing social division of labour. The key insight of the Latin American literature on marginality thus runs diametrically opposed to a view of social exclusion as lack of integration (Faria, Ch. 6). Similarly, in Africa, historical research effectively challenged dualist models of economy and society which posited an excluded sector (traditional, subsistence) and the conventional wisdom which had emerged by the first half of the 1970s was that individuals and communities had been incorporated into the broader economy and society and that what was problematical was their *terms of incorporation*. Since the late 1970s, with spiralling crises, key concepts have been "disengagement" and "withdrawal". People are not suffering from poverty owing to exclusion. Rather, they are excluding themselves from the wider economy and society, and from the burdensome and unequal obligations of citizenship, in order to survive (Gore, Ch. 5).

Whilst the literature reviews raise questions about the value of exporting European concepts to the rest of the world, and in particular to developing countries, they also suggest ways in which the concept of social exclusion might contribute to better analysis of poverty, and ways in which the concept might be rendered of more general applicability.

With regard to the usefulness of the concept of social exclusion, Faria argues that it stems from its potential as "a way of integrating loosely connected notions such as poverty, deprivation, lack of access to goods, services and assets, precariousness of social rights, and of providing a general framework" (Ch. 6, p. 127). De Haan finds that the potential of the approach for understanding poverty lies in the fact that present poverty studies tend to emphasize economic aspects and to pay less attention to political and cultural dimensions of poverty [de Haan & Nayak, forthcoming]. The analysis of the inter-related processes of inclusion and exclusion could help one to understand the interplay between these dimensions. Gore argues that a more explicit social exclusion approach can also usefully inform analyses of socio-economic change in Africa, in particular processes of impoverishment. It does so, first, through directing more attention to the relationships between poverty and agency; and second, by providing a framework to draw together separate literatures on access to land, employment, organization and representation and social services, and to inter-relate them in way which illuminates trajectories of social change. Whilst Yépez argues that the critical general insights of the European literature on social exclusion are "(i) the stress placed on employment... as a central element of social exclusion; and (ii) the importance placed on the spatial dimension, as the locus of both social differentiation and the articulation between different social actors", and she suggests that social exclusion can best be regarded as a "pivotal concept" which "aims less to identify the contours of empirically observed reality than to highlight the relationships between processes, between micro and macro mechanisms, between individual and collective dimensions" [Yépez, 1994, p. 15].

B. *The value of the social exclusion approach*

Taking these insights together, one may suggest that the value and relevance of the social exclusion approach for policy analysis is descriptive, analytical and normative.

As a *description* of a state of affairs, social exclusion closely corresponds to a state of poverty defined as relative deprivation.[3] As such, the concepts of poverty and social exclusion can easily be used interchangeably. The apparent value-added which is derived from using the concept might seem less. But the social exclusion approach reinforces some of the advantages of defining poverty as relative deprivation. Notably it sees individuals as social beings and not simply repositories of utility. It offers a way of defining poverty which is relevant at a global scale given differences in what is considered essential in different societies. And it sees poverty as multi-dimensional rather than in terms of income and expenditure. A particular contribution of the social exclusion approach in this regard is that "the concept of social exclusion goes beyond economic and social aspects of poverty and embraces the political aspects such as political rights and citizenship which outline a relationship between individuals and

---

[3] "People are relatively deprived if they cannot obtain, at all or sufficiently, the conditions of life — that is, the diets, amenities, standards and services — which allow them to play the roles, participate in the relationships and follow the customary behaviour which is expected of them by virtue of their membership of society. If they lack or are denied resources to obtain access to these conditions of life and so fulfil membership of society they may be said to be in poverty." (Townsend [1993, p. 36]).

the State as well as between the society and the individual" [Bhalla & Lapeyre, 1994, pp. 10-11].

Analytically, the social exclusion approach seeks to understand the inter-relationships between poverty, productive employment, and social integration. The approach can be applied in various ways, which in turn lead to different policy conclusions.

Silver (Ch. 3) argues that the different approaches to social exclusion are grounded in different paradigms of citizenship and social integration. She labels the three most important paradigms "solidarity", "specialization", and "monopoly", and she argues that processes of exclusion are conceptualized in fundamentally different ways in each. In the solidarity paradigm, which is rooted in Republican political thought (particularly as it has evolved in France), the emphasis is placed upon the existence of a core of shared values, a "moral community" around which social order is constructed, and processes of assimilation of individuals into this community, and their ability to express their membership through active participation are important. Social exclusion has a particular salience in this paradigm as it represents a rupture of the social tie. In the specialization paradigm, which is rooted in liberal thought, societies are seen as composed of individuals who are bearers of rights and obligations, and who have diverse interests and capabilities. The structure of society is built around a division of labour and exchange in both economic and social spheres. Social exclusion reflects voluntary choices, patterns of interests and contractual relationships between individuals, and various "distortions" to the system — discrimination, market failures, and unenforced rights. In the monopoly paradigm, societies are seen as inherently conflictual, with different groups controlling resources and insiders protecting their domains against outsiders, constructing barriers and restricting access — to occupations, to cultural resources, to goods and services. Within this paradigm it is shown that access to groups affects access to resources and other social goods. Exclusion occurs through "social closure", "the process by which social collectivities seek to maximize rewards by restricting access to a limited number of eligibles" [Parkin, 1979, p. 44], and "usurpation", the process through which "outsiders" resist and seek to overcome their exclusion.

Silver's analysis is extremely helpful in that it contextualizes the use of the term "social exclusion" in French political debates and in the construction of European Union. Moreover it identifies a third possible stream of social exclusion analysis, beyond the solidarist and social rights approaches which are present in European policy discourse — that is, the monopoly paradigm. This is likely to offer significant insights in the study of poverty and employment issues as it emphasizes agency and also does not posit a simple dualism between insiders and outsiders (as in the solidarity model in particular), but a complex hierarchy of inter-related inclusions and exclusions.

One implication of Silver's decoding of social exclusion discourse is that the precise analytical advantages which stem from a social exclusion approach depend on the particular frame of analysis. But what all the paradigms have in common is an emphasis on processes and a concern to examine how people's lives are being affected by the inter-relationships between economic restructuring and social institutions. Moreover, the social exclusion approach does not address these issues in an abstract way. It seeks to address emerging problems associated with globalization. These include: trends since the 1980s which suggest that "within the global system more people are becoming permanently superfluous, irrelevant, or hindrances to its functioning" (Wolfe, Ch. 4); problems associated with increasing, and increasingly blocked, international migration; intensifying competitive pressures which are bringing in their train various actions by social collectivities to curb competition [Crompton & Brown, 1994]; and technological change which is promoting skill polarization and the dualization of labour markets.

Globalization is making national citizenship increasingly salient as a social status. Citizenship has always been important in development policy analysis, but usually as a silent term, implicitly structuring debates and suggesting analytical and policy priorities, though its nature has not been spelled out. A concern with social exclusion makes the significance of citizenship within development debates explicit and it directs attention towards what the condition of citizenship actually is by focusing on situations of incomplete citizenship. The social exclusion approach makes the social institutions associated with citizenship a central issue of development policy analysis and examines how relationships between markets and citizenship affect people's lives.

Normatively, the social exclusion approach has value because it raises questions about the nature of social justice. In his important work on inequality, Amartya Sen has deliberated deeply on the question "equality of what?", and his project of shifting from a utilitarian perspective to a capability approach has had significant operational implications.[4] The notion of social exclusion can serve to direct attention to an equally fundamental question, namely "equality amongst whom?". As Waltzer [1983] argues, concepts of distributive justice assume (usually silently) the

---

[4] See Sen [1992], for a synthesis of many years' work on this issue.

existence of a community within which rights are held, goods shared, and mutual recognition expressed. Logically the right to membership is thus the most basic right, which depends on the admission policies (exclusionary and inclusionary practices) of the group concerned.

But the relationship between social exclusion and social justice may be even more powerful than this insight, which is founded within an individualistic perspective. With an observation pregnant with possibilities, Room [1994, p. 9] suggests that, whereas the Anglo-Saxon notion of poverty is *distributional*, social exclusion focuses on *relational* issues — inadequate social participation, lack of social integration and lack of power. From Silver's decoding of the notion of social exclusion, it is apparent that the term can be used to think of both relational and distributional notions of justice. But seen as a relational concept, it offers a way of completing the shift away from a welfarist view of social disadvantage which Amartya Sen has begun, but which, in the guise of the concept of capabilities, still remains wedded to an excessively individualist, and insufficiently social, view.

The relationship between social exclusion and social justice needs much more conceptual work of the type which Silver has done on the relationship between social exclusion and different views of society. But, to put all the foregoing together, it may be stated that the specific value of the social exclusion approach is that it offers a way of reconceptualizing and understanding social disadvantage as the globalization of economic relations occurs.

C. Global relevance

If this value is to be realized, the concept of social exclusion needs to be fashioned in a way which is not Eurocentric, but relevant globally, in a range of country contexts. Silver's work, by putting the concept as it is used in European policy discourse within a broader framework, offers a vital map for making this intellectual transformation. But the literature reviews also indicate ways in which the social exclusion approach may be modified to take account of regional differences and also global dimensions of processes of social exclusion. At least four are particularly important.

First, the literature on the peripheral integration of Latin American economies and societies into the world capitalist system suggests that processes of social exclusion need to incorporate various international relations — of trade, aid, technology transfers, migration, etc. — and the nature and design of international regimes which underpin them. Some notion of exclusion at an international level is implicit in the opposition between the "centre" and the "periphery" of the world economic system in that literature.

Second, whereas a focal point for the study of social exclusion in western Europe (and research funding of the European Union) is the relationship between labour markets and social exclusion, in the context of developing countries and countries in transition the focus needs to include other factor markets, as well as the processes through which these markets are developing. Access to agricultural land, access to inputs to work that land productively, and access to credit (for peasant production, urban self-employment and the development of micro-enterprises) are all vital bases of livelihood, as well as access to employment through labour markets.

Third, in examining the relationship between rights, livelihood, and well-being, it is important that work in developing countries does not simply focus on social rights as the western European literature has done, but on civil and political rights. This can build on a long tradition of research which examines popular participation in development and has considered the ways in which individuals and groups who were the object of development programmes were excluded from factors affecting their livelihood, as well as newer research which examines the importance of democracy (variously defined) for economic performance. It also gets beyond the institutional specificity of debates about social exclusion in Europe, which are linked to the future of, and alternatives to, the welfare state. It thus addresses Yépez's pointed question about the value of speaking about social exclusion in countries where people have never been integrated through a welfare state system [Yépez, 1994].

Finally, it is important to focus on various social institutions in which rules governing exclusionary and inclusionary practices are negotiated, including households and national States which are focal in European debates, but going beyond them. The African literature, for example, raises questions about the "nationality" of social exclusion, that is to say, the significance of the nation State in the institutionalization of exclusionary practices (Gore, Ch. 5). With globalization, African societies are developing into post-national societies, but this is occurring in societies in which rights and obligations defining access to resources and other social goods have not been fully "nationalized", in the sense that the enforcement of legal rights is not fully effective, and a national culture of expectations and norms has not been in existence for a long time.

By recognizing the international dimension of processes of exclusion, and using insights from literature in developing countries to contribute to the formulation of a concept of social exclusion which is not Eurocentric, the social exclusion approach can be relevant in a range of country settings, including developing countries and countries in transition. But its value must ultimately be assessed, as Faria (Ch. 6) points out, on the basis of fresh knowledge inspired by the concept.

II. Social exclusion as a process: Evidence from country studies

To explore the value and relevance of the social exclusion approach in developing countries and countries in transition, a series of empirical studies has been undertaken. These studies were particularly designed to explore the analytical and policy advantages of viewing poverty, inequality and a lack of productive employment with a social exclusion approach. Studies were undertaken in ten countries: in Latin America (Mexico, Peru); Sub-Saharan Africa (Cameroon, Tanzania); the Arab world (Tunisia, Yemen); South and South-east Asia (India, Thailand); and the former USSR (Russia, Kazakhstan). This sample of countries was selected to provide examples from different regions of the world, as well as a wide range of economic situations. Thus, the countries selected encompass: (i) socialist economies in transition; (ii) newly-industrializing countries; and (iii) least developed countries. They include countries undergoing rapid economic growth and countries facing stagnation or intensive structural adjustment. Taken along with existing material on Western Europe and the United States, this offers the first insights into processes of social exclusion in a global context.

The studies were undertaken within a limited time-frame (approximately one year) in order to ensure that findings were available for the World Summit for Social Development in March 1995. But nevertheless, in most of the studies, primary data were collected to complement available statistics, which were either almost totally absent (Yemen, Kazakhstan) or — more commonly — did not adequately capture the dimensions of exclusion. Multi-disciplinary research teams, including sociologists, anthropologists and economists, were put together by leading national research institutions, in order to explore the variety of processes involved and assess the value of the exclusion approach through different disciplinary perspectives. Within a common agreed frame of reference, the teams collected data on processes of social exclusion, the social status of selected excluded groups, and their perception of exclusion.

The groups which were defined as "excluded" and analysed in each study varied from country to country, reflecting the different priorities of the research teams. But ethnic, racial or caste and gender elements were common in many of the studies. In Yemen, the study was organized around several distinct excluded groups: the *akhdam*, an ethnically identifiable low-status group; migrants, especially return migrants from the Gulf, who have virtually the status of refugees; casual labourers; and inhabitants of remote villages. In Thailand, some attention is given to ethnic identity and migrants, but there is a particular concern to explore the cultural underpinnings of gender discrimination. In Tanzania, the groups chosen included beggars, certain casual or low-income occupations, the landless and near landless. Gender, age and tribal dimensions of all these groups are also investigated. In addition, a special study was undertaken of orphans. The Cameroon study is dominated by ethnic considerations. In Tunisia, a high priority is given to the illiterate unemployed, whilst some attention is given to the gender dimension. In Siberia – the location of detailed sociological investigation of social exclusion in the Russian study – the focus is on rural low-income groups, the long-term unemployed, and downwardly mobile professional workers. In India, the study covers caste, gender and locational elements of the non-realization of rights. In Peru, class groups are identified, with a strong stress also on indigenous groups and migrants. In Mexico, gender issues are considered.

The chapters in Part II of this volume report, in summary form,[5] the major results of these studies in all the research locations except Kazakhstan, where the work began later.

One thing which is immediately apparent in reviewing the summarized findings of the research projects is the fact that the social exclusion approach readily lends itself to being a different language for describing and labelling persistent problems of poverty. This is not bad in itself. We believe that the studies offer an important and eloquent description of the conditions in which people are living in different parts of the world in relation to the three main themes of the World Social Summit, namely poverty, lack of productive employment, and the breakdown of social cohesion. But, beyond this, some of the studies contain valuable insights for the analysis of the links between poverty, productive employment, and social integration and for understanding processes of social exclusion. Moreover, some assess policy experience and discuss the implications of the approach for policy design. It is these analytical and policy insights which are the focus here. The rest of this section of the introduction look at analytical insights, in particular the role of social institutions in processes of social exclusion, whilst the next section considers policy insights.

[5] Full versions of country studies will be published in future.

1. Markets and social exclusion

The analytical insights on the relationship between markets and social exclusion in the case studies can usefully be introduced in relation to Sen's entitlement approach to the analysis of famines and endemic hunger. There is a significant relationship between the entitlement approach and the analysis of social exclusion [de Haan & Nayak, forthcoming]. But the case studies provide clues as to how the latter goes beyond the former, potentially deepening it.

Entitlement analysis focuses on *commodity markets*. A person's entitlement, in this frame of reference, refers to the bundle of commodities over which a person can establish command using the rules of acquirement which govern his or her circumstances. The rules of acquirement encompass legal rights (such as property rights and social rights to health and education services) and social norms. Sen argues that famines arise because of entitlement failures, in which certain sections of the population cannot command sufficient food. In a private ownership market economy, the main ingredients of such entitlement failure are: "endowment loss" (loss of assets), and/or "movements in the exchange entitlement mapping" (the exchange relationships which specify what a person can acquire through production or trade, for any given endowment — for example, the ratio of daily wages for casual work to grain prices). Endemic hunger arises because of food entitlement failures but also from the inability of some people to "convert" their entitlement bundle into adequate nutritional functioning. Such an inability is due to certain personal characteristics, but also to a lack of entitlement to other kinds of commodities which are essential to adequate nutritional functioning — health and medical attention, elementary education, clean water, living space, and basic sanitation.

The entitlement approach directly examines the interplay between livelihood and citizenship rights, and shows how individuals are excluded from commodity markets. Exclusion from basic goods and basic consumption can usefully be analysed within this framework. But whether there is an analytical pay-off simply from substituting the phrase "exclusion from goods and services" for "entitlement failure" is debatable.

There may be an added advantage in recasting entitlement failures as exclusion from basic goods in that an exclusion approach pays greater attention to agency and the role of social institutions, a critical deficiency of entitlement analysis [Gore, 1993]. But the case studies do not illustrate this potential. What they do demonstrate, however, is that the social exclusion approach can go beyond entitlement analysis by looking more deeply at processes behind entitlement failure. It does so precisely by focusing on exclusion from *factor markets*. With this focus it is possible to identify processes of *economic disenfranchisement*.

Analysis of exclusion from markets has been taken furthest in the study of Peru, in which it is argued that two different types of market can be distinguished to clarify how exclusion from markets occurs. In the first type, individuals can buy or sell as much as they wish of a good or service at the prevailing price (so-called "Walrasian markets"); in the second type, prices still influence demand but there is also rationing which arises because the expected quality of the commodity or service demanded or supplied is a function of its price ("non-Walrasian markets"). In the former type of market, people are excluded if they do not have sufficient real income or productive capacity; in the latter type of market, they can be excluded even when they are willing and able to participate.

In Peru, markets such as the potato market are of the first type, while labour, credit and insurance markets are of the second. This is significant in that the latter three markets can be regarded as basic markets, in the sense that they are fundamental for livelihood and security. In these markets, people are excluded because they are considered high credit or insurance risks, or because they belong to stigmatized social groups, regarded by employers or creditors as less reliable, less trustworthy, or less productive. In all these markets, "social assets" play a role in providing signals for the rationing process. Such "social assets" include a person's rights (to property, for example) and social identity (characteristics such as their language, race, sex, kinship, education, occupation, religion and geographical origin).

The exclusionary process is particularly strong in the *credit market*, which in Peru is extremely selective and highly concentrated. Available figures suggest that 70 per cent of formal credit from the banking system serves the modern trade and manufacturing sectors; that more than 80 per cent is allocated to the capital city, Lima; that less than 5 per cent of firms borrow from the formal credit system, and that the top decile of debtors holds 74 per cent of total bank credit. These patterns reflect the fact that formal financial institutions regard the costs of transactions and information as too high for small producers, and that peasant households and urban micro-enterprises are regarded as bad risks. As a result of this exclusion, a segmented credit market has developed, with adverse consequences for those outside the formal market, where interest rates are higher and informal financial institutions are often precarious.

The importance of market exclusion is even more obvious in the *labour markets*. Most of the case studies showed similar (and familiar) broad patterns, in which formal wage employment was expanding insufficiently to absorb new entrants to the labour force or to reduce the numbers of people working in precarious or vulnerable labour situations. They also showed that exclusion from the labour market not only has direct effects on livelihood but also exacerbates other processes of exclusion such as those related to basic rights, social security and identity. This situation has been aggravated by a fall in overall average real income and a deterioration of working conditions in the wage sector in many countries (including Tanzania, Mexico, Russia and Peru among the case studies), involving lower levels of organization, an increase in the proportion of jobs on short-term contracts and decline in the coverage of labour protection schemes.

Three distinct types of labour market exclusion were identified in the studies: those involving open unemployment; those involving precarious types of labour market insertion; and those involving various forms of non-wage employment.

Open unemployment is widespread, even in the lowest income situations. In Peru the current national unemployment rate is around 10 per cent. Long-term unemployment is growing rapidly in Tunisia. Young people seeking enter to labour markets for the first time have often experienced difficulty but, with economic restructuring, and particularly the opening of national markets to international competition through adjustment programmes, the unemployed includes older people who have lost their jobs. In Mexico and Russia, recorded rates of unemployment are low, but for different reasons. In Mexico, published unemployment statistics reflect mainly frictional unemployment, that is, the relatively small number of unemployed who know for sure — or firmly believe — that they will get a job in the long run. In Russia, unemployment is low partly because employers are not making surplus labour redundant as, during privatization, they have pursued a policy of maintaining "worker collectives" against external shareholders.

Precarious forms of wage labour are also widespread, especially casual daily labour. Exclusion from decent working conditions and employment security is reported in most case studies. In such situations, the process is not one of exclusion from employment — indeed there is usually intensification of work, much of it involving unregulated wage work in agriculture or the informal sector. The problem is one of exclusion from the decent jobs, as higher and more remunerative reaches of the labour market depend on access to secondary education at a minimum as well as on networks of contacts, and strong patterns of labour market segmentation emerge, between both public and private sectors, and within the private sector. There is a strong tendency for particular population groups to be subject to exclusion of this sort, for instance ethnic groups such as the *akhdam* in Yemen, indigenous migrants in Peru and women in many countries.

Not all non-wage employment reflects exclusion, but much self-employment is in practice the result of exclusion from wage labour and is strongly associated with poverty. Where it is competitive with formal-sector production it is likely to face administrative obstacles; alternatively, the "self-employed" may be used as low-cost producers of intermediate goods by larger enterprises and so are in reality disguised and unprotected wage workers. Exclusion here may involve exclusion from markets for inputs, markets which are controlled by large firms or particular population groups. Exclusion from credit markets also limits access to more remunerative and more productive sections of self-employment.

An important theory of labour market exclusion, which focuses on processes of "economic disenfranchisement", has recently been put forward by Partha Dasgupta [1993]. This theory can usefully be contrasted with that proposed by Figueroa et al. (Ch. 12) in their discussion of non-Walrasian markets in Peru. Whilst the theory of social exclusion of Figueroa and his associates is elaborated for an "overpopulated economy", and thus requires that rationing takes place, Dasgupta develops his theory for an economy which is neither rich in assets, nor "vastly poor" in assets (which is defined as an economy in which "it is technologically infeasible for *all* citizens to enjoy adequate diet and health care" [emphasis added], or an economy whose "population size exceeds the land's carrying capacity" [ibid., p. 476]). In Dasgupta's analysis, therefore, people are not shut out of the labour market because of rationing and job queues in the labour market (though this situation can be added to the model). Nor are they excluded because of monopsony, which arises through collusion amongst a small number of employers (though this, too, can be added to the model). Labour markets are competitive and cultural identity is not a basis for discrimination. But job seekers include two categories of person: first, landless persons; and second, persons with a small amount of land, whose nutritional needs are partially, though not completely, met through cultivation of that land.

In this situation, Dasgupta argues that there is a tendency for landless persons to become economically disenfranchised "not because they don't wish to work, but because they are unable to offer the labour power the market demands" [ibid., p. 484]. Possessing no physical assets, their one asset appears to be their labour power. But, Dasgupta asserts, what an assetless person owns is *potential* labour power and to convert to actual labour power requires adequate nutrition and health care. Persons with a small amount of land can meet some of their nutritional requirements from their own land but the totally landless must meet their total energy requirements from their earnings from employment. They cannot do so unless they receive a relatively high piece-rate in relation to the small farmer-cum-labourers and, if they get weak, they are driven to eke out a bare subsistence, continuing to live in destitution through the exploitation of common property resources (which require less energy expenditure if they are available) or begging.

The case studies provide little evidence to support (or reject) Dasgupta's theory, although the Tanzanian case suggests that health status is an important determinant of an individual becoming a beggar. However, various case studies found that *educational status*, and particularly illiteracy, was an important cause of labour market exclusion. Like health and nutritional status, educational status is associated with the nature of the labour power being offered for sale by persons without any other physical assets.

The importance of education is identified in the studies of Tanzania, Thailand and Tunisia, and the process of social exclusion and problems of devising policies for labour market reinsertion are particularly considered in the study of Tunisia. These studies suggest that, in a situation of rising educational standards, those with a level of formal schooling which does not go beyond primary level, and particularly those who are illiterate, find it very difficult to find decent employment. Moreover, amongst the unemployed, it is this group which is the most difficult to reinsert into the labour market.

More work is obviously required on both the links between illiteracy and labour market exclusions, and the links between nutritional/health status and labour market exclusions. These links seem to be at the heart of the relationship between exclusion from livelihood and exclusion from social rights. This work needs to include theoretical approaches (such as those of Figueroa and associates and Dasgupta) and also to be sensitive to local situations. An example is the work of Breman [1994] who demonstrates the importance of physical strength and stamina in determining labour market exclusion in situations where there is surplus labour. Studying localities in South Gujarat, India, where unskilled day-labourers gather to seek work each morning and when there are insufficient jobs, those who are not capable of maximum effort and cannot meet the heavy demands on physical strength and stamina will be hired less frequently. In South Gujarat, this applied to men and women over 40, who had literally been used up in the labour process and also younger persons suffering from ailments or malnutrition. A vicious circle operates, in which exclusion from labour markets leads to exclusion from satisfaction of basic nutritional and health needs, which in turn reinforces exclusion from labour markets owing to diminishing capacity to work. This is a common route to destitution for people without land or informal social support or access to common property resources.

With regard to exclusion from *land markets*, the studies suggested that these markets were weakly developed, partly because of the contested nature of property rights, and that exclusion from land resources was strongly influenced by State actions which did not reflect the interests of peasant farmers. This is particularly well-illustrated in the contrasting cases of Thailand (which is considered in more detail in the next section) and Tanzania. In the latter case, various forms of "land-grabbing" by wealthier or more well-connected individuals has occurred during both the period when State ownership was central to the development strategy and under the new neo-liberal policies. During the villagization programme in the 1970s, some landless gained access to land, but village-level land allocation procedures were sometimes unjust, with persistent exclusion of women, and practices which favoured friends, relatives and cronies. With the changes associated with liberalization, settled agriculture or land-intensive tourist development have become more lucrative and this has accentuated a tendency for pastoralists and hunter-gatherers to lose land. This reflects the economic priority given to agriculture over pastoralism, and is rationalized by describing pastoralists' land as "unutilized".

2. States, citizenship rights and social exclusion

One of the crucial advantages of a social exclusion approach is that it inserts the condition of citizenship directly into development policy analysis. Although Silver's work makes it very clear that there is no single conception of citizenship, the case studies tend to work with a particular notion of citizenship. This is not a participatory notion of citizenship (which informs Wolfe's discussion of the paradoxes of social exclusion, Ch. 4). Rather, most of the case studies (implicitly) are based on a conception of citizenship which sees individuals as bearers of rights.

The analytical insights of the case studies in relation to exclusion from citizenship rights can be usefully introduced in relation to Marshall's classic discussion of citizenship. Marshall argued that

> Citizenship is a status bestowed on those who are full members of a community. All who possess the status are equal with respect to the rights and duties with which the status is endowed. There is no universal principle that determines what those rights and duties shall be, but societies in which citizenship is a developing institution create an image of an ideal citizenship against which

achievement can be measured and towards which aspiration can be directed [Marshall and Bottomore, 1992, p. 18].

He divided citizenship rights into *civil rights* (liberty of the person, freedom speech, the right to own property and to conclude valid contracts, the right to justice), for which a key institution was courts of justice; *political rights* (to participate in the exercise of State power), for which the key institutions are central and local government; and *social rights*, "to a modicum of economic welfare and security...and to live the life of a civilized being according to the standards prevailing in the society" [ibid., p. 8]. Moreover, drawing extensively on the British experience, he saw the development of rights as a movement towards the possession of citizenship rights by increasing numbers of people in the community, greater equality in the possession of rights and the possession of an increasing range of rights. In the British situation, the historical development involved an expansion from civil rights, to political rights and, in the twentieth century, to social rights.

Within this Marshallian framework, social exclusion can be seen as *incomplete citizenship*, which is due to deficiencies in the possession of citizenship rights (in relation to the ideal of citizenship, of that society or elsewhere) and inequalities in the status of citizenship. Critical analytical questions are the ways in which the range of citizenship rights are increased and reduced; the inter-relationships between different types of rights; and the inter-relationships between the norm of equality in the status of citizenship and the social inequalities associated with the functioning markets. Some clues to answer these questions are found in Marshall's own work. But it is particularly based on the British experience and it can potentially (and unhelpfully) be interpreted in a a teleological way. Much work, which is likely to go beyond Marshall's analysis, needs to be done.

One route is to make international comparisons of citizenship rights and identify conditions of incomplete citizenship in relation to *global norms*. This is an emerging area of analysis, but the case studies follow another path. They contain four main types of information. First, some of the studies describe the range of rights and pattern of inequality in their possession within a national frame of reference. Second, some analyse the macro-dynamics through which citizenship rights are extended or contracted in relation to the development strategies of countries. Third, some also focus upon the micro-dynamics through which rights are negotiated, realized and denied. Finally some of the studies provide material for thinking about the effects of the globalization of markets on the condition of citizenship. Some insights are made into the inter-relationships between different types of citizenship rights, but the work is of a very preliminary nature and does not reflect the complexity of the issue.

A. Range and inequality of citizenship rights

Information within the studies showed the limited range of citizenship rights which nationals of low-income countries possess and also identified patterns of inequality. The studies confirm that analysis of social exclusion in a developing country must include civil and political rights, as well as social rights, which are the focus of the West European literature. In Peru, available statistics show that 37 per cent of the peasantry had no legal title to their land in 1984, and 43 per cent of people living in shanty towns had no legal title on their urban plots in 1991.

Amongst the studies, the case of India provides the most complete delineation of social rights. A particular finding of that study, which is replicated in other studies, is that many aspects of social protection are linked with regular wage employment, which is obtained by only a minority of the workforce. Despite obligations written into the Indian Constitution to provide (within the limits of economic capacity and development) for the right to work, to education and to public assistance in the case of unemployment, old age, sickness and disablement, entitlements have been concentrated on "organized workers" who number less than 10 per cent of the workforce, and implementation of social assistance schemes for other population groups has been patchy. In Peru, only 42 per cent of the economically active population is affiliated to the social security system. One consequence is that two-thirds of the population aged 65 and above have no retirement pension. Labour rights, in terms of organization, protection and acceptable conditions of employment and of work are effectively enforced only in a part of the economic system, which, in the case of economies such as Yemen and Tanzania, is only a very small part. More generally, labour rights are often contested in practice even when they are admitted in theory. In many countries, attempts have been made by both State and private employers to undermine labour organizations promoting such rights.

With regard to the inequality of citizenship rights, rural populations are seen to be particularly disadvantaged in a number of the studies, including Yemen and India. Similar patterns of exclusion are important in Mexico and Peru and are compounded there by discrimination against ethnic minorities dominant in marginal regions. In Siberia, the breakdown of institutions which provided such goods and services outside the market is of vital importance. In rural areas, access to housing, child care facilities, health care and many other social services was linked to participation in collective or State farms. The breakdown of the old universalist systems has led to a growth of patronage and a race for personal enrichment, based on formerly collective resources. This leads to situations of extreme deprivation and insecurity, with rights to housing a critical issue.

B. Macro-dynamics of exclusion from rights

There are major variations between countries, *and* in the same countries over time, in terms of: the set of citizenship rights which is legally recognized; the capacity of governments to enforce and make rights effective, and of individuals, groups and organizations to defend their rights; and the measure of equality in the realization of rights. An important stream within current development literature is concerned with the relationships between economic performance, development strategy and the provision and realization of civil, political and social rights.

Aggregate statistics show that there are no straightforward correlations between economic growth and social, civil and political rights at the national level. This has led to the important insight that it is possible to extend entitlements to health, education and social assistance without waiting for a general rise in affluence. Increasing command over commodities and services can be achieved through development strategies which aim for "growth-mediated security" or "support-led security" rather than development strategies of "unaimed opulence" [Drèze & Sen, 1989].

The case studies do not confirm or deny these ideas. But they show how different forms of social exclusion from citizenship rights are related to the economic logic of a growth strategy. This is a very promising area of research and policy design, whose potential is perhaps best illustrated in the already published literature by an analysis of the dilemmas of securing and maintaining citizenship entitlements in Eastern Europe [Fitzgerald, 1991]. This analysis identifies the central problem of transition in the semi-industrialized economies in the region as precisely how to achieve the imperative of modernizing industry to compete in international markets in a situation in which the population is used to a high standard of social provision and wishes to defend that standard.

The relationship between citizenship rights and macro-economic strategy is most clearly shown in the case of Mexico. Current social exclusion processes are interpreted as being related to "the breakdown of the inclusive development model, based on a corporatist social covenant, which prevailed in the country from the 1940s to the early 1980s, and its replacement with a neo-liberal project which is being implemented through structural adjustment programmes" (Gordon Rapoport et al., Ch. 13, p. 215). In the inclusive development model, various sectoral groupings were linked to the official party (PRI) and to the government and the State mediated the demands of their members. There was a strong link between economic and social policies and social expenditure was conceived as a part of the development project as, with import substitution industrialization, consumption was promoted to expand the domestic market. Agriculture also had a definite role in the process of economic growth. The social policy sought to give welfare benefits to as many people as possible, without attempting to implement a comprehensive welfare state.

This development model was imperfectly inclusive, very unequal, and by the 1960s was beginning to prove unsustainable. But it increasingly included population groups. With the implementation of an export-oriented industrialization strategy, the expansion of domestic consumption is no longer integral to the growth model, the guarantee of cheap labour is a crucial element of the strategy, and the agricultural sector has been simply exposed to international competition. There has been increasing informalization of labour following the dissolution of collective contracts between workers and employers, the introduction of several new *Pactos Económicos*, and the break-up of regional and national trade unions and their replacement with firm-level unions. The adoption of the neo-liberal reforms is reinforcing old patterns of inequality and discrimination and leading to new exclusions which reflect the particular trajectory of economic restructuring.

The relationship between the role of agriculture in the growth model and social exclusion in rural areas is also noted as significant in another newly-industrializing economy, namely Thailand. This identifies the structural underpinnings of dispossession of peasants of land in the fact that the utility of the rural sector to the current development model is primarily as a source of labour.

Other studies point to the complex set of forces, economic and political, which both enable and entrain the expansion and effective delivery of rights. The Peruvian study, with a phrase which bears deeper consideration, argues that "the culture of inequality" is one aspect of the demand for rights whilst, on the supply side, the delivery of rights depends on the production capacity of the economy, the preference of the ruling classes to allocate resources for the provision of rights in the form of public goods, and international agreements. The factors underlying basic needs satisfaction are considered in some detail in the Indian study. In that case, underlying the expansion of the provision of public goods in the health and education sector, and also improvements in water supply and sanitation, is a general commitment to promote economic growth. This has been complemented with: specific State interventions to augment the asset base of poorer sections of the population and to provide employment; efforts to move towards more universal provision and higher standards of the services for which the government has accepted prime responsibility; and mandatory reverse discrimination and affirmative action in favour of Scheduled Castes and Scheduled Tribes facing historically accumulated disadvantages. The study argues that the progress which has been made in reducing exclusion from such basic needs reflects two major countervailing tendencies. On the one hand, mass electoral politics based on adult franchise has been important in increasing the political clout of the poor. On the other hand, the effectiveness of programmes targeted at the poor has been reduced by mis-targeting, leakages, corruption, and lack of accountability. Moreover, as special programmes have been implemented, additional groups have also begun to demand special treatment. The politics of caste have become more conflictual in recent years.

A common, though not surprising, finding of some of the studies is that programmes of structural adjustment have undermined the capacity of States to provide health, education and social services. In Peru, for example, per capita real public expenditure on education, health, housing and employment in 1992 was just 30 per cent of the 1980 level. In Tanzania, per capita real public expenditure on health in 1990-91 was 41 per cent of 1977-78, whilst for education it was 34 per cent. Between 1981 and 1987 in the same country, the gross primary school enrolment rate fell from 98 to 78 per cent, and the cumulative drop-out rate in primary schools rose from 16 per cent in 1977 to 25 per cent in 1989 and was even higher for girls.

What is perhaps more important than this finding itself is the observation that these adjustment programmes seek to intensify the integration of national economies into the world economy, and that they have been implemented, particularly in the poor countries of Africa, with multiple and binding conditionalities. A question which arises following Fitzgerald's line of thought is whether these programmes necessarily require regression in the realization of rights.

C. Micro-dynamics of exclusion from rights

Some of the studies examine the micro-dynamics of social exclusion from citizenship rights. They emphasize the gap between the provision and the realization of rights, noting the importance of poverty in engendering that gap. They also show that negotiation between individuals and groups is an important element in the realization of rights. This is particularly clear in the studies of both Russia and Thailand, which focus on the micro-dynamics associated with *property rights*.

In countries in transition there is likely to be particular confusion over property rights, but mechanisms for defending ones' rights may at the same time be more difficult. In the case of rural Siberia, it is observed that the transition to new forms of ownership and management, which occurred as members of a former State farm (*kolkhoz*) became a Peasant Farm Association with land shared out between members, was nominal rather than real. Each member theoretically had a right to set up in private ownership and was free to work elsewhere, but disputes over claims to housing, in a situation where former managers of the State farm continued to exercise managerial authority and were doing so in their own interests, effectively prevented the realization of these new-found freedoms. The earlier party committees, through which the poor could express their grievances, were disbanded and the only way people could defend their rights was through the courts. However, very few people brought their cases to court because of general legal illiteracy, transportation and time expenditures required (the court was seated in the city), and the general tradition of long suffering.

In Thailand, rapid growth and industrialization has made areas of land designated by the government as "forest reserves" a major source of conflict between business interests and peasants. The former seek to establish eucalyptus plantations to supply the growing pulp industry, whilst the latter, some of whom were earlier encouraged to settle in the forest and many of whom were living in the forest areas before they were officially designated as such, seek to retain access to the natural resources on which their livelihoods are based.

This conflict was dramatized with the short-lived implementation of the *Kho Jo Ko* programme in 1991-92. In this programme, the government sought to rent out "degraded" forest land for reforestation under eucalyptus on 15-30 year concessions at cheap rates. The programme envisaged the relocation of more than five million peasants. It was implemented initially in the north-east of the country where people are very poor and are sometimes regarded as inferior minorities. It was shoddily planned and implemented with violence. In some villages, peasants, with the help of NGOs and students, successfully resisted exclusion and, with a change of government in 1992, the programme was abandoned. However, similar, if less crude policies excluding peasants from land resources continue as the old momentum of peasant expansion comes into conflict with new forces of expansive urban capitalism, and State policy is founded on a top-down approach.

With regard to *social rights*, the studies focused more on macro-dynamics, as indicated in the previous section. However, the Tanzanian study includes a particular survey of how the plight of the increasing numbers of AIDS orphans in north-west Tanzania is worsening. Customary systems of care, which used to provide some kind of safety-net for the most disadvantaged, are under stress as economic opportunities and incomes decline in the region, and there is an increasingly narrow definition of the immediate family. The interplay between local community-based systems of rights and obligations and national citizenship rights should prove an interesting area for future analysis of the micro-dynamics of social exclusion from rights. Another avenue to explore is to build upon Schaffer's work on the way in which the negotiation of the rules of access to public goods, particularly education and health services, affect the realization of social rights.[6]

D. Globalization and incomplete citizenship

Possession of the status of national citizen is becoming more important as a basis for social exclusion as increasing numbers of people move across international boundaries. In general, persons defined as "aliens" of various kinds (who might be international migrant workers or refugees) are denied rights available to members of the national community and they may be subject to the insecurity associated with the possibility of sudden expulsion [Cohen, 1987]. A good illustration is found in the study of Yemen. It shows the situation in which international migrant workers can find themselves if they are suddenly forced to leave the country to which they have migrated. After the outbreak of the Gulf War, over one million persons returned to Yemen, increasing the population by about one-eighth. Almost half of the returnee emigrants are illiterate and three-quarters do not own housing or land in Yemen. Almost two-thirds have been out of the country for more than ten years and, with their arrival, the unemployment rate increased from 7 per cent to 25 per cent. Four years after the War about 75,000 families still remain permanently in camps with little social infrastructure and restricted access to local labour markets.

---

[6] See the theme issue of *Development and Change*, 1975, Vol. 6, on "The problem of access to public services"; and Schaffer & Lamb [1981].

There is often ambiguity over what constitutes the "national community", and the full exercise of citizenship may also be linked to acceptance of a dominant cultural or political mode of behaviour, including language, customs and way of life. In Thailand, for example, while minority groups such as Malay Moslems in the South do obtain the identity cards which give them full legal and economic rights, the right to cultural and religious differences suffers in the process. The rights of indigenous peoples to identity and the maintenance of their own way of life is widely threatened by unrecognized property rights, coupled with development and population pressure.

One feature of the situation facing developing countries, as the globalization of markets occurs, is that at the same time as the status of national citizenship becomes more salient, the capacity of governments to control the productive basis of the economy, on which the delivery of citizenship rights depends, is becoming increasingly eroded. Also, developing countries are increasingly subject to international regimes which directly seek to influence patterns of rights provision within their national territories. Both aid conditionality and, more recently, threats of trade sanctions, are influencing patterns of exclusion from rights in developing countries.

This is happening in perverse ways. Countries are finding themselves subject to both human rights conditionality, which encourages countries to extend certain civil, political and social rights (which are regarded externally as universally valid) to national citizens, and macro-economic conditionality which can, in the short term at least, undermine their ability to extend the realization of social and political rights. This difficult situation reflects, amongst other things, a failure to understand exclusions from citizenship rights in relation to development paths.

3. *Social exclusion and civil society*

The case studies show that institutions of civil society are also important in regulating exclusionary practices and in enabling resistance to social exclusion.

The relationship between civil society and social exclusion is particularly apparent in the studies of Cameroon and Thailand, with the former considering the relationship between ethnic identity and individual economic advancement, and the latter gender discrimination. The Cameroon study examines various voluntary associations, which include ethnic associations, professional and religious associations. These associations act as an informal social security system and a parallel financial system to official banks. They support poorer individuals excluded from economic resources and legal rights. But paradoxically "in regrouping the excluded, the associations also exclude" (Inack Inack et al., Ch. 14, p. 235). Savings are a particularly important function of these associations and informal credit associations (*tontines*), often rooted in ethnic solidarity, are an important source of finance enabling their members to acquire goods and services which they could not normally acquire. However, one ethnic group, the Bamileke, has a more developed associational life and has used the *tontines* more effectively in advancing their business interests. As a consequence, they dominate lucrative trading activity.

The Thailand study examines the cultural and religious beliefs which lead to the formation of unequal gender relations and the exclusion of women, particularly those who are young and poor, from their right to equal recognition as human beings. It shows the importance of certain Buddhist practices and the legacy of the male-dominated *sakdina* culture which prevailed in nineteenth-century Thailand. The analysis raises difficult questions about the types of policies which can reduce exclusionary practices which are deeply rooted in civil society.

The institutions of civil society intertwine with markets and States to reinforce social exclusion. But these institutions also can offer a resource for individuals and groups to resist exclusion, although the studies do not identify many grounds for confidence in this regard. They show that people respond to social exclusion in various ways, which range from passivity and a sense of shame and despair on the one hand, to group action to reverse particular processes of exclusion or to alter the political balance of forces within a country, on the other. These responses are rooted in everyday experience, different perceptions by people of their situations, different expectations of the effectiveness of political action, and the existence of different organizational capabilities. But often passivity prevails.

In studies in settings as different as Siberia and Yemen, particular groups experience a sense of worthlessness or impotence which compounds and reinforces their social exclusion. In Yemen this was apparent in the case of the returnee emigrant workers. They initially selected representatives to follow up with the government on promises to provide housing, employment and other social services to help them to reintegrate into the country. Over time, however, they ceased to do this, and responded to the limited ability of the government to help them by giving up hope that they could get support and by withdrawing from political activity. In Siberia, it was found that, amongst the long-term unemployed who had formerly worked as professionals, the sense of shame associated with their transition in status from persons "who earn by their own labour" to being "social dependants" was engendering psychological depression, and feelings of uselessness and inferiority. One person in this situation responded to a question about their participation in public activities by asking the interviewer "What is the essence of public activity for a 'useless' person?", capturing in that rhetorical question the wider sense of isolation and separation from society associated with long-term unemployment.

Some of the studies, particularly in the least developed countries, showed that people living in situations of extreme material poverty did not necessarily view themselves as "excluded" or "marginalized". This was found in particular in Tanzania, where it was suggested that people are so used to a hard life and material deprivation that they do not always see it. None of the studies focused on social groups which were actively resisting inclusion and integration into national society because they wished to preserve their way of life.

Resistance to exclusion through group action was observed most clearly in situations where people were dispossessed from assets which they regarded as rightfully theirs and on which their basic livelihood depended. In the case of the peasant farmers in Thailand, resistance initially took the form of public irony to shame the military regime with the establishment of "Thai refugee camps" for Thai peasants who had been evicted from their villages without proper resettlement. Government attempts to suppress this form of protest included violent intimidation and the arrest of leaders, but this only reinforced the protest movement, which was also supported by NGOs and students. Protest demonstrations escalated and eventually, after the fall of the military government, the programme was abandoned. In this case, group resistance was linked to specific processes of exclusion and was, on the side of the protesters, non-violent.

In general, social exclusion seems to be more often associated with resignation and a sense of worthlessness paralyzing action rather than resistance. The most common response to exclusion is the active improvisation of household survival strategies. In various studies, a trade-off was observed between effective democratic politics and everyday survival, with excluded groups unable to develop longer-term political strategies to alter the setting which has excluded them because of the unrelenting compulsion to find work and acquire food.

One important finding, articulated in the Yemen study, was that people perceive the problem of their exclusion as a problem of the family or the community as a whole and not as a problem limited to the individual. This is one reason why in the Yemen study it is argued that women there do not perceive themselves as individually excluded, even if they participate less in the economic domain than do men. A similar perspective was apparent in the study of Cameroon, where ethnic identity is an important idiom of belonging.

4. Some conclusions[7]

Markets institutions, citizenship rights and the associations of civil society interact in complex ways in processes of social exclusion. Underlying, and intertwined with, market exclusions there are exclusions from citizenship rights. For example, one consequence of the poor being excluded from property rights is that they cannot use property as collateral for credit. Informal contracts and informal markets, with higher transaction costs, inevitably arise. The possibility of people realizing their rights may itself be diminished through poverty. Moreover, the precise implications of rights associated with the legally constituted status of citizen depend crucially on the norms and expectations of civil society.

The case studies suggest that, starting from a situation characterized by wide inequalities in endowments and extreme poverty, the exclusionary and inclusionary practices and processes, regulated through the institutions of markets, States and civil society, can best be understood as the expression of the interplay between four basic underlying determinants.

The *first* is the increasing transnationalization of social and economic life, with intensifying flows of capital, labour and ideas. Associated with this trend, there has been a loss of decision-making capacity by nation States. This process is occurring to different degrees in different regions according to their position on the international scene but, in general, the economic policies and situations of more industrialized countries are having increasingly intense economic effects on less industrialized countries.

The *second* is the changing availability and distribution of assets in situations of increasing scarcity associated with population growth, radical economic transformation and, in recent years, widespread recession and even, in some regions, a disturbing trend of economic decline. The assets with which people participate in social and economic life are of three types: economic assets, which refer to productive resources such as land and other physical capital, and financial and human capital; political assets, which refer to the access of people to universal rights established by society; and cultural assets, which are defined by the social values attached

---

[7] Much of this section is based on a discussion by representatives of all the research teams which took place at a workshop held in Cambridge, England, in July 1994.

to individuals' personal characteristics such as sex, race, religion, and education.[8]

The *third* is the diverse social and political structures, which encompass the institutions through which power is exercised and specific cultural values which reflect and reproduce the balance of power between social groups and also determine their status. These structures and institutions in turn depend on the dominant paradigm of social integration which exists in given national societies. The paradigms discussed by Silver are thus not simply alternative ways in which researchers can define and understand social exclusion. They represent ways in which societies *themselves* understand exclusion. Whether solidaristic or liberal, they give rise to patterns of behaviour and influence for different social actors which are central to understanding who excludes whom, and how.

The *fourth* is the nature of the development regime adopted by the national government, including the relative role of State and markets as allocation and accumulation mechanisms; the policies for growth, poverty reduction and structural transformation; and the short- and medium-run programmes aimed at economic adjustment and stabilization.

Many dimensions of exclusion were considered by the case studies, including livelihood, basic needs, productive assets, labour markets, social and political participation, civil rights, dignity and security. The exclusion mechanisms to which the studies pointed as being important in relation to these dimensions are: *(a)* the organization of markets, and particularly processes of economic disenfranchisement associated with factor markets; *(b)* the functioning of governmental and inter-governmental institutions, in particular where they are characterized by limited accountability, the presence of corruption, non-universal enforcement of the law, mismanagement, the centralization of policy- and decision-making, and the monopolization of information and of the power to allocate resources; and *(c)* the presence of discrimination, particularly vis-à-vis the following social identities — gender, caste, ethnicity and race. Such discrimination is paradoxically found in both the accentuation of particularlistic distinctions and also attempts to achieve cultural homogenization through national integration plans.

The studies show that in each country there is a hierarchy in the importance of the different dimensions of exclusion. This hierarchy exists in three senses. First, some exclusions are more important than others in terms of their effects on poverty and inequality. Second, some exclusions

---

[8] This model derives from the study of Peru (Figueroa et al., Ch. 12).

are perceived to be more important than others by members of society, perceptions which may vary between social groups. Thirdly, there are inter-relationships between the different dimensions of exclusion. The failure to command particular resources, to obtain particular rights or to enter particular markets results in exclusion in other dimensions. For example, it was observed in one country that for particular rural groups, the process of economic exclusion from the natural resources on which they depend for a livelihood results also in cultural exclusion from their traditional practices and communities and also sometimes in political exclusion as they become labelled dissidents.

The case studies invariably found that inter-relationships existed between exclusion in different dimensions. Also, some social groups — with particular identities, social assets and property endowments — experienced multiple and self-reinforcing exclusions and faced persistent, rather than temporary, disadvantages, which were transferred from generation to generation, often through the nexus of poverty, child labour and under-education. Early labour market entry prevents acquisition of the qualifications which are essential for access to regular, protected work, so early labour market entry is a source of lifetime exclusion from adequate livelihood.

Bearing in mind that the choice of groups studied reflects the researchers' perceptions, the studies suggest that ethnic, racial or caste elements are involved in exclusion in most circumstances (the issue was not treated in Russia or Tunisia) and is sometimes pervasive (Cameroon). Gender-based exclusion is also very widespread. It also seems likely that certain characteristics which were not examined in all studies, notably physical disability, are also widespread and important. Children and young people constitute a particularly important group, subject to some very specific exclusions. Migrants constitute another group subject to many forms of exclusion. International migrant workers are increasing in numbers and they are particularly vulnerable to political and policy changes.

Excluded groups are identified in the studies on the basis of their exclusion (e.g. the unemployed or the landless) or on the basis of an identity which is assumed to lead to exclusion (e.g. gender, ethnicity). One important methodological finding of the research project is that the first method of identifying groups restricts the analytical insights which can be derived from a social exclusion approach. It is almost tautological, since we identify the excluded, from the outset, by the nature of their exclusion. In this approach, the research task can easily get reduced to describing the living conditions, particularly the deprivations of the "excluded". However, particular dimensions of exclusion may also become characteristics which identify groups subject to other forms of exclusion; for instance, a fixed residence or a job may be needed to obtain social rights or public goods. The unemployed or the landless may be stigmatized and gradually marginalized.

The second basis for defining excluded groups is more promising analytically because identities associated with such attributes as age, sex, and ethnicity are socially constructed, and the ways in which identities are constructed are integral to processes of exclusion. Some attributes are fixed and others are modifiable, a distinction which is important as individuals may escape exclusion through migration or investing in skills. But often, the groups most vulnerable to exclusion are simply those which are most readily identified as different, which are most readily exploited, or which have a particular initial disadvantage which is multiplied through a social process.

From a methodological point of view, deeper understanding of social exclusion is likely to come from a focus on the processes and practices of exclusion, and the social institutions which regulate exclusion, rather than the groups which are affected. But examining which groups are excluded under different circumstances can also help to understand the processes through which they are excluded. Particular situations — youth; lack of work experience; physical handicap; dependency within the household; lack of command of the dominant language; low position in an established social hierarchy — may be directly responsible for vulnerability and so may facilitate exclusion even if they do not directly cause it.

It is difficult to detect regional variations in processes of social exclusion in different parts of the world on the basis of the studies. Nevertheless, two generalizations on regional variation seem valid. First, the studies confirmed that the degree of development of labour markets, and their nature, are pivotal in understanding the relative importance of, and the inter-relationships between, different dimensions of exclusion. In agrarian and predominantly peasant societies, access to land and labour, and to other inputs required to render them productive, are vital. Complex interactions arise between access to labour markets (both rural and urban) and access to land, with exclusion from labour markets, and particularly their more remunerative segments, becoming increasingly significant as urbanization and industrialization occur. In industrialized countries, whether market or transition economies, exclusion is very much associated with long-term unemployment, the loss of rights associated with work and the process of breakdown of social ties and disaffiliation which often comes with this situation.

Second, the studies suggested that the ways in which the institutions of civil society are interlinked with the State and markets in processes of social exclusion varies between countries. Institutions of civil society are particularly important where citizenship rights are not "nationalized", in the sense that the enforcement of legal rights is not fully effective and a national culture of expectations and norms has not been in existence for a long time, and where livelihoods are less dependent on impersonal market relations.

Social exclusion appears to occur within all economies and societies, but manifests itself in different forms, with different intensities and with different degrees of salience to members of society or their representatives. What is critical in one country may not be so perceived in another.

III. Policy issues

It is possible to take two broad routes to elaborate the policy implications of a social exclusion approach in developing countries and countries in transition. The first is to describe and evaluate the policy initiatives to combat exclusion which are being implemented in Europe and to consider their applicability and relevance elsewhere. The second is to conduct analyses of social exclusion outside Europe, and to infer policy conclusions in the light of the approach and existing policy experiences to counter poverty, deprivation and discrimination. Both routes are followed here.

1. The nature and broader applicability of European policy experience

In Europe, the social exclusion approach is leading to new policy initiatives to prevent and remedy social disadvantage in the face of economic restructuring. The measures specifically targeted on those who are considered to be socially excluded are various and include: (i) income support tied to social and professional insertion; (ii) training programmes for unemployed adults and youth; (ii) territorially-based cross-sectoral initiatives to improve physical infrastructure, services, community organization, and enterprise development at the local level (which are generally focused areas suffering multiple disadvantages in cities); and (iv) the establishment of micro-enterprises and community associations to reorientate for work those deemed unemployable (such as ex-convicts, substance abusers, homeless persons) (Silver and Wilkinson, Ch. 17). A particularly important initiative in France is the *revenu minimum d'insertion* (minimum income of integration — RMI), which combines an income allowance with an "insertion contract" which pledges the recipient to take actions (e.g. moving towards a job, undertaking training) which will facilitate the economic integration of the individual. This measure "links the right to the satisfaction of basic needs with the aspiration for social and professional insertion" (Rodgers, Ch. 16, p. 258).

Existing evaluations of this policy experience are not wholly favourable (see Silver and Wilkinson, Ch. 17). Also, in assessing its relevance to "low-income settings" Rodgers argues that *some* items of the European policy agenda can be relevant in *some* situations — for example, "policies such as the RMI might be relevant in some higher-income countries in Latin America and East Asia, where meaningful 'integration' contracts might be designed" — but as "low-income settings" are diverse, there are other situations where European experiences will be inappropriate (Rodgers, Ch. 16, p. 266). Devising policy against exclusion, he argues, must be seen in a framework which encompasses actions at the international, national and regional/local levels, and in relation to groups vulnerable to exclusion.

In considering what lessons, if any, might be learnt from the European experience, it is important to examine both the policies themselves and the principles and perspectives which underlie policy. In this light, the European experience suggests six main insights.

First, if policies to combat social disadvantage are marginalized as purely social policies, they will tend to have a welfarist orientation, providing assistance to socially marginal persons. Policies based on a social exclusion approach combat social disadvantage through socio-economic policies which manage the relationship between social dependency and isolation on the one hand, and economic integration (particularly insertion in the labour market), on the other hand.

Second, a participatory bias (either individualist or communitarian in orientation) is inherent to policies based on a social exclusion approach. This is because participation is, in itself, a form of integration. With its participatory bias, the social exclusion approach leads to policies which are not welfarist and which seek to transform the disadvantaged from passive recipients of social assistance into active agents in society and the economy. The approach leads to policy measures which create new partnerships between the public and private sectors.

Third, there is a wide variety of policies which can be derived from a social exclusion approach. The difference between these policies basically reflects different views of social integration. The three basic paradigms of society underlying policy are "solidarity", "specialization" and "monopoly" (see Silver, Ch. 3). These do not in themselves constitute specific institutional types, but they are foundational understandings of the relationship between the individual and society, on the basis of which various "integration regimes" develop. "Integration regimes" can be considered analogous to the concept of "welfare regimes", which has usefully illuminated discussion of welfare state systems [Esping-Anderson, 1990]. In Europe, France and the United Kingdom offer contrasting examples of "integration regimes".

Fourth, one consequence of the multi-dimensional nature of exclusion is that different professions, agencies and levels of government have to cooperate in administering insertion policies. This can lead to a confusing multiplication of agencies concerned with combating social disadvantage.

Fifth, a territorial approach, with a local focus, offers a possible way of reducing these implementation problems. This focus is also important because local community resources, services and relationships can act to short-circuit processes of social exclusion.

Sixth, initiatives to promote economic and social integration may be counteracted by macro-economic strategies, including fiscal, monetary, trade and labour market policies. Special initiatives based on a social exclusion approach will have limited effectiveness in the absence of significant market-driven employment growth (Silver and Wilkinson, Ch. 17).

In general, the European experience shows that policies to reduce social exclusion can be used for a variety of political purposes and they are not necessarily a panacea. They can distract attention away from a widespread rise in inequality, insecurity and unemployment towards small groups ("the excluded") who are "ghettoized" in risk categories under a new label (Silver, Ch. 3, p. 78).

2. *Policy conclusions of case studies*

The case studies conducted as part of the IILS-UNDP project include a number of preliminary policy conclusions which are derived directly from the application of a social exclusion approach to developing countries and countries in transition. The studies suggest that a social exclusion approach provides new justifications for some long-standing policy proposals which go beyond the dominant orthodoxy about what kinds of development policy can effectively reduce poverty. Moreover, they point towards the need to devise mutually reinforcing policies in different dimensions.

The way that the social exclusion approach leads to different policy conclusions to the current orthodoxy can be illustrated in relation to what Lipton and Maxwell [1992] describe as the "new poverty agenda" — the new conventional wisdom amongst international development agencies about how to reduce poverty in developing countries. In the new agenda, poverty reduction is seen as helping people to achieve a secure and sustainable livelihood. The three essential elements of a poverty reduction strategy at the national level are: (i) promote labour-intensive growth, in order to make use of the poor's most abundant asset (labour); (ii) increase the access of the poor to social services, particularly basic health and full primary education; and (iii) put in place effective welfare safety nets which are targeted at the poorest and most vulnerable to shocks. At the international level, poverty reduction is enhanced through "an appropriate trading environment", more debt-relief for low-income countries, and better targeted aid programmes.

The case studies would agree with (ii), but they question how much this can be achieved through budget prioritization when public expenditure on social services is being cut back. They also go further to suggest some alternative policy proposals to the "new poverty agenda" at the national level.

First, they direct attention to the importance of the redistribution of basic productive assets (a matter on which the new poverty agenda is damagingly shy, according to Lipton and Maxwell), as well as expanding employment opportunities. Land reform and access to credit can be essential to prevent economic disenfranchisement, as well as education and training. Second, they direct attention to the importance of measures to influence the development of social institutions. This encompasses changes in market structures (creating markets), changes in administrative structures and bureaucratic practices, new institutional forms embedded in civil society (such as solidarity banks), and education programmes oriented to change attitudes and cultural values. Markets, States and civil society are all equally seen as part of the problem of social exclusion, as well as part of the solution to it. Third, they draw attention to complex relationships between livelihood and citizenship rights and they suggest that civil and political rights are important in securing and sustaining livelihoods. Fourth, they replace welfarist targeting to catch the casualties of economic restructuring with a participatory and active approach to integrating people in economic life. An important policy for achieving this is the adoption of measures to improve the associational and organizational skills of individuals and groups.

The alternative policy ideas emerging from the social exclusion approach in the case studies are best illustrated in the Peru case which argues that "Policies must be addressed to change the market structure and the initial distribution of assets, which are the factors at the base of the exclusion mechanisms" (Figueroa et al., Ch. 12). Basic markets (labour, credit, and insurance) need to be created or expanded in the entire economy, particularly rural areas (rather than liberalized on the assumption that markets already exist). New economic assets must be redistributed, universal rights and duties secured and cultural values must, through education, be changed. Economic and cultural assets can be redistributed through the promotion of rights. But this is not costless and rights (for example, to education and health) which can increase other assets should have priority.

The policy recommendations contained in the case studies by no means exhaust the possible policy recommendations which can be derived from a social exclusion approach. The studies do not consider global relationships, apart from stressing that adjustment programmes have often had the effect of tearing the social fabric. They do not consider technology policy. There are many complex issues to be explored, such as the relationships between changes in legal rights on paper and the realization of rights, and the economic costs of redistributing assets through affirmative action. Both the Malaysian case [Lim Teck Ghee, forthcoming] and measures to assist Scheduled Castes and Scheduled Tribes in India indicate possibilities and limitations. A major area of analysis will be to explore the potential of a social exclusion approach at a macro-level, understanding the relationships between capital accumulation, the pursuit of productivity improvements through allocative and technical efficiency, and social integration.

IV. Outline of the book

The book is divided into three parts. The first part deals with conceptual issues. Rodgers presents a clear statement of the value of a social exclusion approach. Silver decodes the meaning and deployment of the concept of social exclusion in advanced capitalist democracies in terms of three paradigms of social integration and citizenship, thus providing a map of how to interpret both analyses of social exclusion and policies of social integration. Wolfe, focusing on the situation of developing countries, situates the analysis of social exclusion in relation to processes of globalization. He considers the paradox of a style of development in which increasing numbers of people are being incorporated into wider economic relations under conditions of exploitation and powerlessness, whilst at the same time increasing numbers are also becoming superfluous to the functioning of the global economy. Gore examines how the literature on socio-economic change in Africa south of the Sahara can contribute to the formulation of a concept of social exclusion which is not Eurocentric, and also considers how a social exclusion approach can usefully inform debates about processes of impoverishment on the continent. Faria assesses the Latin American literature on poverty, deprivation and marginalization, and considers what a social exclusion perspective might add.

The second part reports the results of case studies undertaken to explore the potential of the social exclusion approach in developing countries and countries in transition. Five of the studies are synoptic, focusing on patterns and processes of social exclusion in each country; four of the studies examine specific issues in relation to social exclusion in particular countries.

The synoptic country studies include one country in transition (Russia), two newly-industrializing countries (Thailand, Tunisia), and two least developed countries (Tanzania, Yemen). In each of the studies of Russia, Thailand, Tanzania and Yemen, special attention is paid to the macro context of exclusionary processes and the micro-dynamics of exclusion in relation to specific excluded groups and/or specific dimensions of exclusion (land, employment, etc.). The Tunisian study pays more attention to the subjective aspects of exclusion, considering how exclusion is seen by persons who might be identified by researchers and planners as "excluded", and discussing in some detail policies to combat exclusion. The Tunisian study is important as it is an example of how European-type thinking on exclusion and insertion can be translated into policy initiatives in a newly-industrializing economy.

The four issue-oriented country studies consider the relationship between social exclusion and social inequality (Peru), social exclusion and economic restructuring (Mexico), social exclusion and ethnic solidarity (Cameroon), and social exclusion and basic needs deprivation (India). The Peruvian study bears particular attention because it contains theoretical propositions about exclusion from markets, as well as important policy proposals.

Many of the case studies include sections on the policy implications of their analyses. But the third part of the book specifically considers policy issues. Rodgers opens the question of the design of policy to combat exclusion in a variety of country settings, providing a framework for future work. Silver and Wilkinson present a comparative study of integration policies in France and United Kingdom.

Finally, the present introduction, as the reader is aware by now, provides a synthesis of the ideas in the book, situates these ideas in relation to existing literature on analysis of social disadvantage and policy design to reduce it, and indicates what we have learnt from the IILS/UNDP research project, thus far, about the value of a social exclusion approach.

Bibliographical references

Bédoui, M. Forthcoming. *Bibliographie de l'exclusion dans les pays arabes du Maghreb et du Machreq (Afrique du Nord et Moyen-Orient)*. Discussion Paper Series No. 80. Geneva, IILS.

Bhalla, A. S.; Lapeyre, F. 1994. "A note on exclusion". Geneva, IILS, mimeo.

Breman, J. 1994. "Labour nomads in south Gujarat", paper presented at the second workshop of the IILS/UNDP project on "Patterns and causes of social exclusion and the design of policies to promote integration", Cambridge, United Kingdom, 14-18 July.

Cohen, R. 1987. *The new helots: Migrants in the international division of labour*. Avebury.

Crompton, R.; Brown, P. 1994. "Introduction", in Brown, P.; Crompton, R. (eds.): *Economic restructuring and social exclusion*. London, UCL Press.

Dasgupta, P. 1993. *An inquiry into well-being and destitution*. Oxford, Clarendon Press.

Drèze, J.; Sen, A. K. 1989. *Hunger and public action*. Oxford, Clarendon Press.

Esping-Anderson, G. 1990. *The three worlds of welfare capitalism*. Cambridge, Polity Press.

Faria, V. 1994. *Social exclusion in Latin America: An annotated bibliography*. Discussion Paper Series No. 70. Geneva, IILS.

Fitzgerald, E. V. K. 1991. *Economic reform and citizen entitlements in Eastern Europe: Some social implications of structural adjustment in semi-industrial economies*. UNRISD Discussion Paper No. 27, June.

Gore, C. 1993. "Entitlement relations and 'unruly' social practices: A comment on the work of Amartya Sen", in *Journal of Development Studies*, Vol. 29, No. 3, April, pp. 429-460.

—. 1994. *Social exclusion and Africa south of the Sahara*. Discussion Paper Series No. 62. Geneva, IILS.

Haan, A. de; Nayak, P. Forthcoming. *Social exclusion and South Asia* Discussion Paper Series No. 77. Geneva, IILS.

Lim Teck Ghee. Forthcoming. *Effectiveness of policies aimed at the social and economic integration of different ethnic groups in South-east Asia, with special reference to Malaysia: Review of the literature and empirical material*. Discussion Paper Series No. 82. Geneva, IILS.

Lipton, M.; Maxwell, S. 1992. *The new poverty agenda: An overview*. Institute of Development Studies (University of Sussex), Discussion Paper No. 306.

Marshall, T. H.; Bottomore, T. 1992. *Citizenship and social class*. London, Pluto Press.

Parkin, F. 1979. *The Marxist analysis of class: A bourgeois critique*. London, Tavistock.

Room, G. 1992. *Observatory on National Policies to Combat Social Exclusion. Second Annual Report*. Brussels, Directorate General V, Employment, Social Affairs, and Industrial Relations, Commission for European Communities.

Room, G. 1994. "Understanding social exclusion: Lessons from transnational research studies", paper presented at the conference on "Poverty studies in the European Union: Retrospect and prospect", Policy Studies Institute, London, 24 November, mimeo.

Schaffer, B. B.; Lamb, G. 1981. *Can equity be organised?*. Farnborough, Gower.

Sen, A. K. 1992. *Inequality re-examined*. Oxford, Clarendon Press.

Silver, H. 1994. *Social solidarity and social exclusion: Three paradigms*. Discussion Paper Series No. 69. Geneva, IILS.

Touraine, A. 1992. "Inégalités de la société industrielle, exclusion du marché", in Affichard, J.; de Foucauld, J.-B.: *Justice sociale et inégalites*. Paris, Editions Esprit.

Townsend, P. 1993. *The international analysis of poverty*. New York, Harvester Wheatsheaf.

Waltzer, M. 1983. *Spheres of justice*. Oxford, Blackwell.

Yépez, I. 1994. *Review of the French and Belgian literature on social exclusion: A Latin American perspective*. Discussion Paper Series No.71. Geneva, IILS.

Part I: Conceptual issues

2 What is special about a "social exclusion" approach?

Gerry Rodgers[1]

The term "exclusion" has become part of the political vocabulary in Europe. Like "poverty" or "unemployment" it is one of those words which seems to have an everyday meaning, an underlying sense. Social scientists may demand a precise definition but, increasingly, the term is used as if its meaning were self-evident. Social exclusion is seen in the growth of homelessness or urban slums, the declining hopes of the long-term unemployed, the lack of access to jobs and incomes of migrants and some ethnic minorities, the increasingly precarious nature of jobs on offer to new labour market entrants. The European Commission (EC), a major figure in debates on social exclusion and how to overcome it, insists on the diversity of situations, including groups varying from former prisoners to street children, from ethnic minorities to single-parent families, and on the diversity of the social factors concerned: employment, health, housing, education. Many words may be found to express these different problems but the European Commission argues that the notion of social exclusion is particularly appropriate because it describes not just a situation, but also focuses attention on a process which excludes. Excludes who from what? Implicitly, the EC is concerned with the exclusion of groups and individuals from rights, livelihoods and sources of well-being to which all should have access (exclusion of "part of the population from economic and social life and from their share of the general prosperity" [CEC, 1993, p. 7]; "social exclusion refers, in particular, to inability to enjoy social rights without help, suffering from low self-esteem, inadequacy in their capacity to meet their obligations, the risk of long-term relegation to the

---

[1] This chapter regroups parts of a paper published in the IILS Discussion Paper Series prepared by Gerry Rodgers [1994], including contributions by José B. de Figueiredo, Charles Gore, Frédéric Lapeyre and Hilary Silver. But many other project participants, who are undertaking empirical studies in countries around the world, have contributed directly or indirectly to this work.

ranks of those on social benefits, and stigmatization..." [ibid., p. 10]. But the perspective which it proposes, which in turn is grounded in the analysis of major French sociologists such as Alain Touraine [1991], relates such exclusions to the way in which society functions. An individual may be excluded from the labour market, or indeed from a country club, but this is not the point: it is rather that societies and economies systematically marginalize some and integrate others, and distribute rewards in ways which both include and exclude.

Social exclusion, then, is seen as a way of analysing how and why individuals and groups fail to have access to or benefit from the possibilities offered by societies and economies. It is at heart a normative, heavily value-laden notion, evoking negative responses, in contrast to the positive image of inclusion or integration. As such it provides an important justification for social policy, and was used as such by the European Commission under Jacques Delors, even appearing explicitly in the social chapter of the Maastricht Treaty.

In other parts of the world, the concept of social exclusion has not been widely used. But a great deal of attention has been paid, particularly in developing countries, to related issues such as poverty, inequality, entitlements, marginalization or deprivation. Does the concept of social exclusion add anything which cannot be provided by analysis within more conventional frameworks? Might the analysis of social exclusion offer a new way to approach the structural problems of poverty and extreme inequality in developing countries? Or is this simply a relabelling of an old problem?

For the concept to be useful in more than a political sense, first it is necessary to dissect the idea of exclusion and in particular to consider more carefully the question, exclusion from what?

I. The pattern of exclusion

Three types of exclusion in particular appear to be responsible for heightened public awareness in Europe: exclusion from the labour market, reflected in rising numbers of long-term unemployed and increasing difficulty of initial labour market entry; exclusion from regular work, through the growth of precarious and part-time employment relationships; and exclusion from decent housing and community services, reflected in the *banlieue* phenomenon (which also has ethnic or migrant connotations).

In low-income settings, these three types of exclusion are also widely found, but the forms which they take vary. Moreover, there is a need to cast the net more widely, and encompass levels of living, means of livelihood, social rights and broader linkages with the pattern of development. Levels of living are reflected in exclusions from goods and services. Exclusions from livelihood take diverse forms. For some this involves exclusion from land, from other productive assets or from markets for goods. For others, it is labour market exclusions which dominate: unemployment, exclusion from secure jobs or exclusion from social protection in work, exclusion from opportunities to develop skills. These patterns of exclusion are linked to the process of development — if the latter is organized around a small modern or formal production system, development itself will create exclusions at the same time as it creates inclusions.

1. Exclusion from goods and services

Poverty is usually seen in terms of low consumption levels, and measured in relation to a basket of goods and services, including some which may be provided through public channels such as education and health care. In this framework, exclusion from consumption is mainly a result of inadequacy of purchasing power (or of entitlements, in Sen's framework), and one needs to look further back, in the reasons for low purchasing power, to find the principal mechanisms of exclusion. However, some aspects of consumption can be legitimately interpreted directly in terms of exclusion. The visible growth of mass consumption among affluent minorities clearly intensifies the sense of exclusion among other groups even if absolute poverty does not increase. As Wolfe [Ch. 4] expresses it, there is exclusion from the consumer society, from a high-consumption way of life. Housing may also play a direct part in exclusion, as the clustering of the poor in areas without sanitation, good water, recreational facilities, reliable electricity and other services may directly promote exclusion — residence in a particular locality may stigmatize, may lead to poor health, may make community integration difficult. Spatial segregation has become a major concern in the French literature on exclusion, and one can see parallels in the literature on slums in low-income settings.

In general, the expectation is that public goods will be distributed less unequally than other forms of consumption, but many factors also generate exclusion. Exclusion from public goods is often a question of location. Services may also be most readily available to those with the knowledge or the connections to have access to them. In the case of many public goods, ability to pay is also a constraint, especially where opportunity costs of time are concerned — this is particularly true of education; even when universally available in theory, the income sacrifices demanded of the poor are such that their children are more likely to be excluded from schooling.

2. Labour market exclusions

The understanding of many processes of social exclusion comes through the understanding of the mechanisms at play in the labour market. For most households, and especially for the poor, labour earnings are the major source of income. Employment provides social legitimacy as well as access to income. At the opposite extreme, unemployment and casual, insecure jobs lead to rejection from both material and symbolic spheres of society. Open unemployment, persistently high in Western Europe and growing rapidly in many Third World cities, is increasingly becoming a crucial factor excluding young people not only from jobs and incomes but also from social identity. The struggle for the limited resources available becomes intense. While politicians continue to promote solidarity or consociational models, the segmentation of the economic system, and the barriers which are erected to protect sources of livelihood, suggest that the monopoly paradigm (see Silver, Ch. 3) is widely applicable. Exclusion from the labour market may be associated with increasing violence and insecurity, with a growth of marginal and unproductive forms of income generation, with individual anomie and helplessness. Some is visible, as groups of youths while away the day on the streets, but much is hidden within the home — for instance, women who drop out of the labour force and do not appear in the unemployment statistics.

Open unemployment refers to exclusion from the labour market, but there is also exclusion within the labour market. One of the important contributions of research on the segmentation of the labour market has been to show that some groups are trapped in segments where jobs are insecure, ill-paid and low-skilled. The underlying issue here is the dualization process with, on one side, the "bad" jobs with easier access but where poverty is concentrated and, on the other side, the "good" jobs with restricted access and which provide a degree of security and acceptable working conditions. This implies that there are different levels of exclusion, so it is possible to be included in the labour market and at the same time excluded from the "good" labour market. Labour market segmentation tends to be built around readily identified groups (notably on the basis of gender, race and nationality) and so exclusion from livelihood becomes associated with other forms of social exclusion.

3. Exclusion from land

Exclusion from land is a critical issue in many developing countries, and widely associated with poverty and insecurity — but land is a source not only of livelihood but also of social integration in a broader sense. Literature reviews examining the relationship between social exclusion and access to land have shown that this link is strong even in apparently land-abundant settings. One reason is declining availability of productive land to the bulk of the rural population because of land degradation or because of rapidly increasing land concentration in the hands of a few individuals or enterprises. State intervention by no means always leads to less exclusion, for it may involve the ejection of local residents in favour of logging companies or tourist developments. Access to land is usually obtained through discriminatory modes. In much of Africa, for instance, this process may be controlled by particular groups, identified ethnically or demographically (sex and age). In this respect, women are particularly vulnerable to exclusion in that they tend to have not a direct but rather a derivative access to land due, for instance, to their status in the family. Moreover, access to land does not necessarily mean control over the use of land, as there is often an obligation associated with its use, notably for family subsistence purposes.

This aspect of exclusion has been effectively absent from the industrialized country literature on exclusion (except in so far as land for housing is concerned). But the exclusion approach applies forcefully to this domain.

4. Exclusion from security

Security has a number of different dimensions. One is physical — security of the person, in terms of safety, freedom from risk of physical violence. To this might be added freedom from environmental insecurity. A second concerns security of livelihood. A third involves protection against contingencies — accident, ill health, death. This issue, which has been taken up strongly by UNDP in recent years (see, for instance, UNDP [1994]), is one to which the analysis of exclusion can be usefully applied. Insecurity of livelihood is linked to the exclusions from land and labour markets discussed above, but focuses on risk — risk of loss of land or of employment, and the possibilities for finding alternative income sources. In comprehensive social security systems, unemployment insurance or social assistance programmes provide a safety net, but these are rare in low-income countries. Instead, informal sharing mechanisms at the community or family level, sometimes structured as pooled resources in mutual credit funds provide a — usually unsatisfactory — fall-back. Protection against contingencies through social insurance is more widespread, but it is usually those who are least well placed to withstand the contingencies who are least well insured. Appasamy et al. (see Ch. 15) highlight the ways in which inadequacies in social security coverage reflect and lead to exclusion in India (see also Guhan [1994]). They argue that this issue is underemphasized in policy design and that, with appropriate promotional, insurance and social assistance measures, an acceptable degree of security can be attained.

5. *Exclusion from human rights*

A major advantage of the notion of exclusion is that it permits one to consider both rights and welfare within a single framework. The attainment of a living standard adequate for health and well-being in fact forms part of the Universal Declaration of Human Rights but, in practice, inadequate consumption standards are usually analysed in welfare terms. Nevertheless, it makes a great deal of sense to link these two perspectives, for the attainment of particular basic human rights may well be a precondition for overcoming economic exclusion. Thus, the right to freedom of assembly and expression is surely important as a basis for effective mobilization and organization, in turn a precondition for overcoming other forms of exclusion. Where competing interests are at stake in the struggle against exclusion, equality before the law is also a powerful weapon in the hands of the less powerful.

The reverse relationship is also true, as economic and social exclusions affect the attainment of other rights. Extreme need leads to abuse and forces individuals to abandon rights to legal protection or freedom of association. The exclusion of minority groups from full participation in modern economies may render them vulnerable to exploitation and diminish their ability to defend their assets and their civil rights. These exclusions are interdependent with exclusions which are more economic in nature. For instance, the exclusion of populations from land may start with a process aimed at restricting other rights.

On the other hand, it is often argued that premature attainment of certain rights may be inconsistent with economic advance. In particular, workers' rights (to strike, to negotiate collectively) are often restricted in the name of promoting competitivity and growth. This was the case in the Republic of Korea for many years, for example. It was argued there, and continues to be argued in Malaysia and Singapore, for instance, that this is the most efficient long-term route towards social and economic progress

[Mahathir bin Mohamad, 1994]. In all three cases the model is organicist, arguably State corporatist, and worker demands have been channelled through enterprises or subject to central decision-making. Rising wages and employment have apparently made it much easier to obtain the acquiescence of workers in restricting organization and industrial action (though industrial unrest contributed to the overthrow of authoritarian rule in Korea in 1987).

There is a basic question of citizenship here. Yépez [1994] quotes Marshall's [1973] notion that the rights of citizens in modern societies have been progressively extended and consolidated, starting with civil liberties, continuing with democratic participation and finally extending to social rights. This provides a framework for integrating citizenship, rights and welfare; but the content of social rights remains ambiguous. Those which need to be addressed, in order to establish their linkage with other forms of exclusion, include rights to equality before the law, to freedom of organization and expression, to security, dignity and identity.

6. Exclusion and macro-economic development strategy

A central aspect of the analysis of exclusion is the idea that it is embedded in the way societies function. Thus, differences in development paths and in macro-economic and structural adjustment strategies, imply equally varied patterns of social exclusion. Similar aggregate economic growth records may lead to quite different patterns of income inequality, quite different patterns of distribution of the benefits of growth. In this the institutional arrangements which mediate between economic and social development are crucial. They may include or exclude, limit gains to a few sectors or groups or spread advantage widely. Institutionalists within the *régulation* school, such as Robert Boyer [1994], show how a mutually interdependent set of institutional mechanisms underlies any particular growth path, generating the economic incentives for investment and production at the same time as they provide the social underpinnings of growth by setting the terms on which different groups participate in and benefit from development. Such arrangements therefore determine the pattern of both inclusions and exclusions.

An important application of this line of thinking is to the analysis of the social costs of structural adjustment. The retreat of the State and the restructuring of production systems to adapt to a more market- and externally-oriented economy have generated new patterns of inclusion and exclusion, notably in terms of access to social rights, to employment or to the best jobs in the labour market. Analysing the pattern of exclusion as an outcome of the interaction between economic and institutional mechanisms may provide significant contributions to the design of adjustment strategies which are more inclusionary than those in the recent past.

II. Special features of the approach

1. A multi-dimensional, multi-disciplinary view

The notion of exclusion links together both social rights and material deprivations. So it encompasses not only the lack of access to goods and services which underlie poverty and basic needs satisfaction, but also exclusion from security, from justice, from representation and from citizenship. A central idea is that exclusion has much to do with inequality in many dimensions — economic, social, political, cultural. This broad framework not only helps to identify the most important mechanisms and dimensions of exclusion, which vary from one situation to another, but also provides the basis for an effective interdisciplinary approach.

While the different dimensions of exclusion interact they are not necessarily congruent. In other words, individuals and groups may be excluded in some ways and some senses and not in others. Labour in parts of East Asia, for instance, has been described as economically included but politically excluded. In many societies, citizenship has multiple dimensions and individuals participate to differing degrees in these different dimensions. Another implication of the multidimensional approach is that exclusions and inclusions may coincide, indeed may feed on one another. For instance, premature labour market inclusion — child labour, for instance — may be the basis for exclusion from acquisition of skills and self-development. Forced economic inclusion of ethnic minorities may at the same time imply their social exclusion.

2. A focus on process

Social exclusion may describe a state, but its particular advantage, in comparison with most work on poverty, for instance, is that it focuses attention on process. It captures both situations of poverty and deprivation and the mechanisms which lead to them. In this it is important to distinguish two quite different situations: one of permanent exclusion, in which groups live on the margins of society; and one in which exclusion is created and recreated by the operation of social and economic forces, so that individuals move from vulnerability to dependence to marginality, or groups are constantly restructured, subject to deliberate actions to maintain their dependency. The assets over which different individuals and groups have claims determine their ability to resist exclusion — assets extending beyond the economic to include the social, political and cultural.

This perspective is particularly important in understanding the links between deprivation and development. Particular patterns of development have exclusion built into them, in that economic growth is concentrated on particular regions or groups, the gains are captured by national or international elites, the need for cheap and docile labour leads to the suppression of rights, the restructuring of older systems of production and exchange leads to the suppression of institutions for sharing and participation. To understand the persistence of poverty, an understanding of such mechanisms of exclusion is likely to be fundamental.

3. *A focus on social actors and agents*

There are processes which include and exclude, but there are also social actors who both include and exclude. An important aspect of the treatment of social exclusion is to identify these actors, and understand how and why they exclude others. Social groups actively defend their domains against outsiders. The State may play the role of umpire, controlling the exclusion of one group by another, or ensuring that different groups stay in their place and work together. But this positive view of the State can be misleading, for State actions may also lead to the exclusion from services and opportunities of those on whom it is not dependent, or to the forcible inclusion of groups against their will — indigenous groups forced into the market and unable to maintain traditional land rights, or peasants forced into plantation wage labour by taxation or coercion. Other important actors here are enterprises, the military, local authorities, religious bodies and local elites. Enterprises create jobs and incomes and so include some in new economic opportunities, but if their search for competitiveness takes no account of social objectives, they may actively exclude workers from social protection. Academics and international agencies are not innocent, for their work focuses attention and sets priorities.

The same logic implies a stress on the role of the excluded in promoting their own inclusion. Exclusion from effective participation is a dimension of exclusion but, because of the importance of agency, it is also a fulcrum around which other aspects of exclusion turn. Participation here includes issues of organization and representation, political voice, empowerment and more general participation in social interchange.

This perception of agency in exclusion has important implications for the design of policy. Attention turns to the behaviour of the "excluders", and how it may be controlled; and to the ways different groups may organize to promote inclusion. A wide range of actors may be involved in intervention to prevent or reverse exclusion; the State will be one, but not the only one, and perhaps not dominant.

4. An impact at many levels

Exclusion can be understood at several levels: nations, regions, institutions, social groups, individuals, the world as a whole. The question is not one of exclusion within countries alone, for it makes little sense to consider exclusions within national boundaries without considering the greater exclusions beyond them. This is particularly important when we come to policy issues, for a purely national perspective on social exclusion is liable to promote inclusion by either redrawing the mental boundaries around the populations concerned — so that immigrants can be conveniently forgotten or regarded as responsible for their own exclusion — or, in the case of many industrialized countries, by shifting the burdens of exclusion onto populations beyond those boundaries. A transnational view is needed.

Below the international level, exclusion may have a national, regional, group or individual character. Regional exclusion may reflect lack of integration of particular ethnic groups in society, or may reflect the inadequate social and economic infrastructure of areas which have insufficient resources for participation in the mainstream of development and merely constitute a labour reserve.

5. The terms of inclusion

Implicit in most of the foregoing is the idea that inclusion is good, exclusion is bad. But there are many possible forms of integration. The dominant economic models may be rejected by large groups, notably in former colonial settler countries with substantial indigenous populations, who are none the less coerced into inclusion. Inclusion in the labour market is not necessarily to the advantage of groups who are forced out of alternative sources of livelihood. There is a widespread trend for increasing wage labour by women but on terms which are inferior to those of men. Rural-urban migrants may become incorporated in a process of industrial development but with little social protection and a loss of community support networks.

The basic issue is the terms on which inclusion occurs. The notion of exclusion is closely bound up with ideas of inclusion or integration. This by no means simplifies the problem. Integration is as ambiguous as exclusion, for there can be many degrees and facets of inclusion. Inclusion can be voluntary or forced, may involve rights or responsibilities at various levels, above all means entirely different things in different types of society. In other words, thinking about integration means conceptualizing the nature of social relationships, the nature of the society in which integration takes place. It is therefore important to consider how social exclusion occurs and is interpreted in different models of society, as is done by Silver (Ch. 3).

III. Operational value

Ideas are weapons and, like other weapons, their value lies in the use to which they are put. An "exclusion" discourse is possible from many political perspectives. It can be a call for radical restructuring of society, but it can also be a way of rendering major social problems innocuous by breaking them down, so that unemployment becomes not a problem for society as a whole, but a problem for the underskilled, for the handicapped, for migrants and for other specific groups. It may be used to support a return to traditional values of solidarity, just as it may be used to promote the empowerment of groups which have suffered systematic discrimination and deprivation.

But the danger that the notion of social exclusion may be captured by particular ideologies or political groups should not distract attention from its very real advantages for analysis and policy. Some of these advantages have been suggested above. They include a direct focus on the processes which lead to deprivation and disadvantage, rather than a simple description of a problem; a focus on agents of exclusion and inclusion, offering perspectives on the ways in which exclusion may be overcome; and a broad framework which brings together economic, social and cultural aspects of livelihood and rights. The analysis of exclusion points to the linkage between deprivation and injustice on the one hand, and the waste of resources on the other. It also promotes thinking about inequality, not as an abstract, theoretical concept, but in terms of its practical implications for people's lives.

Social exclusion has become a mainstream policy concern in the countries of the North, in Europe at least. In the South, its relevance remains to be established. If the problem is essentially one of widespread absolute poverty associated with low productivity, then addressing the problem of social exclusion is likely to be helpful only in so far as it helps to solve the basic problems of the production system. But if the aim is to create a broad-based process of development which is built upon participatory institutions and a general sharing of the benefits of development, the analysis of social exclusion and how it may be overcome is likely to be important. And beyond the design of policy at the national level, the global problems of inequality in access to livelihoods and to markets are in large measure problems of exclusion.

An important aspect of the approach through social exclusion is that it helps to reconsider the role of the State. In liberal thinking, the ineffectiveness and the negative externalities of active State social policies are highlighted, and policies for economic growth are stressed, in the expectation that growth will increase the welfare of the entire population. The analysis of exclusion, however, shows that there exist mechanisms that exclude many groups from markets and from public goods and services, limiting their access to the benefits of growth. To the withdrawal of the State and reactive policy, we may oppose the possibility of effective proactive social policy based on the understanding of exclusionary mechanisms. Actions on the labour market seem to be crucial, given the socializing function of labour and its ability to provide social legitimacy and social identity as well as income. Such policies require an active role for the State. But, at the same time, the moral authority of the State is bounded; it cannot effectively represent the interests of excluded groups against other groups on which it depends, indeed acts itself as an excluder in some domains. Excluded groups have to be able to formulate their own needs and to integrate them in the process of policy definition. Institutions are required which promote their effective representation and provide them resources, autonomy and influence. One purpose of such institutions would be to build consensus around a "social project" which would determine the social policies to be implemented. Far from an administrative and centralized logic, the new social policies would rely on empowerment and entitlement and assign a key role to civil society.

From the ILO perspective, and perhaps more generally from a perspective which focuses on the relationships between exclusion and poverty, the link between livelihood and rights is the core issue. Exclusions from the labour market, from productive assets, from the capacity to work productively and gain an adequate income are the issues around which other exclusions are structured. And policies for integration in productive and rewarding work, under socially desirable conditions, are likely to constitute the most important elements in the fight against both social and economic exclusion and poverty. But such policies acquire value, indeed become feasible, only if they are linked to the effective achievement and exercise of rights — rights to security, to protection, to identity and full citizenship.

Bibliographical references

Boyer, R. 1994. "Do labour institutions matter for economic development? A 'regulation' approach for the OECD and Latin America, with an extension to Asia", in Rodgers, G. (ed.): *Workers, institutions and economic growth in Asia*. Geneva, IILS.

Commission of the European Communities (CEC). 1993. *Towards a Europe of solidarity: Intensifying the fight against social exclusion, fostering integration*. Brussels.

Guhan, S. 1994. "Social security options for developing countries", in *International Labour Review* (Geneva, ILO), Vol. 133, No. 1.

Mahathir bin Mohamad (Prime Minister of Malaysia). 1994. *Vision of the future of social justice: Essays on the occasion of the ILO's 75th anniversary*. Geneva, International Labour Office.

Marshall, T. H. 1973. *Class, citizenship and social development*. New York, Greenwood Press.

Rodgers, G. 1994. *Overcoming exclusion: Livelihood and rights in economic and social development*. Discussion Paper Series No. 72. Geneva, IILS.

Touraine, A. 1991. "Face à l'exclusion", in *Citoyenneté et urbanité*, ouvrage collectif. Paris, Edition Esprit.

United Nations Development Programme (UNDP). 1994. *Human development report*. New York, Oxford University Press.

Yépez, I. 1994. *Review of the French and Belgian literature on social exclusion: A Latin American perspective* Discussion Paper Series No. 71. Geneva, IILS.

3 Reconceptualizing social disadvantage: Three paradigms of social exclusion

Hilary Silver[1]

All changes coming to a head at this time — technological, economic, demographic, political, ideological — affected the poor to a greater degree than any other class and made their poverty more conspicuous, more controversial, and in a sense less "natural" than it had ever been before... The changes affecting the poor were changes in kind as well as degree, in quantity, in ideas, attitudes, beliefs, perceptions, values. They were changes in what may called the "moral imagination" (Himmelfarb [1984, pp. 18-19], referring to England circa 1760).

Since the mid-1970s, the advanced capitalist democracies have been undergoing a process of profound economic restructuring. As a consequence, new social problems have emerged that appear to challenge the assumptions underlying Western welfare states. While universal social policies still insure against risks predictable from a shared life-cycle, career pattern, and family structure, the standardization of the life course can no longer be assumed. More and more people suffer insecurities, have become dependent upon "residual" means-tested programmes, or are without social protection altogether. In the European Community, 50 million people live below the poverty line of one-half the national median income, and 16 million people, or 10.5 per cent of the workforce, are officially unemployed. Over half the latter have been unemployed for over a year [CEC, 1994].

How are we to understand these changes? A historical perspective shows that earlier economic and social upheavals brought about a shift in

---

[1] This is an abbreviated, revised summary of Silver [1994] in which a complete list of references can be found. The long version of the paper discusses the deep historical context of recent French debates on social exclusion and also examines the application of the three paradigms of social exclusion in studies of citizenship and national identity, race and ethnic relations, and long-term unemployment.

the "moral imagination", and led to the introduction of new concepts. The idea of "poverty" emerged in the Great Transformations associated with industrialization in late-eighteenth century Britain. It was at this time that "the poor" were first set apart from the rest of society. By the end of the nineteenth century, those suffering from economic dislocations came to be distinguished from undeserving "paupers" who rarely, if ever, worked, lived on alms, and lacked direction and self-respect. The notion of "unemployment" first emerged as a political issue in Britain in the 1880s. It was "perceived as a problem distinct from poverty, caused by factors other than moral failings, deserving of public sympathy and remedial action by the state... Much attention was subsequently focused on the need to separate the 'efficient' unemployed, who could and should be helped into the labour market, from the 'unemployables' or 'inefficients' who should be removed from it" [Burnett, 1994, pp. 145-148]. With the rise of Anglo-American "social liberalism," rights to social insurance were legitimated on the basis of contributions made during employment. Unlike means-tested programmes, insurance implied an obligation of the able-bodied to work when economic conditions allowed. Pauperism was slowly restricted to a small segment of the poor unable to work — the "Fourth World", as Père Wresinski called them [Paugam, 1993a]. Since the "poverty" addressed by means-tested benefit programmes came to be regarded as a residual problem, its meaning progressively narrowed to denote an insufficiency of income.

Just as in the past, today's economic and social transformations are giving rise to a shift in the "moral imagination", new conceptions of social disadvantage, and the introduction of new terminology into public debates. In some countries, the new social problems have been taken as symptoms of a growing "underclass". In other contexts, they imply the development of a "new poverty". But, particularly in France, these social transformations are said to reflect "social exclusion".

The discourse of "exclusion" is rapidly diffusing. For example, in 1989, the Council and Ministers of Social Affairs of the European Community passed a resolution to foster integration and a "Europe of Solidarity" by fighting "social exclusion" [CEC, 1993; Room, 1991]. The preamble to the European Community Charter of Fundamental Social Rights also stated: "it is important to combat every form of social exclusion and discrimination, including discrimination on the grounds of race, color, and religion". The European Commission's White Paper, *Growth, competitiveness, employment*, called for fighting exclusion and "the poverty which so degrades men and women and splits society in two". Today, Germany, Denmark, Portugal, Italy, and especially Belgium, as well as France, have introduced new institutions to discuss or act on social exclusion. Even United States President Bill Clinton took up the rhetoric of exclusion in late 1993 when, speaking of inner city problems, he remarked "It's not an underclass any more. It's an outer class".

This paper focuses on what precisely is meant by social exclusion, and what implications the introduction of this new conceptualization of social disadvantage might have for social policy.

I. Defining exclusion: A strategy

The approach of this paper is not to set out a single unambiguous definition of "social exclusion". Existing efforts to do this have only shown that the term seems to be loaded with numerous economic, social, political and cultural connotations and dimensions. One European Community document, for example, conceded that "it is difficult to come up with a simple definition" [CEC, 1993, p. 10]. An EC Poverty 3 Programme debate over the meaning of exclusion also "did not lead to firm conclusions with respect to the concepts but highlighted some relevant aspects". Trying to clarify the concepts underlying exclusion "without sufficient precision as to their meaning" only resulted in "a reading of the implicit indications that may be picked up", listed as the notion's "main ingredients" [Andersen et al., 1994]. Similarly, a recent review of sociological theories of exclusion [Weinberg & Ruano-Borbalan, 1993] concluded:

> Observers in fact only agree on a single point: the impossibility to define the status of "the excluded" by a single and unique criterion. Reading numerous enquiries and reports on exclusion reveals a profound confusion amongst experts.

Even the *Commissariat General au Plan* (CGP) in France, which is responsible for designing and evaluating policies to combat exclusion, has recognized how difficult it is to define the term and to synthesize existing theories. The CGP's Commission on Social Cohesion and the Prevention of Exclusion concluded that:

> Every attempt at typology is necessarily reductive, particularly when it concerns populations which are either excluded or in the process of becoming excluded. The factors causing exclusion — individual, familial, or socio-economic — are multiple, fluctuating, interacting and finally often cumulative.

Despite attempts at official definition:

> In the final analysis the notion of exclusion is saturated with meanings, non-meanings, and counter-meanings; finally one can make almost anything of the term, as it signifies the resentment of those who cannot obtain that which they claim [Freund, in Xiberras, 1993, p. 11].

The term "social exclusion" is so evocative, ambiguous, multidimensional and expansive that it can be defined in many different ways. Yet the difficulty of defining exclusion and the fact that it is interpreted differently in different contexts at different times can be seen as a theoretical opportunity. The discourse of exclusion may serve as a window through which one may view political cultures. From this perspective, the multiple meanings of the term are not problematical, but rather inherent to a concept which is "essentially contested" , in the sense that its proper use "inevitably involves endless disputes" [Gallie, 1956].

Rather than putting forward a single definition of exclusion, this paper offers a way of understanding the disputes surrounding the term "exclusion" and understanding its usage in different contexts. It does so by tracing the history of the idea in France and decoding the multiple meanings of the term in a variety of national contexts in advanced capitalist democracies.

The argument of the paper can be briefly summarized as follows. The multiple meanings of the term firstly reflect the range of empirical referents of the idea of "exclusion". The concept is often conflated with the new poverty and inequality, discrimination and the underclass; and it is associated with a variety of terms like superfluity, irrelevance, marginality, foreignness, alterity, closure, disaffiliation, dispossession, deprivation and destitution. Moreover, the answer to the question "exclusion from what?" can generate multiple responses. Virtually any social distinction or affiliation will exclude somebody. In the United States, for example, the term calls to mind "exclusionary" immigration policy, "exclusionary" zoning, and "exclusionary" social clubs. Consider also just a few of the things the literature says people may be excluded from: a livelihood; secure, permanent employment; earnings; property, credit, or land; housing; minimal or prevailing consumption levels; education, skills, and cultural capital; the welfare state; citizenship and legal equality; democratic participation; public goods; the nation or the dominant race; family and sociability; humanity, respect, fulfilment and understanding.

But, more important than the multiple empirical referents of the term, the uses and meanings of "social exclusion" are embedded in conflicting social science paradigms and political ideologies. This is because at the heart of the question "exclusion from what?" is a more basic one, the "problem of social order" under conditions of profound social change. Just as the great transformations of earlier centuries gave rise to the ideas of poverty and unemployment, and also to the first social scientific accounts of social order to address them, so does the notion of exclusion attempt to address the issue of social inclusion under contemporary conditions of rapid transformation. In this case, theories of "insertion," "integration," "citizenship," or "solidarity" provide a point of reference for understanding different meanings and usages of the term "social exclusion", making it possible to identify different paradigmatic approaches to exclusion.

On the basis of an analysis of the literature on exclusion in Western Europe and the USA, the paper elaborates a threefold typology of the multiple meanings of exclusion which are situated in different theoretical perspectives, political ideologies, and national discourses. Founded on different notions of social integration, I call these types the *solidarity*, *specialization*, and *monopoly* paradigms. These paradigms "specify not only what sorts of entities the universe does contain but also, by implication, those that it does not" [Kuhn, 1970, p. 7]. In effect, they are ontologies that render reality comprehensible and mingle elements of what "is" and what "ought to be". Moreover, when different paradigms are adopted, practitioners speak from "incommensurable viewpoints" and use the same language to mean different things.

Each of the three paradigms attributes exclusion to a different cause, and is grounded in a different political philosophy: republicanism, liberalism, and social democracy (Table 1). Each provides an explanation of multiple forms of social disadvantage — economic, social, political, and cultural — and thus encompasses theories of citizenship and racial-ethnic inequality as well as poverty and long-term unemployment. All three paradigms are cast in relief when contrasted with conservative notions that see social integration in organic, racial, or corporatist terms and with neo-Marxist conceptions of the capitalist social order which deny the possibility of social integration to begin with.

Identifying these paradigms is not simply an academic exercise. Specifying what exclusion means necessarily entails the adoption of particular values and world views. Prior to recasting "social exclusion" as a general phenomenon or a scientific concept transcending national and political contexts, the values underlying its usage should be made explicit. This serves to clarify the implicit objectives of any policies introduced to combat exclusion.

Table 1: Three paradigms of social exclusion

	Solidarity	Specialization	Monopoly
Conception of integration	Group solidarity/ Cultural boundaries	Specialization/ Separate spheres/ Interdependence	Monopoly/ Social closure
Source of integration	Moral integration	Exchange	Citizenship rights
Ideology	Republicanism	Liberalism	Social democracy
Discourse	Exclusion	Discrimination Underclass	New poverty, Inequality, Underclass
Seminal thinkers	Rousseau, Durkheim	Locke, Madison, utilitarians	Marx, Weber, Marshall
Exemplars	de Foucauld Xiberras	Stoleru, Lenoir, Shklar	Dahrendorf, Room, Townsend
	Schnapper Costa-Lascoux	Allport, Pluralism, Chicago School	Balibar, Silverman
	Douglas, Mead	Murray	Gobelot, Bourdieu
Model of the new political economy	Flexible production Regulation School	Skills Work disincentives Networks Social capital	Labour market segmentation

II. The history of "exclusion" discourse in France

The identification of the paradigms of exclusion can appropriately begin with the history of exclusion discourse in France. The term has become a keyword in French discourse on poverty and inequality, and is providing the impetus for new social policies. Some now deem exclusion to be "the principal challenge confronting French society" (*Esprit*, 1991, p. 6).

Exclusion discourse began to appear in France during the 1960s. Politicians, activists, officials, journalists and academics made vague and ideological references to the poor as "the excluded". However, the coining of the term is generally attributed to René Lenoir, who, in 1974 (when he was *Secretaire d'Etat à l'Action Sociale* in the Gaullist Chirac government), estimated that "the excluded" made up one-tenth of the French population: mentally and physically handicapped, suicidal people, aged invalids, abused children, substance abusers, delinquents, single parents, multi-problem households, marginal, asocial persons, and other social "misfits". All were social categories unprotected under social insurance principles at that time.[2] During the 1970s, the French Left also began to distinguish between objective and subjective exclusion. The latter, drawing upon Sartre's existentialism and the participatory ideology of Catholic social action, referred to alienation and the loss of personal autonomy under advanced capitalism. In stressing subjective exclusion, discourse moved away from political expressions of class conflict towards the struggles of mass urban and social movements. Exclusion meant being treated as an object, a condition which could apply to virtually any individual or group.

Exclusion discourse became widespread in the 1980s. As successive social and political crises erupted in France, "exclusion" came to refer to more and more types of social disadvantage. In the early 1980s, the use of the term "insertion" in political discourse shifted from a focus on the handicapped to youth leaving school without adequate skills to obtain a job. By the mid-1980s, both the Right and the communist opposition blamed the socialist government for rising unemployment and what was being called the "new poverty". In symbolic politics, the power to name a social problem has vast implications for the policies considered suitable to

[2] Since the mid-1970s, the government has introduced numerous policies explicitly designed to combat exclusion of this sort, so that today single mothers and the handicapped, for example, tend to fall outside the purview of commissions of integration and exclusion rhetoric.

address it. Thus, in response to the opposition's emphasis on the new poverty and inequality, the socialist government spoke of "exclusion." The term referred not only to the rise in long-term and recurrent unemployment, but also to the growing instability of social relations: family instability, single member households, social isolation, and the decline of class solidarity based on unions, the labour market, and the working class neighbourhood and social networks. It encompassed not only material but spiritual and symbolic aspects. In sum, exclusion became a new way to describe the difficulty of establishing solidarities between individuals and groups and the larger society.

The prototypical definitions of "social exclusion" can be found in the publications of the *Commissariat Général au Plan* (CGP) which has recognized the State's responsibility to nourish "social cohesion". For example, the current *Commissaire au Plan*, Jean-Baptiste de Foucauld, argues that preventing exclusion requires a different conception of social justice than the one underlying the post-war social compromise which simply insured the population against predictable risks [Foucauld, 1992a; b]. The welfare state must bind itself to the ethical and cultural values that make citizenship live not only in the form of rights, but as a particular relation to the other. A more personalized, participatory welfare state should rest on new principles of social cohesion, insertion, sharing and integration [Nasse, 1992]. In another CGP account, exclusion is a metaphor for the social polyphony of post-modern society, a lack of communication or mutual incomprehension of individuals and groups, preventing them from negotiating on common recognition and belonging. The long review of the sociological literature upon which this diagnosis was based [Xiberras, 1993] itself defined exclusion as a progressive rupture of the social and symbolic bonds — economic, institutional, and meaningful — that normally attach each individual to the society. This rupture is seen to entail a risk for each individual in terms of material and symbolic exchange with the larger society and also, adopting Durkheimian rhetoric, a threat to society as a whole in terms of loss of collective values and destruction of the social fabric.

Within this viewpoint, insertion and integration are seen as the appropriate responses to exclusion. This is reflected in the names of a wide variety of new social programmes introduced in France during the 1980s. For example, those who advocated the *revenu minimum d'insertion* (RMI) adopted the Republican rhetoric of "solidarity", "cohesion", "social ties" and, in a Rousseauian sense, a "new social contract". The discourse was so compelling that, by the 1988 presidential campaign, the electoral programmes of both the Right and the Left included a minimum income proposal to promote insertion.

New political crises continued to expand the meanings of exclusion and insertion. The rise of the *Front National* set off a debate over immigration law. The *Front National*'s claims that North African and Moslem immigrants were "unassimilable" provoked the formation of new anti-racist and ethnic movements like *SOS-racism* and *France Plus* which mobilized mass anti-racist demonstrations. Some argued that the Jacobin State was too strong and inflexible to recognize the legitimate solidarities of ethnic groups. One began to hear about a *racism d'exclusion* which provided a rubric under which the anti-racist movement could criticize all kinds of "exclusion" — national, ethnic, cultural, religious, linguistic, sex, social status, and physical appearance. Finally, exclusion encompassed the issue of the *banlieues* (suburban housing estates).

The inter-related rhetoric of immigrant integration, youth problems, and economic exclusion was spatially fixed after a series of violent incidents in suburban housing estates, starting in Les Minguettes in 1981 and peaking in Vaulx-en-Velin, Sartrouville, and Mantes-la-Jolie in 1991. Increasingly, residents of the *banlieues* were described as the excluded. Through ongoing State decentralization and reform of social and housing services, juvenile delinquency policies, the *Développement social des quartiers* (DSQ) programme, and the 1991 creation of a full-fledged *Ministère de la Ville*, the State sought to combat "urban exclusion". Again, programmes were couched in Republican terminology: *prêts locatifs aidés d'insertion*, *fonds de solidarité logement*, and *programme développement-solidarité*", to name but a few.

Much of the rhetoric of exclusion in France is embedded in French Republican thought. But there is a stream of literature which has a social democratic perspective. This school of thought sees the main problems of the *banlieues* as economic exclusion, aggravated by spatial, generational, and political exclusion. In general, for these interpretations, the real problem is not race and ethnicity, but social exploitation in an era when class-based movements and organizations have decisively weakened.

III. Three paradigms: An introduction

Given the embeddedness of the concept of social exclusion in French political rhetoric, and the varied usages of the term even in that single national context, one might rightly wonder whether it is possible to recast "social exclusion" as a general phenomenon or as a scientific concept transcending national and political contexts. The term does not refer just to poverty or inequality or unemployment or citizenship, but also to social status, identity and isolation. Its meaning keeps expanding and yet it is contextually and ideologically embedded. How can social exclusion become an object of social scientific research when it is a value-laden moving target?

This paper clarifies the different meanings and values attached to the term through identifying the major paradigmatic approaches to exclusion, namely "solidarity", "specialization" and "monopoly". These approaches permeate the existing literature on exclusion in Western Europe and North America. National exclusion discourse in France centres on the debate between republicanism and social democracy and hence between the solidarity and monopoly paradigms, though the former is dominant. In Britain the debate is between social democracy and liberalism (the specialization paradigm) while, in the USA, discourse and debate on social exclusion tends to take place within liberal ideological assumptions.

1. *Solidarity*

In French Republican thought, exclusion is the rupture of a social bond (*lien social*) between the individual and society, referred to as social solidarity. Adumbrated by Rousseau and exemplified by Durkheimian sociology, the "social" order is conceived as external, moral and normative, rather than grounded in individual, group or class interests. A national consensus, collective conscience, or general will ties the individual to the larger society through vertically inter-related mediating institutions.

The traditional moral discourse of "social solidarity" rejects Christian charity, liberal individualism, socialist class conflict and strictly political citizenship as sufficient bases of social integration. Rather, it offers a "third way" to reconcile individual rights with State responsibility. Solidarity is less organic than humanist in its reconciliation of social interdependence and the feeling of belonging to the collectivity with the demand for individual fulfilment. In republican ethics, individual citizens are less bearers of rights than participants in a communal "civility", a public life of fraternity. Such moral unity and equality requires incorporating mediating institutions that might compete with the State for citizens' loyalty. The Jacobin State — strong, unitary, centralized, egalitarian, universalist and secular — actively assimilated regional, national, and religious cultures into a single, distinctive conception of citizenship and national civilization. Rather than accepting cultural and political pluralism, separate interests and memberships are reconciled and synthesized into a unitary whole.

Thus, the solidarity approach lays heavy emphasis on the ways in which cultural or moral boundaries between groups socially construct dualistic categories for ordering the world. Exclusion, like deviance or anomie, both threatens and reinforces social cohesion. The inverse of exclusion is thus "integration" and the process of attaining it, "insertion".[3] In a Durkheimian sense, this implies assimilation to the dominant culture. But most recent usages are "post-modernist" in that they incorporate multi-cultural or cultural pluralist notions about the reconfiguration of the basis of solidarity as the dominant culture adjusts to minority culture.

This paradigm draws heavily on anthropology, sociology, ethnography, and cultural studies more generally. It focusses attention on the exclusion inherent in the solidarity of nation, race, ethnicity, locality and other cultural or primordial ties that delimit group boundaries. Yet applications go beyond analyses of Republican citizenship, ethnic conflicts, and deviance to discussions of cultures of poverty and long-term unemployment and of trends toward "flexible specialization" in political economy.

2. Specialization

In Anglo-American liberalism, exclusion is considered a consequence of *specialization*: social differentiation, economic division of labour, and the separation of spheres. It assumes that individuals differ, giving rise to specialization in the market and among social groups. It is thus individualist in method, although causation is situated not simply in individual preference but also in the structures created by cooperating and competing individuals — markets, associations and the like. It thus conceives of the social order, like the economy and politics, as networks of voluntary exchanges between autonomous individuals with their own interests and motivations.

Specialized social structures are comprised of separate, competing, but not necessarily unequal spheres which become interdependent through exchange. Social groups are voluntarily constituted by their members, and shifting alliances among them reflect differentiated interests and desires. Liberal models of citizenship emphasize the contractual exchange of rights

[3] Nasse [1992] maintains that liberal individualist conceptions of society use *insertion* to mean making room beside others or placing side by side, while Durkheimian cultural and normative conceptions use the term *intégration* to mean *assimilation*. However, a content analysis of ten years of the French press found that the term *intégration* was used synonymously with *insertion* and *adaptation* with little reference to who was being integrated to what [see Barou, 1993]. *Insertion* also has multiple meanings.

and obligations and the separation of spheres of social life. Thus, exclusion results from inadequate separation of social spheres, the application of rules inappropriate to a given sphere, or barriers to free movement and exchange across spheres.

Because of the existence of separate social spheres, exclusion may have multiple causes and dimensions. The same individual may not be excluded in every sphere. Nor are social spheres and categories necessarily ordered hierarchically in terms of resources or value. Specialization protects liberties and may be efficient, as long as "excluded" individuals have the right to move across boundaries. Individual freedom of choice based on diverse personal values and psychological motives for engaging in social relations should give rise to cross-cutting group affiliations and loyalties, integrating the society. To the extent that group boundaries impede individual freedom to participate in social exchanges, exclusion is a form of "discrimination". However, the liberal State's protection of individual rights as well as group and market competition impede this form of exclusion.

In social science, liberal individualism is often reflected in methodological individualism which treats group memberships as individual attributes. It underlies neo-classical economics, theories of political pluralism, rational and public choice theories, and "mainstream" sociology. It encompasses two streams of thought: libertarian or "neo-liberalism", and "social" or "communitarian" liberalism.

3. Monopoly

Finally, the third paradigm, influential among the European left, sees exclusion as a consequence of the formation of group *monopoly*. Drawing heavily on Weber and, to a lesser extent, Marx, it views the social order as coercive, imposed through a set of hierarchical power relations. In this social democratic or conflict theory, exclusion entails the interplay of class, status and political power and serves the interests of the included.

This paradigm's fullest expression descends from the work of Max Weber. It treats group boundaries — "status" — as a source of domination potentially independent of social class. Orthodox Marxism privileges class solidarity and denies the potential for true social integration in class-based societies. It aspires to universalism. In contrast, this paradigm assumes that the unequal power underlying more general group monopolies can be mitigated with inclusive "social democratic" citizenship, especially as defined by T. H. Marshall.

Weber's theory of status groups assumes that social action is motivated by "material and ideal interests," by structure and culture, constraint and autonomy. Status groups are a manifestation of power relations; they claim social honour and esteem, and have their own consciousness, consumption patterns, and style of life. Material, legal or other forms of monopoly maintain the status group's exclusivity. Social classes may be status groups to the extent that they can exclude non-owners from competing for valuable resources. However, there is nothing necessary about this process. Indeed, one of Weber's most influential theses is that, if the social closure of *status* groups creates monopoly and thus inequality, it does not follow that social *classes* are always status groups.

Those who do not have to exchange in markets have power over the terms of exchange, i.e. a monopoly. Weber used the term "closure" to refer to a process of subordination whereby one group monopolizes advantages by closing off opportunities to outsiders whom it defines as inferior or ineligible. Any convenient, visible characteristic, such as race, language, social origin, religion, or lack of a particular school diploma, can be used to declare competitors to be outsiders. By restricting access to opportunities and resources, closure allows collectivities to maximize rewards. The group of insiders share a common culture and identity and hence, norms legitimating exclusion.

Weber also recognized that such social closure may cause the excluded to react and resist exclusion. When excluded groups successfully usurp in-group privileges, however, they may redraw boundaries in such a way as to exclude groups even less powerful than themselves, in a process Parkin [1974] calls "dual closure". Indeed, this monopoly paradigm does not assume that a society — however open — can include everyone and everything.

Social "closure" is achieved when institutions and cultural distinctions not only create boundaries that keep others out against their will, but are also used to perpetuate inequality. Those within bounded social entities enjoy a monopoly over scarce resources. The monopoly creates a bond of common interest among otherwise unequal insiders. The excluded are therefore outsiders and dominated at the same time.

The particular boundaries of exclusion may be drawn within or between nation States, localities, firms, or social groups. Processes of social closure are also evident in labour market segmentation. Whatever the nature of the boundary, the overlap or coincidence of group distinctions and inequality is at the heart of the problematic of this paradigm. As Gobelot argued, "every social demarcation is at once a barrier and a level" [Gobelot, 1925/1967]. Paradoxically, every level distinguishes and every distinction levels. The very barrier that demarcates class distinction, however exaggerated and imaginary, also creates equality within class boundaries.

IV. Three paradigms: Some clarifications

Several remarks about these paradigms are in order. *First*, they are, of course, ideal types. In reality, different societies and cultures define belonging in different ways. Moreover, at different times, national debates emphasize some aspects of exclusion and not others:

> Sometimes the emphasis is on migration and refugees (e.g. Belgium, Germany), sometimes on long-term or extremely long-term unemployment and exclusion from the labour market (e.g. Denmark, France, Netherlands); or on the problem. of low income (Portugal). Discussion is sometimes directly linked to specific policy-making, as is the case with the minimum income (France, Spain) or can be part of more general consideration of the functions of the welfare state (United Kingdom: Citizens' Charter) or discouraging the passivity engendered by certain forms of social protection (Denmark, Netherlands, United Kingdom). It is sometimes fuelled by association or media campaigns focusing on particularly visible problems or those which in any case catch the public's attention, such as the homeless (UK, France), drugs (Italy), child labour (Portugal), and inner city crisis (France) [CEC, 1993, p. 32].

Although recognizing the cultural embeddedness of the concept of exclusion makes the development of legitimate cross-national indicators more difficult than measuring poverty or unemployment, the paradigms illuminate the reasons behind the contested and selective meanings of the term. Choosing one definition means accepting the theoretical and ideological "baggage" associated with it.

Second, as is appropriate for a social scientific analysis, each paradigm conceives of exclusion as a social relationship between the included and the excluded. That relationship may certainly be conceived as social action, as the activity of excluding, and thereby, calls attention to the actors responsible. But does exclusion refer only to a change in the condition of those who are at one time integrated, or can it refer to the constant condition of excluded people who want to be included? To the extent that exclusion is viewed as a process, analysts should specify its beginning as well as its end. Similarly, the extent to which differences produce exclusion depends on such issues as the permeability of boundaries, the extent to which membership is freely chosen, and whether social distinctions have any social benefits. Indeed, some marginal or deviant individuals may not even want to be included. Rather than define these issues away, they should be explored.

Third, exclusion can be viewed macro-sociologically or micro-sociologically. Weinberg and Ruano-Borbalan [1993] distinguish between macro and micro causes in contrasting exclusion from "above" and "below". "Top-down" perspectives view exclusion as an employment crisis, or a crisis of ineffective social and immigration policies, or as a crisis of integrative social institutions of the nation more generally. In contrast, local and communitarian "grass-roots" perspectives cast exclusion as a crisis of community solidarity and social regulation. Both macro- and micro-sociological trends may contribute to the process of exclusion.

Fourth, the distinctions among paradigms should not be confused with institutional classifications, like welfare state typologies. Institutions are historical accretions that bear the imprint of past conflicts between ideologies and paradigms. To say, for example, that the French Republic institutionalized Republican ideas implies that, during a particular period of institution-building, a popular coalition was formed around a particular ideological consensus. However, other coalitions contested these ideas and, to the extent that they, too, had influence, the law, the welfare state, and other social institutions embed opponents' ideas as well.

Fifth, all three paradigms must be distinguished from *organic* approaches to social integration. Like those paradigms, organic models are empirical, normative, and methodological; they describe social reality, provide conceptions of what a good society should be, and offer a selective strategy of analysis. Organic models can thus be seen as a further paradigm, or family of paradigms, for analizing social exclusion. However, the solidarity, specialization, and monopoly paradigms of social integration fall within the spectrum of mainstream sociological thought which attributes greater scope and autonomy to civil society relative to the State and market than do other paradigms. Indeed, the discipline of sociology and its central concern with integration arose to provide an alternative explanation of the social changes brought about by the democratic and industrial revolutions than those offered by utilitarian liberalism and socialism, as well as reactionary thought.

However, where democracy and industrialization came late, as in Germany, Italy, Iberia, and many less developed countries, other conceptions of social integration took hold. In some places, traditional conservative, preindustrial, and corporatist notions of integration degenerated into justifications for authoritarianism and fascism. In contrast, Christian democracy and "societal" corporatism, particularly in the postwar era, tempered organicist thought with a recognition of individual rights and tolerance of ideological and religious rivals. Indeed, some analysts classify France in this category, eliding Republican ideology with Christian Democratic or neo-corporatist thought (see, for example, Esping-Andersen [1990]).[4] Finally, some "plural societies" developed a form of stable consociational democracy in which elites compromise and check one another's power on behalf of distinct social segments. These alternative notions of social integration took hold in both European and Third World contexts.

What most distinguishes organic approaches is less their politically conservative or centrist tendencies than their concern to construct a social order based on groups, be they functional, regional, or primordially based. As mentioned, within this broad range of thought there are three streams: Christian Democratic (societal or neo-corporatist); State corporatist; and consociational. Although they differ in the emphasis they accord to individual rights and group autonomy, all reject extreme individualism and collectivism. Rather, they reflect the principles of "community" and "subsidiarity".

Unlike liberalism, Christian Democracy is "personalist" rather than individualist and, unlike socialism, it is "pluralist" rather than collectivist. Similarly, consociationalism, by checking the power of majorities, guarantees groups the autonomy to run their internal affairs within nation States. And corporatism, or organic-statism to use Stepan's [1978] terminology, rests upon official State recognition or "chartering" of mediating associations which are thus centrally coordinated and controlled for the public good, unlike their free, competitive, interest-based operation in liberal pluralism or their suppression under command socialism.

Christian principles of social integration provide a distinctive perspective on the issue of exclusion. On the one hand, the State has the responsibility to ensure personal development and thus, social, political, and civil rights for all. On the other hand, the inequality inherent in

---

[4] In the comparative politics literature, France is usually portrayed as an ideologically and religiously divided polity, lacking the political consensus of the Anglo-American democracies. Based upon its history of reaction and fascist collaboration and its fragmented party and union structures, many assume that the State suffers from democratic immobilism. Based upon the electorate's lack of party loyalty and periodic rebellions against central authority, it is concluded that representatives are not accountable and unresponsive. However, most of these generalizations are based on politics prior to the Fifth Republic and neglect the rise of a "political class," the increasing importance of the central bureaucracy, and expansion of the welfare state.

horizonal pluralism — "sovereignty in one's own circle" — is also justified. Thus, if the pre-capitalist "corporatist-statist legacy" — feudal paternalism, patronage, and clientelism; corporativism of cities, guilds, and friendly societies; and Bismarckian statism — justified the earliest welfare states, it also shaped the tendency of Christian Democratic social policies to preserve differentials between social classes, occupations, and status groups as well as support the traditional family [Esping-Andersen, 1990]. Thus, this viewpoint recognizes the social exclusion of those not organically integrated into the various smaller, autonomous units of society that make up the greater whole — families, communities, classes, nation States, and so on — but is less cognizant of gender and economic inequality as individual expressions of exclusion.

In contrast, Roman law recognized no individual freedom of association. The only legal organizations were those officially recognized by the State on the basis of *lex specialis*, or "privilege" [Stepan, 1978, p. 38]. In this view, the State may legitimately shape the structure of civil society so that functional parts are integrated into an organic whole. In return for a corporate charter, associations also have an obligation to the State to perform a public service. In this, organic-statism differs from republicanism. Indeed, in the second preface to *The division of labour in society*, Durkheim rejected State corporatism because controls on worker and other associations made them part of the official administration, restricted meaningful participation, and precluded moral, rather than coerced integration.

Several weaknesses of organic-statist integration produce what might be called "social exclusion." First, the model provides no clear justifications for recognizing some groups rather than others. For example, the model privileges or "over-franchises" functional groups relative to groups based on primordial, e.g. ethnic, religious, regional, or linguistic identities, which are thus excluded. Second, it is unclear why vertical functional associations, with elite representatives, are privileged over horizontal, decentralized, participatory and membership organizations, like movements and community groups. The latter can be viewed as excluded. Third, if functional groups are indeed granted autonomy, there is little to prevent some groups — particularly those with initial power — from gaining control over others, undermining the presumption of organic harmony. Thus, inequality in civil society can also produce social exclusion. Finally, while the State's concern with the integration of the parts of society can lead to top-down control of functional groupings, undermining their autonomy, dependent States cannot integrate multinational capital within national corporatist structures. This "excludes" workers in the export sector from bargaining rights. These definitions of exclusion differ markedly from the three perspectives under discussion.

Sixth, the solidarity, specialization, and monopoly paradigms address more than one dimension or aspect of exclusion — economic, sociological and interactional, cultural and political — and thus cut across the social sciences. This interdisciplinary approach differs from prior classifications of theories of exclusion which focus on conditions in one country, usually France, or on one discipline, especially sociology. Although each paradigm includes theories drawn from economics, political science, and anthropology, I, too, stress sociological theories because the concepts of exclusion and integration are central to that discipline.

Seventh, even when empirical studies define social exclusion in "global" terms, research tends to be more "sectoral". By focusing on a specific population identified as being "at risk" of exclusion, studies often draw on more than one paradigm. The research literature on exclusion includes studies of the following specific social categories:

(a) the long-term or recurrently unemployed;

(b) those employed in precarious and unskilled jobs, especially older workers, or those unprotected by labour regulations;

(c) the low-paid and the poor;

(d) the landless;

(e) the unskilled, illiterate, and school dropouts;

(f) the mentally and physically handicapped and disabled;

(g) substance abusers;

(h) delinquents, prison inmates and those with criminal records;

(i) single parents;

(j) abused children, those who grew up in problem households or were abused;

(k) youth, especially with no work experience or diploma;

(l) child labourers;

(m) women;

(n) foreigners, refugees and immigrants;

(o) racial, religious, linguistic and ethnic minorities;

(p) the politically disenfranchised;

(q) recipients of social assistance;

(r) those needing, but ineligible for, social assistance;

(s) residents of deteriorated housing or disreputable neighbourhoods;

(t) those with consumption levels below subsistence (the hungry, the homeless, the Fourth World);

(u) those whose consumption, leisure, or other practices (drug or alcohol abuse, delinquency, dress, speech, mannerisms) are stigmatized or labelled as deviant;

(v) the downwardly mobile;

(w) the socially isolated without friends or family.

These absolute and relative social disadvantages may be inter-related. Indeed, the extent to which these dimensions overlap is a frequent subject of research on exclusion [Wuhl, 1992]. Some find very weak *correlations* among the types of exclusion. But others conceive of exclusion as the *accumulation* of such disadvantages, as the last stage in a process of social disqualification [Paugam, 1993b]. For example, those born into particular groups, with a particular upbringing, education, family or work history may in a sense be doubly or triply excluded. However, the disproportionate representation among the "excluded" of people with these social characteristics does not imply that these characteristics *determine* whether any given individual is excluded. One needs to examine the incidence of these attributes in the included population as well. Some individuals with such characteristics do make their way into secure, well-paid employment, stable families, political participation and so on. Depending on turnover, there need be no "hard-core" group of excluded people or families trapped in a "vicious cycle".

V. Conclusion: Exclusion, politics and social policy

In this chapter, I have presented three major paradigms of exclusion, each grounded in a different conception of integration and citizenship. In the solidarity paradigm dominant in France, exclusion is the rupture of a social bond between the individual and society that is cultural and moral, rather than interested in orientation. Cultural boundaries give rise to socially constructed dualistic categories for ordering the world, defining the poor, unemployed and ethnic minorities as deviant outsiders. However, Republican citizenship, by wedding national solidarity to political rights and duties, imposes an obligation on the State to aid in the insertion of the excluded. By posing as a "third way" between liberalism and socialism, the Republican notion of solidarity weds economic to social concerns. Similar emphases can be found in new schools of political economy stressing normative regulation.

In the specialization paradigm, exclusion reflects discrimination. Social differentiation, economic divisions of labour, and the separation of spheres should not produce hierarchically ordered social categories if "excluded" individuals are free to move across boundaries and if spheres of social life governed by different principles are kept legally separate. Cultural pluralism, like political pluralism, rests upon voluntary membership and group competition. Liberal models of citizenship emphasize the contractual exchange of individual rights and obligations and the tensions between the sphere of civil society based on liberty and the public sphere based on equality and democracy. Liberal assumptions are embedded in micro-sociology, with its emphasis on small groups, and in neo-classical economics and other social sciences characterized by methodological individualism.

Finally, the third paradigm sees exclusion as a consequence of the formation of group monopolies. Powerful groups, often with distinctive cultural identities and institutions, restrict the access of outsiders to valued resources through a process of "social closure." The same process is evident in labour market and enterprise segmentation which draws boundaries of exclusion between and within firms. At the heart of this paradigm is the necessary overlap of group distinctions and inequality, "the barrier and the level", to adopt Gobelot's terminology. Inequality is mitigated by social democratic citizenship which, in T.H. Marshall's formulation, entails full participation in the community.

In whatever way they are conceived, the empirical manifestations of rising exclusion in the advanced countries call into question the adequacy of existing welfare state arrangements. Means-tested categorical programmes designed to serve small constituencies are growing rapidly. For more and more people, the assumption underlying post-war social insurance programmes of a uniform life-cycle, career pattern, and family structure no longer applies. The growing types of social disadvantage appear to be "new." Demands to address these newly identified social problems have increased as well.

Moreover, once-quiescent beneficiaries are politicizing under the banner of "demographic identities", forming non-profit groups, and pressuring local governments in areas where they are concentrated. Concerned less with transfers than with unpopular and residual social services (e.g. drug rehabilitation, assistance for refugees or immigrants, urban programmes), this "politics of consumption" introduces distributive conflicts not only between productive and unproductive citizens, but between cultural groups as well. The demand for differentiated services tailored to socially marginal groups also challenges the principle of universalism that once legitimated the post-war welfare states.This crisis in social policy requires a rethinking of the notions of "citizenship" and "solidarity."

While the manifestations of "exclusion" have led to new social policy approaches, especially in France, any large-scale recasting of welfare state institutions will require a broad political consensus. It is useful to recall that the initial establishment of national welfare states was a process of "institutional searching" for political compromise. To achieve such compromise, it was necessary to formulate political ideas that blended pre-existing nation-specific norms and practices. As the paradigms illustrate, such ideas are still reflected in existing welfare state institutions. Today, as new social problems call for major social policy reforms, the importance of new ideas to forge political consensus would appear to be just as important. Does the notion of exclusion offer a new formula to achieve the political compromises necessary to meet these challenges?

As I have indicated, fighting "exclusion" means different things to different people. But only at the extremes of the political spectrum is one likely to find those who are in favor of exclusion. Given the multiple connotations of the term, it might provide a political opportunity to cement a broad-based alliance in favour of new social policies. For example, the importance that French observers attach to distinguishing "exclusion" from other terms denoting social disadvantage suggests that the concept does have political significance. By defining exclusion as a thoroughly new, multidimensional problem touching those at all levels of the social hierarchy in some respects or at some point in their lives, it may become easier to build large, cross-class coalitions to combat it. Most people have suffered from some kind of rejection or misery in their lives, and apprehension about it has become widespread. As the connotations of exclusion expand to encompass the dashing of extravagant aspirations, "each individual will finally consider him- or herself as an excluded person" [Xiberras, 1993].

For example, a widely-reported December 1993 survey by *CSA/La Rue*, a newspaper sold by the homeless, found that 55 per cent of French adults and 69 per cent of 18-24-year-old youth fear they themselves will become "excluded" and three-quarters worried that one of those close to them would be [André, 1994]. That feeling of vulnerability is not confined to France. The Families and Work Institute found that 42 per cent of American workers report their companies are reducing their workforces temporarily or permanently [Gans, 1993]. That near majorities perceive a clear threat of exclusion — in the broad sense of a loss of social status — may account for the term's wide appeal and its increasingly broad application.

Exclusionary discourse also mobilizes opposition. Examples are the outrage provoked by Jean-Marie Le Pen and by the Paris mayor and former Prime Minister Jacques Chirac, who set off a furore after expressing sympathy for the French working-class family who must put up with the "noise and smell" of living next door to an immigrant with three or four wives and 20 children and who receives 50,000 FF a month in social assistance without working.

However, whether public apprehension and indignation will be sufficient to mobilize strong political support for new social policies remains to be seen. For example, during the March 1994 demonstrations against the second minimum wage for those under 25 years old, students debated whether to focus on what a CGC union member called the "Kleenex youth, which one utilizes and throws away", or to extend their goals to fighting the Pasqua immigration laws and to demanding youth programmes for the unskilled. If the common fear of exclusion may cement an alliance among those differentially placed in the social hierarchy, it may not be enough to overcome other social cleavages.

Indeed, to the extent that exclusion is understood in the liberal, individualistic terms of the specialization paradigm, it may become a euphemism for stigmatized, isolated, or scapegoated groups. Its meaning may narrow to those with multiple disadvantages. From a monopoly perspective, the university student protests against declining employment prospects may simply reflect a defence of their traditional prerogatives and a demand for protection from increasing competition. Terms like exclusion, the new poor, or the underclass — by identifying the victims of economic restructuring and the end of full employment — may even justify majority resistance to redistributive taxation and expenditures [Room, 1990]. Targeted social policies will then entail no sacrifice by the privileged, and dualism will be reinforced.

Thus, while the idea of exclusion could be useful to reformers who want to point to the inadequacies of current welfare states, it might conversely serve to distract attention from the general rise in inequality, general unemployment, and family dissolution that is affecting all social classes. By "ghetto-izing" risk categories under a new label and publicizing the more spectacular forms of poverty requiring emergency aid, policies to combat "exclusion" may make it easier to re-target money on smaller social categories like the homeless or long-term unemployed. It may even undermine the universal social insurance programmes that traditionally protected the working and middle classes. To conclude, just as the idea of exclusion has many meanings, it can also serve a variety of political purposes.

Bibliographical references

Andersen, J. et al. 1994. *Contribution of Poverty 3 to the understanding of poverty, exclusion and integration*. Brussels, EEIG, European Commission DG V/E/2.

André, C. 1994. "La France des pauvres", in *Alternatives économiques*, No. 114, February.

Barou, J. 1993. "Les paradoxes de l'intégration: de l'infortune des mots à la vertu des concepts", in *Ethnologie française*, Vol. 23, No. 2, April-June.

Burnett, J. 1994. *Idle hands: The experience of unemployment, 1790-1990*. London, Routledge.

Commission of the European Communities (CEC). 1994. *White Paper: Growth, competitiveness, employment*. Luxembourg.

—. 1993. *Towards a Europe of solidarity: Intensifying the fight against social exclusion, fostering integration*. Brussels, 12 December.

Esping-Andersen, G. 1990. *The three worlds of welfare capitalism*. Oxford, Polity Press.

Foucauld, J.-B. de. 1992a. "Exclusion, inégalités et justice sociale", in *Esprit*, No. 182, June.

—. 1992b. "Vouloir faire, savoir faire", in Affichard, J.; Foucauld, J.-B. de (eds.): *Justice sociale et inégalités* Paris, Editions Esprit.

Gallie, W. B. 1956. "Essentially contested concepts", in *Aristotelian Society Proceedings*, No. 56.

Gans, H. 1993. "From 'underclass' to 'undercaste': Some observations about the future of the post-industrial economy and its major victims", in *International Journal of Urban and Regional Research*, Vol. 17, No. 3.

Gobelot, E. 1925/1967. *La barrière et le niveau: Etude sociologique sur la bourgeoisie française moderne*. Paris, Presses universitaires de France.

Himmelfarb, G. 1984. *The idea of poverty: England in the early industrial age*. New York, Alfred A. Knopf.

Kuhn, T. 1970. *The structure of scientific revolutions*, 2nd edition. Chicago, University of Chicago Press.

Nasse, P. 1992. *Exclus et exclusions: connaître les populations, comprendre les processus*. Paris, Commissariat général au Plan, January.

Parkin, F. 1974. "Strategies of social closure in class formation", in Parkin, F. (ed.): *The social analysis of class structure*. London, Tavistock.

Paugam, S. 1993a. *La disqualification sociale: essai sur la nouvelle pauvreté*. Paris, Presses universitaires de France.

—. 1993b. "La dynamique de la disqualification sociale", in *Sciences humaines*, 28 (mai).

Room, Graham. 1991. *National policies to combat social exclusion. First annual report*. Brussels, Commission of the European Communities, Directorate General V: Employment, Social Affairs and Industrial Relations.

Room, G. 1990. *"New poverty" in the European Community*. London, St. Martin's Press.

Silver, H. 1994. *Social exclusion and social solidarity: Three paradigms*, Discussion paper Series No. 69. Geneva, IILS.

Stepan, A. 1978. *The State and society: Peru in comparative perspective*. Princeton, Princeton University Press.

Weinberg, A.; Ruano-Borbalan, J.-C. 1993. "Comprendre l'exclusion", in *Sciences humaines*, No. 28, May.

Wuhl, S. 1992. *Les exclus face à l'emploi*. Paris, Syros.

Xiberras, M. 1993. *Théories de l'exclusion sociale*. Paris, Méridiens Klincksieck.

4 Globalization and social exclusion: Some paradoxes

Marshall Wolfe

The term "social exclusion" represents a relatively recent way of conceptualizing or at least labelling a range of situations and trends already visible as "problems", or threats to a self-evidently desirable future of "social integration" or "solidarity".[1] (It also harks back to debates of the 1960s in Latin America over "marginality"). As with all such efforts its users must struggle uneasily with their own criteria for "inclusion". Social exclusion can easily become a catch-all for most of the phenomena that seem menacing or ethically intolerable within the globalized capitalist order. As policy prescribers should have learned by now, a changing of labels does not go far toward the curing of social ills. To what extent does the term help to clarify real mutations in human interaction within the present order and in ideological frames of reference for international discourse on "development"? To what extent are the phenomena of social exclusion under way in the industrial or post-industrial societies comparable to those in the so-called "developing" societies?

When the UNRISD Research Programme on Popular Participation in 1979 used the word "excluded" in its working definition of the issues to be explored ("the organized efforts to increase control over resources and regulative institutions, on the part of groups and movements of those hitherto excluded from such control") it hardly had in mind the broader implications now attached to "social exclusion" [Stiefel & Wolfe, 1994]. The groups and movements in question were envisaged as excluded from control over factors affecting their livelihood and their place in society. They were being expelled or lured from previous forms of livelihood and being incorporated under conditions of exploitation, insecurity and impoverishment into ways of life functional to the "development process".

---

[1] The first European Community text to contain the notion of "social exclusion" was a resolution of September 1989. See CEC [1993].

The focus, then, should be on the terms of their incorporation, on their ability to influence these terms through "organized efforts".

It was only in the course of reporting on the field research that the "hitherto excluded" emerged first as a convenient umbrella label for the peasants, proletarians, slum-dwellers, indigenous or "tribal" people and women who were under consideration; and then as a way of conceptualizing an increasingly prominent trait of real processes of economic and social change since the 1970s: exclusion in the sense of superfluity rather than incorporation under conditions of exploitation and powerlessness. Exclusion in the sense of superfluity now seemed to be threatening not only the impoverished rural and urban groups previously labelled "marginal", who were indeed growing more rapidly than ever, but also much of the population that previously participated in "development" with some degree of control over the terms of its incorporation: the industrial labour force and the salaried middle strata. Many kinds of "newly excluded" were joining the "hitherto excluded".

This new face of exclusion did not reduce the relevance of the original focus of the inquiry into participation. "Exclusion" is an active concept like "exploitation". Someone or something bars out or drives out someone or something else, which reacts as best it can. The excluded in some settings may become practically invisible to the power-holders — the "policy-makers" — improvising minimal survival strategies and unable to conceive promising tactics vis-à-vis the social order that excludes them. For the most part, however, there can be no clearcut distinction between struggles over terms of incorporation, that is, against exploitation, and struggles to resist exclusion and open new channels for incorporation. The changing settings generate responses that are in part unprecedented, responding to the globalization of communications and cultural stimuli, in part adaptations of pre-existing organizational forms, and in part resurgences of bases for solidarity that seemed to have dwindled in importance with modernization, the welfare state, and socialism (religious and ethnic ties). Ways of livelihood proliferate that represent unresolved mixtures of dependent functional integration into the dominant style of "development" (sweatshop production, home piecework, street vending), refuge from it through networks of production and exchange among the excluded, and parasitism upon it. Associational ties combine mutual aid, clientelism, clannishness, intimidation, extortion and other worldly hopes.

The most dramatic aspect of the struggle against exclusion at present is the expansion of migration across national frontiers in the face of rising barriers against such migration. Tens of millions of people are enduring hardships and also showing exceptional persistence and ingenuity to escape from perceived exclusion in their countries of origin into situations of exploitation and insecurity in new countries. Many of them eventually achieve satisfactory terms of incorporation and even save the economies of their countries of origin from collapse through their remittances.[2]

The adoption of "social exclusion" as a valid concept through which to view the diverse and contradictory trends now emerging implies a critical but not radically negative assessment of the style of "development" that has come to dominate the world and that since the 1980s has become for some countries a style of disintegration. This style lures and forces the whole of the world's population toward inclusion in a global system of production, consumption, expectations, political and cultural norms, while at the same time barring out the majority in many different ways and degrees and continually changing the rules of the game. At the same time, use of the concept by policy-oriented institutions implies that once governments or other agents turn their attention to social exclusion they can devise remedies that will make the system function for social integration. Remedies that can mitigate certain extremes of exclusion can readily be imagined, but the fundamental paradoxes of the system seem at present to be beyond the understanding or control of any agent, and one might be justified in pinning more hope on the improvisations emerging within societies through the interplay of exclusion and integration.

People who are excluded within one set of norms and expectations can often achieve some kind of inclusion once they accept different norms, generally implying, at least for a time, intensified exploitation and insecurity. That has been happening throughout human history. It may well be, as trends since the 1980s suggest, that within the global system more people are becoming permanently superfluous, irrelevant, or hindrances to its functioning. Under foreseeable conditions of rates of population increase positively correlated with poverty, accelerating environmental degradation, technological innovations divorcing productive capacity from labour needs, and eclipse of the great alternatives for ordering human society in a spirit of social justice, it is hard to see how exclusion can fail to become more pervasive and intractable. The globalized system generates exclusion through its logic as well as through its precariousness. However, historical trends rarely work themselves out in ways foreseeable to observers at a given time. The recent past has been full of surprises and the future will bring its own surprises, for better or worse.

---

[2] The United States Population Fund [1993] estimates 100 million international migrants, including 37 millions fleeing disasters, and US$ 66 thousand millions in remittances to their countries of origin.

A survey of current transformations focusing on exclusion risks over-emphasizing the explanatory power of this concept. It also needs to guard against a propensity to suppose that all bad things go together: that exclusion necessarily generates anomie, anti-social behaviour, resort to the fanatical extremisms that continue to plague humanity. These phenomena, however, seem just as likely to emerge from group competition over the prizes associated with modernization and rising consumption levels, or from defence of traditional power relationships and life styles that are threatened by democratization and changing gender and age-group roles, as from social exclusion.

Let us try to differentiate the main dimensions of exclusion as they interact with each other and with the forces making for incorporation or integration.

I. Exclusion from livelihood

Up to the 1960s, discourse on development commonly singled out as a central problem the "commitment" of people from peasant societies to wage work in industry and other "modern" activities. It was assumed that the demand for wage labour would continue to exceed supply until a late stage of development, and that the supply would be insufficiently committed and of low productivity owing to lack of appropriate work habits, lack of education, poor physical condition and various cultural traits, summed up in one version as absence of "achievement motivation". In the earlier stages of "development" directed by colonial powers or national oligarchies, various forms of compulsion were recommended and applied. At later stages, with substantial urban and plantation wage labour forces already in being, positive inducements came to the fore: education, subsidized food supplies, social welfare and housing schemes linked to industrial employment. In their approaches to recruitment and stabilization of an industrial labour force the "real socialist" States were rather similar to the capitalist "developing" countries.

When it became evident that the supply of people anxious to work for wages was in most settings exceeding demand and that the excess was finding refuge in "marginal" or "informal" occupations it could still be argued that this was a remediable deficiency of the rate or pattern of economic growth, or simply the formation of an "industrial reserve army" functional to such growth.

In much of the world, the processes that in the past generated a labour force for industrialization are continuing and are fulfilling the same function: expulsion from small-holding agriculture and efforts by peasant youth to escape a life of poverty and drudgery. (In Latin America, these processes have receded to secondary importance, as rapid urbanization has reduced the rural population to a static or shrinking minority). To a large extent, the international transfers of productive activity in search of lower labour costs are still providing real openings. In most of East and Southeast Asia, labour absorption is probably still keeping pace with supply, and in the oil-producing States labour shortages are still attracting millions of migrants, who are incorporated in livelihood opportunities while being radically excluded in other dimensions to be discussed below.

Exclusion from livelihood became more clear-cut and extensive during the 1980s in the countries most burdened by debt and forced into structural adjustment policies, mainly in Africa and Latin America. Import-substitution industries collapsed. Mining was hard-hit by falling mineral prices and rising costs. Governments became unable to support the institutions they had acquired, which had long served as the main job sources for university graduates. Inflation reduced the incomes of these latter groups to levels violently excluding them from accustomed life styles, while campaigns of privatization and debureaucratization eliminated the jobs of many, or at least threatened their job security. For workers and salaried middle strata alike, exclusion meant inclusion in a world of precarious survival strategies and blurring of class self-identification.

Comparable, although less traumatic, trends were emerging in the high-income countries, partly through economic slowdown and transfer of some productive activities to lower-cost countries, partly through curtailment of welfare state activities, but more ominously through technological and organizational innovations that were increasingly divorcing production from the need for a large and relatively stable labour force. Traditional heavy industries such as steel and auto production and mining had for some time combined rising production with declining numbers of workers. More recently, computerization began to eliminate some areas of white-collar employment. Industries as well as commercial and financial enterprises increasingly began to hire temporary workers at lower rates of pay, lesser health and social security protection, and no job stability, so as to reduce costs and strengthen flexibility. Exclusion now threatened even corporate executives.[3]

---

[3] According to a recent summing up applying to the United States, "Companies struggling through a weak economy are pushing profits up by pushing employees out. Very few good new jobs are being created to replace the ones that are being lost. All types of workers are affected, from gung-ho men and women at the highest levels of the corporate

Pressures toward exclusion from certain preferred lines of employment derive not only from the creative-destructive logic of capitalism but from overdue public efforts to modify this logic, particularly by curbing environmentally unsustainable industrial and extractive activities and by winding down military forces and armaments production. In the high-income countries, as well as elsewhere, pressures toward exclusion from livelihood combine inextricably with challenges to seek and qualify for new livelihood opportunities that are undoubtedly emerging, with increased exploitation, and with changing tactics for organized self-defence against exclusion and exploitation. In the well-paid technological and cultural specializations that are expanding, arduous educational qualifications are needed, and demands for such specializations may continue to change as unpredictably as they have in the recent past. The services that are least susceptible to rationalization but indispensable to the consumer society continue to offer abundant job opportunities but at wages unacceptable to those displaced from industries and white-collar occupations, as the chorus of complaints at dead-end jobs serving hamburgers indicates.

Meanwhile, migrants find opportunities for inclusion and future prosperity in occupations that the "newly excluded" reject. Women have been able to incorporate themselves into the labour force at all levels, partly through greater independence from traditional family roles, partly through pressure to earn so as to maintain family consumption standards, partly through employer preference for them in the occupations most susceptible to exploitation. While young people have been most acutely affected by exclusion from traditional industrial opportunities, and for some exclusion seems to have become practically total except for illegal and dangerous activities such as drug peddling, others have benefited from education to gain privileged access to the newer and more attractive forms of livelihood.

It would be premature to conclude that exclusion from livelihood is bound to become more radical and pervasive, qualitatively different from the painful adaptations that all societies have experienced since the industrial revolution. However, insecurity over exclusion from culturally defined standards of livelihood is on the rise in most of the world, and this has much to do with the other dimensions of exclusion to be discussed below.

---

hierarchy to kids fresh out of high school and college." ("Looking for work", *New York Times,* 1 August 1993). See also "Service jobs fall as business gains: Automation's impact shrinks employment in New York", *New York Times,* 18 April 1993; and "Temporary workers on the increase in nation's factories", *New York Times,* 6 July 1993.

II. Exclusion from social services, welfare and security networks

Up to the 1980s, popular expectations concerning social rights and services to be guaranteed by the State had been rising over a long period, in poor countries as well as rich. The right to education and basic health services for all; to a social safety net against destitution; to shelter, safe water and waste disposal; and to the satisfaction of various other needs had become internationally accepted responsibilities of the modern State. Now the State's capacity to meet these responsibilities and public confidence in the effectiveness and legitimacy of its efforts to do so have been eroded. In the upper-income capitalist or mixed-economy countries resistance to redistributive taxation and bureaucratic paternalism have mounted, while the diversity of interest groups crusading for different conceptions of rights has become unmanageable. Elsewhere, similar factors have combined with the drying up of external aid and loans, the net outflow of public funds to meet debt obligations, the associated structural adjustment policies, unfavourable export markets and, in some instances, a nearly complete breakdown of the legitimacy and authority of the State.

In the upper-income countries the outcome thus far has been contradictory, with curtailment of some services and continued expansion of others, with some groups of beneficiaries, particularly the aged, holding their own while others, particularly single mothers and their children, have increased in numbers and become paradoxically more dependent on services that seem to confirm their exclusion and generate resentment in other strata of society. The most striking change, particularly in the United States, has been the emergence of significant numbers of families and individuals practically excluded from shelter.

In many of the poorer countries, particularly in Africa and Latin America, and also in the former "real socialist" countries, where State social responsibilities were previously most ambitious, the breakdown in such responsibilities has been more far-reaching. As State ability to finance and administer services and subsidies has dwindled, access to the former has come to depend increasingly on the recipient's ability to pay, in part through privatization and changing of fees for services previously free, in part through illicit but unavoidable payments to functionaries whose salaries have fallen below subsistence levels. Subsidies to urban food supplies (formerly at the expense of peasant producers) and to urban transport fares have dried up. Policies "targeting" public social expenditures to the most needy, as recommended by various international agencies, are in some countries beginning to modify these trends, but in general exclusion of the neediest probably continues to predominate over compensatory targeting.

The state-supported services fashioned on the models of the upper-income countries and aspiring to universality have in practice always had a propensity to "restricted equity". That is, they became enforceable rights for urban minorities (industrial workers, public employees, other categories of white-collar employees and professionals) while rural majorities and the more marginal urban sectors were de facto excluded. (Restricted equity also emerged in the "real socialist" countries, in relation to State and party bureaucracies.) Now access for the former groups has become more restricted, in spite of their efforts to defend acquired rights, partly because of shrinkage of State capacities, partly because of loss of the employment status on which rights were based. The sentiment of exclusion and injustice is very likely stronger among these groups than among those who previously expected little from the State.

Access to the few public services that were really on the way to universalization has been curtailed both by declining coverage and by declining quality. This can be seen most clearly in the case of education, which has been at the same time the most prized means to social integration and mobility and a widely-used device for social differentiation and exclusion. Almost everywhere education has come to absorb very high proportions of public resources. In a good many countries free higher education has become a right even before universal primary education has been achieved. The quality of such higher education was precarious at best, owing to inadequate State financing, sudden "massification", and poor preparation of most students. Now access is being narrowed in various ways, by charging of fees and by inability of the children of the "newly excluded" to meet costs of subsistence while studying. Meanwhile, the rewards expected from such education have diminished with the shrinkage of bureaucratic and other white-collar employment, while openings in the new technological and professional specializations are increasingly restricted to graduates of more prestigious private institutions.

At the other extreme of the educational system, elementary schooling, which had come close to universalization in many countries, at least in quantitative terms of enrolment, has lost ground, with its already poor quality deteriorating further, with miserably paid teachers deserting,[4] and with pupils even more handicapped than before by malnutrition, family insecurity, and obligations to contribute to family livelihood.

[4] In the Philippines, for example, thousands of trained school teachers have left the system to work as maids in Hong Kong, Singapore and elsewhere, for wages several times those offered by the public schools.

For the rural areas that are least promising for modernized commercial agriculture, and in which combinations of self-provisioning peasant farming with migration to earn cash incomes continue to prevail, the withdrawal of State responsibilities is particularly excluding. Such areas have benefited, irregularly and insufficiently, from schools, basic health services, road building, water supplies and other State activities. The activities are in many cases shrinking while capacity for self-provisioning declines with population increases and land deterioration, terms of trade for local produce and handicrafts become more unfavourable, opportunities for migrant labour stagnate, and, in some areas, returning former residents displaced from the cities must be absorbed. Relative neglect of such rural localities is evident even in newly-industrializing countries where the State has remained strong and resources adequate; here there is a natural propensity to concentrate public resources on activities and localities that seem most promising for economic growth.

The people of many of the enormous urban agglomerations of Asia, Latin America and Africa are approaching a kind of environmental exclusion from the possibilities of minimally satisfying life styles at the same time as economic changes are excluding them from previous sources of livelihood. The problems of these agglomerations have been studied over a good many years, with dire prognostications as to their future viability, but at least until recently they have shown remarkable resilience and capacity to continue attracting and absorbing migrants. Public services were inequitably distributed in different urban zones according to power and income, but to some extent they reached even into the peripheral shanty towns. Original and promising forms of community organization emerged, generally combining self-help and self-defence with national or municipal government cooperation.

Now, in many cities, the inadequate infrastructure seems to be reaching a state of terminal decay. Electric power, transport, water supply and waste disposal systems are breaking down together. Violent crime reaches unprecedented levels and is simultaneously combated and abetted by police extortions, torture and summary executions. Air pollution has risen far above the limits supposed to be tolerable. The better-off minorities protect themselves against some of the menaces by living in walled and guarded compounds with their own services, water supply and power generation, but cannot escape the polluted air, the threat of epidemic disease, or the possibility of robbery or kidnapping once they emerge from their strongholds. The proliferation of automobiles has a multiple excluding impact. It forces the authorities to concentrate resources on remodelling the urban space to accommodate them, exacerbates the sense of exclusion of the majority unable to acquire automobiles, and hinders any policy to provide efficient and affordable public transport.

In regard to shelter, the urban authorities have generally abandoned past policies of publicly-financed or subsidized construction, a change that affects mainly the "newly excluded", since the poor practically never had real access to such housing. Programmes to regularize and provide services to the squatter settlements and unregulated land sub-divisions through which the disadvantaged have met their own needs for shelter have continued but have been overwhelmed by the dimensions of the problem and the curtailment of public resources.

As with most other dimensions of exclusion, various forms of exclusion from the amenities previously expected from modern urban life have become ominously visible in many of the great cities of the high-income countries as well as elsewhere. It is evident that the inadequacies of societal efforts to cope with such forms of exclusion are not determined solely by scarcity of public resources and administrative capabilities nor by uncontrollable influxes of impoverished rural migrants. It would be beyond the scope of the present text to comment further on this particularly complex set of issues.

III. Exclusion from the consumer culture

The concept of social exclusion represents, among other things, an attempt at a more operational view of the question of poverty, which has generated such an unassimilable mass of statistical studies, diagnoses, and policy proposals in recent years. For a large part of the world's population, exclusion obviously means destitution, inability to satisfy the most basic needs for food and shelter. For even larger parts, however, exclusion from consumption is a more complicated matter. People throughout the world are now exposed to messages concerning diversified and continually changing norms for consumption. They have internalized such norms to an extent that could hardly have been expected a few decades ago, when the "revolution of rising expectations" became a current cliché, and that is altogether out of keeping with the capacity of the majority to respond. The present felt needs include packaged foods and beverages that are revolutionizing diets and distribution of family expenditures. They include the durable goods that are largely responsible for spreading the consumerist message, first the transistor radio, then television and various electronic devices. They include the automobile, with its devastating effects on the urban environment and its insatiable demand for roads, parking spaces and cheap fuels. They include many artifacts that are reducing household drudgery and making life easier, particularly for women, and that transform the possibilities for family and community interactions from the local to the global.

They provide major stimuli for "popular participation" in innovation and in the quest for more remunerative employment. They have practically negated the possibility of popular acquiescence in styles of development emphasizing austerity and capital accumulation, on the one side, and styles emphasizing satisfaction of narrowly-defined basic needs, social equality and environmental protection, on the other. Under these circumstances, economic liberalization policies have consistently encountered surges in consumer goods imports out-running increases in the exports needed to pay for them. Government-sponsored social pacts calling for shared sacrifices in consumption have been unable to restrain the groups committed by their organizations. This has happened repeatedly in Latin America and most recently in China, where the forces of pent-up consumer demand have pushed aside the egalitarian and collectivist traits previously admired by advocates of "another development", and generated a troublesome trade deficit.

It would be pointless simply to deplore these phenomena or use the negative features as a stick to beat free-market capitalism. For present purposes, the important question is the role of unrealizable consumerist aspirations in exacerbating the frustrations of exclusion from livelihood, exclusion from public services and security nets, and exclusion from meaningful political choice. Although many people are still excluded through isolation, extreme poverty, or cultural resistances, even these forms of exclusion are being penetrated in incongruous ways by elements of the consumer culture, as numerous accounts of present-day village life demonstrate. More commonly, exclusion today generates a determined quest for expedients to enter the consumerist paradise, in its more ostentatious manifestations a paradise for minorities that can exist only as long as the majority is excluded. A Latin American joke divides the population into three groups: those who have credit cards, those who want credit cards, and those who have never heard of credit cards. The middle group is growing and the third dwindling. In some countries the drug traffic has notoriously become the most accessible channel for entry into consumerism.

Since new areas of consumption quickly become cultural necessities and the possibilities for further diversification are unlimited, sentiments of exclusion can be strong at any income level. Majorities in the "rich" countries have achieved levels of consumption that can never be universalized, and that are already entering into contradiction with resource limits and environmental sustainability. However, a few years of relative economic stagnation have generated alarm, not only at immediate job and other insecurities, but also by challenging the conviction that each generation has a right to live better than its predecessor. One result can be a stronger propensity to exclude or ignore the claims of supposed competitors, particularly migrants and ethnic minorities. Similar frustrations and propensities to exclude are more segmented in the "poor" countries, and more likely to bring about violent group conflicts.

IV. Exclusion from political choice

In this area the trends are particularly paradoxical. The previous forms of exclusion from political choice through dictatorships and oligarchies are far from extinct. In a good many countries, even if formal democracy and competing political parties are present at the national level, the experience of most people, especially in the countryside, is of arbitrary rule by local bosses, landowners, military forces and police. In still other countries, the breakdown of central authority and endemic civil war have made the idea of political choice nearly meaningless. At the same time, people in more countries than ever before are able to participate in relatively free elections, have access to varied sources of information and argument, and are able to voice their preoccupations openly. International recognition of pluralist democracy as the only legitimate source of authority of the State has strengthened and manifested itself in support for elections and political rights. The plausibility of infallible leaders or vanguard parties entitled to choose for the people in the name of democracy is at a low ebb.

Under these circumstances, however, realities and sentiments of exclusion from meaningful political choice do not disappear. The well-known oligarchic and bureaucratic traits of mass political parties are as conspicuous as ever, and confidence in their ability to present issues honestly and respond to popular choices is also at a low ebb. The capacity of even the largest and most powerful nation States to decide on and adhere to coherent and autonomous policies has dwindled with the emergence of the globalized economic order, the hegemony of market-oriented anti-State ideologies, and the eclipse of the socialist and populist ideologies that previously offered hope of a better life through political participation. Elsewhere, countries that have not been able to take advantage of the opportunities offered by the globalized economy face the recognition of necessity in the form of structural adjustment policies, with notorious consequences for exclusion and insecurity in their populations.

If the excluded then choose candidates who promise to give priority to their perceived needs, the most likely outcomes, to judge from recent experience, will be either repudiation of the promises immediately after the election, when the "victor" faces up to the constraints set by the world system and the domestic balance of power, or policy voluntarism and incoherence followed by economic crisis. In a few cases, the political leadership has been able to maintain broad support and a degree of economic recovery through coalition-building, convincing explanations of the constraints, and measures alleviating the impact of structural adjustment on the excluded. Elsewhere, the consequences include shifting combinations of political apathy and sullen resentment, extreme shifts in voting patterns to punish incumbents, violent reactions to immediate threats to livelihood and consumption norms, corruption on the part of politicians and administrators who have lost hope of accomplishing anything positive, and diversion of political preoccupations toward scapegoats of ethnic and religious exclusivisms.

V. Exclusion from bases for popular organization and solidarity

Exclusion from meaningful political choice leads back to the question of "organized efforts" for "control" emphasized by the definition of participation quoted above. The "resources and regulative institutions" that the "hitherto excluded" might hope to control, partly through organized intervention in the political process, partly through organized bargaining with employers or produce buyers, and even the forces with which they might have expected to struggle for control, have either been losing relevance or receding to spheres in which popular control based on a rational vision of present needs and future potentialities is hard to imagine.

The organizations and less formal expressions of solidarity through which people have struggled to overcome exclusion are based on: *(a)* their source of livelihood (trade unions, peasant unions, vendors' associations, etc.); *(b)* their consumption and credit needs (cooperatives, credit unions, etc.); *(c)* their relationships to State services or services provided through municipal or voluntary channels (parents' associations, pensioners' associations, etc.); *(d)* their local community or neighbourhood; and *(e)* their religious or ethnic affiliations. In all of these areas, as research has demonstrated, popular innovations in organization and solidarity are ongoing. However, increasing insecurity and instability in the bases for organization test innovativeness to the limit, narrow the benefits that can be hoped for from organization, and exclude large groups altogether. If stable employment in traditional industries declines, trade unions must turn to new clienteles that for many reasons are harder to organize, or give way to localized and precarious groupings in the informal sector. If large numbers of men migrate in search of work their main possibilities for association may be through networks that exploit or even terrorize them in exchange for assistance, while women have to evolve their own forms of collective action in the villages, urban neighbourhoods and sweatshops. Youth, for better or worse, evolve their own ties and goals with few relevant lessons from the organizational experiences of their elders. Religious and ethnic bases for solidarity become more important as other bases weaken.

VI. Exclusion from understanding of what is happening

People from all classes and backgrounds are in a sense excluded from confidence in being able to grasp the implications of the scientific, technological, economic, political, cultural, demographic, environmental and other transformations of the world today, while they confront these transformations in their daily lives and are bombarded by presentations, interpretations and warnings concerning them through television and many other sources, including word-of-mouth rumour. Information becomes more varied and accessible than ever before while the requisites for keeping up with the information revolution become more formidable. According to one formulation, societies are experiencing a transition from social relations organized on the basis of work to social relations based on modes of information [Calderón, 1993; Carnoy et al., 1993]. Inability to use a computer becomes a form of exclusion. Even the best-prepared suffer from what Alvin Toffler some years ago labelled "future shock". For some, this means an unprecedentedly wide range of choices in life styles, gender and age group identifications, and an equally wide range of causes that can be embraced so as to achieve some sense of influencing change and warding off specific menaces. For others, it means an unprecedented range of possible survival strategies, all of them subject to unforeseeable risks. For still others, it offers vicarious satisfactions in the form of exhaustive information on sports events, the private lives of celebrities, etc., to the practical exclusion of more unsettling information.

In the face of future shock and the disintegration of previous expectations, most of humanity adapts as best it can, without becoming traumatized, anomic, or frantic through inability to interpret what is happening. Even in the extreme cases of war-torn societies and mass expulsion of populations, or in the cases of sudden reversal of political systems, eclipsing doctrines that claimed monopoly capacity to explain societal change and also eclipsing the elites that derived power from these claims, some kind of reintegration can be expected to emerge. However, the understandably widening appeal of simplistic, irrationalist, and exclusivist substitutions for participation in the information revolution complicates the picture of exclusion-inclusion that we have been building up.

VII. Policy issues and proposals

For persons of goodwill it might well seem obvious that social exclusion is an intolerable evil, not only in its consequences for the "excluded", but also in its implications for the "included": the permanent threat of being pushed into the ranks of the excluded by incomprehensible and uncontrollable economic and technological transformations; the permanent threat of reactions from the excluded that will become radically incompatible with political and economic stability and personal security. "Social integration" then becomes a tempting slogan for the opposite of exclusion. But how can societies move toward integration and away from exclusion if the globalized capitalist style of "development" cannot help generating exclusion and if the momentum of exclusion has become so great and so complex? Can integration advance without genuine empowerment of the excluded? Can the included welcome or tolerate such empowerment in view of their status strivings, their insecurities, their convictions of restricted equity and the ever-widening gap between consumerist aspirations and capacities to satisfy them? Can national governments and intergovernmental political and financial institutions devise remedies that are more than expressions of good intentions?

As the preceding pages have suggested, the pressures toward integration or incorporation are as strong as pressures toward exclusion and paradoxically intertwined with them. Resolution of the contradictory pressures, within the likely future limits of resources, technologies, population growth, human capacities for rational action and human propensities to irrationality and parochial selfishness, can hardly be more than partial and provisional. Advances in this direction seem to require transformations not only in present economic, political and cultural trends, but also in the ways of thinking about such trends.

Discourse on these questions has long been divided into two main currents, with the ideas in both currents changing and diverging over time.

On the one side is the establishment discourse emphasizing the positive aspects of what is happening, looking to an accessible future of social integration and equity if correct economic policies are followed, if scientific and technological innovations are freed to recognize their full potential, if barriers to trade and investment flows are done away with, if population growth slows down, and if popular majorities come to understand and accept these requisites. At one time this line of discourse favoured State-managed development planning and investment (in capitalist and socialist variants), then exclusive reliance on free markets, and now seems to be turning back to endorsement of State social interventions to correct deficiencies of the market.[5]

The other line of discourse, also with many variants, sees mainly mounting human suffering, alienation and future catastrophe in the trends and policies that the establishment discourse labels "development". Some participants continue to put forward proposals for "another development" on a national or global scale, but have poorer prospects than a few years ago of influencing the centres of power or enlightening and mobilizing the excluded. To a large extent, hopes for plannable transformation have become muted in the face of apparent triumph of a style of development judged humanly disastrous. The following prognosis for Mexico may serve as an example of this frustration: "... perhaps from the new 'common sense' of a freshly constituted democratic political culture new alternatives for egalitarian economic development, as yet impossible to imagine, will also emerge. If we observe in the foreground only the overwhelming power and wealth of the core and the cold logic of capital accumulation in the abstract, the future of Mexico seems dark indeed" [McCaughan, 1993]. The globalization of the processes that generate exclusion and shape the struggles for inclusion have practically ruled out past hopes that some national societies, through "de-linking" from the world system, might find original paths reconciling social integration with sustainable development. It is now evident that past advocacy of such national experiments generally exaggerated achievements and ignored weaknesses that eventually brought them to an end. The few national efforts at de-linking are caught in traps of siege mentality and dogmatism, incurring human costs at least as high as the exclusions and exploitations occurring elsewhere.

Other versions of rejection of globalized capitalist development pin their hopes on the localized and partial de-linkings that persist and re-

[5] The annual *World Development Report* issued by the World Bank constitute the most systematic efforts to elaborate this discourse and at the same time grapple with the real contradictions and inequities associated with "development".

emerge as group survival strategies in many settings.[6] It hardly seems likely, however, that such strategies will become either accessible or acceptable to most of the excluded, who are by now cut off from the cultural roots and values from which cooperative self-limiting life styles would have to grow, or who are striving against all odds for access to modern consumption norms and a political voice. The universalized vision of human nature about to free itself from the aggressions and delusions of "development" is no more convincing as a mobilizing myth than the economic developers' vision of individualistic economic man triumphing over the barriers of tradition.

Can approaches be proposed, at least in very general terms, that recognize the constraints on societal intervention in the paradoxical and poorly understood transformations now under way, that eschew prescriptions wanted neither by the dominant forces nor by most of the excluded, but that point in the direction of social integration? If plausible approaches are at hand, what agents are likely to act on them? Can the dialectical clash of crusaders for development and crusaders for anti-development lead to a synthesis rather than a permanent dialogue of the deaf? The author of a paper such as the present has a certain obligation to end with positive proposals. The following are thrown out in full awareness that they go only a little way toward resolution of the contradictions and that they evade the question left unanswered by innumerable generalized policy proposals: Who listens?

First, a rethinking is overdue of the functions of employment to correspond to the real de-linking between productive capacity and human efforts in some areas, the rising demand for highly skilled and continually evolving technological specializations in others, the proliferation of low-pay and generally low-productivity jobs in still others, and the growth of population residues either excluded altogether from employment or restricted to activities clashing with their cultural and income expectations. In view of the increasing heterogeneity of employment situations, the divorce between work effort and productivity, and the contradictions between what is done for the sake of income and for the sake of individual, family and community needs, the policy goal of "full employment" might well give way to a conception of "meaningful activity for all".

The main functions of employment up to the present can be summed up as follows:

[6] For provocative denunciations of development mythology combined with hopes of this kind, see the contributions to Sachs [1992].

(a) to produce goods and services and perform the social roles valued by the society;

(b) to give individuals and families access to income enabling them to satisfy their needs and wants;

(c) to enable people to enter into relationships with the social order, interpret personal interests in its maintenance or transformation, associate themselves with a class or interest group, and acquire organizational ties;

(d) to enable the individual to meet psychological needs for meaningful activity, self-realization, creativity, and status as family breadwinner.

It hardly needs saying that the ways of livelihood of most people throughout history have combined these functions erratically and contradictorily. In principle, the technological and informational revolutions should mean almost unlimited possibilities for redistributing the ways in which human beings spend their time and for diversifying their choices. In some respects this is happening, in the midst of exclusion, forced improvisation, and choices that the observer might well find deplorable. The gradual shortening of labour time, diversification of work environments, and diversification of leisure activities that seemed socially positive trends a few years ago have been pushed aside as policy goals by globalized economic competition and the widening gap between consumerist aspirations and capabilities. Renewed efforts in these directions seem feasible as well as highly desirable. It might be naïve to expect that such changes will ever lead to ideally harmonious social orders, but if advances can come in regard to other requisites for social integration to be discussed below, the objective of meaningful activity for all might come closer to realization.

Second, the rethinking that is now under way concerning the division of responsibilities between the world system, nation States, local administrations and organizations of the civil society should combine an awareness of the indeterminacy of the future and the imperfections of all human institutions with a striving to strengthen the possibilities for rational political choices and a renewed challenge to the economicist insistence on One Right Way to Develop. This effort must involve many levels of human interaction and participation, but it is more hopeful to seek social integration through changes in the world system than through attempts to withdraw from it, whether at the level of the nation State or the level of the local community.

At the same time, a reaffirmation of the planning and redistributive responsibilities of the State is needed that takes into account the lessons of past policy over-reaching while also confronting the excluding and concentrating traits of the dominant style of "development". Economic and ideological changes throughout the world have left States with fewer carrots and flimsier sticks. State social programmes and regulations, in poor countries as well as rich, have lost a good deal of their legitimacy in the eyes of the public for their inefficiencies, inequities, corruption and bureaucratic paternalism, but their curtailment has contributed to the exclusion of large groups that were beginning to obtain from them some degree of protection and help toward social integration. In many respects, centralized State programmes can be replaced with advantage by decentralized initiatives of municipal authorities and voluntary organizations but this is no more a panacea than past illusions of the welfare state planning to meet all human needs. The poorest localities have least capacity for such initiatives and the most excluded groups have least capacity for representing their interests in municipal administrations or for participating in organizations. The geographical mobility of most peoples today makes ties of local solidarity precarious. The voluntary organizations that try to redress the balance, while they have proliferated and evolved remarkably in recent years, are active in only a small fraction of the localities now forced to meet their own needs as best they can. Any system of decentralization, if it is to contribute to social integration rather than abandonment of the weak, leaves the State with at least two irreplaceable functions: first, it must try to compensate, at least in part, for the enormous differences in the resources that local groups and communities can mobilize for social purposes. Second, it must set and enforce rules of the game for local authorities and voluntary organizations with social purposes, in spite of the obvious dangers inseparable from such a function. Commonly, one of the most serious reasons for the erosion of State legitimacy has been the gap between the overt purposes of State action and the behaviour of its functionaries, generally in alliance with local power holders. In many settings, decentralization might simply shift arbitrary power from State functionaries to self-serving local cliques. Obviously, the State cannot prevent this by regulations and bureaucratic oversight alone, but a combination of realistic regulations, a government genuinely concerned to apply them, and organized popular participation expressing grievances and making demands can constitute a permanently tense but essential condition for progress toward social integration.

The international agencies that have been the main proponent of structural adjustment policies have, as the consequences of State withdrawal of services and subsidies in the midst of economic crises became notorious, turned to recommendations and financial support for renovated State social action. They have urged that the State concentrate what resources it can afford to allocate to social purposes on the poorest population groups rather than continuing to aim at universalization of services. Up to a point, such "targeting" policies might constitute legitimate reversals of "restricted equity" in previous distribution. However, the approach also has negative implications for social integration. The "hitherto included", themselves undergoing traumatic adjustments, would naturally resent and resist the shift. The political viability of targeting would thus be small, unless governments were prepared to mobilize the hitherto excluded, or some of them, to offset the better organized defenders of restricted equity. Another proposal modifying the original insistence on targeting envisages mutually beneficial coalitions between "the poor and certain non-poor groups that have an interest in reform", but such coalitions might lead back to the kinds of clientelistic and populist policies that structural adjustment was intended to bring to an end.[7] In any case, a number of governments (Brazil, Mexico and Peru, for example) have embarked on sizeable programmes targeting the most impoverished groups and designed to compensate for the impact of structural adjustment. The management of such programmes is bound to influence the political dimension of coming struggles over exclusion and integration.

Third, one must grapple with the production and consumption incentives that have dynamized "development" and the contradictions between popular consciousness and the intellectual criticisms of their future viability. This is one of the hardest topics to confront realistically and with full appreciation of the momentum of the processes that are under way. The "right to development", in the sense of the right of all societies to achieve the levels of production and consumption of the present high-income societies, and the right of the peoples of these latter societies to achieve higher levels with each generation, are mirages, with consequences inherently excluding as well as well as environmentally unsustainable. At the same time, there is no prospect of voluntary acceptance of austere egalitarianism and, since China's recent real cultural revolution, no plausible idea as to how a society giving priority to this could function. Consumerism has been paradoxically liberating and integrating as well as excluding and alienating. There may be no accessible alternative to a flight

[7] "Policies that help the poor but impose costs on the non-poor will encounter resistance whether or not they increase national income... Giving the poor a greater say in local and national decision- making would help to restore the balance. But since political power tends to reflect economic power, it is important to design poverty-reducing policies that will be supported, or at least not actively resisted, by the non-poor" [World Bank, 1990].

forward through permanent revolutions in technology, information, and social relationships to consumer societies that generate equivalent satisfactions without unsustainable demands on resources and with an ebbing of competition for conspicuous consumption. Any number of published utopias and dystopias point the way.

Bibliographical references

Commission of the European Communities (CEC). 1993. *Towards a Europe of solidarity: Intensifying the fight against social exclusion, fostering integration*. Brussels, 12 December.

Stiefel, M.; Wolfe, M. 1994. *A voice for the excluded: Popular participation in development*. UNRISD, Zed Books.

Calderón, F. G. 1993. "Pasado y perspectivas del sistema sindical", in *Revista de la CEPAL*, 49, April.

Carnoy, M. et al. 1993. *The new global economy in the information age: Reflections on our changing world*. Pennsylvania State University press, University Park.

McCaughan, E. J. 1993. "Mexico's long crises: Toward new regimes of accumulation and domination", in *Latin American Perspectives*, Sage Publications, 20, 3, Summer.

Sachs, W. (ed.) 1992. *The development dictionary: A guide to knowledge as power*. London, Zed Books.

United States Population Fund. 1993. *State of World Population Report*.

World Bank. 1990. *World development report, 1990*. Washington, DC, Oxford University Press.

5 Social exclusion and social change: Insights in the African literature

Charles Gore[1]

This paper has two aims. The first is to examine how the literature on socio-economic change in Africa south of the Sahara can contribute to the formulation of a concept of social exclusion which is not Eurocentric, but rather capable of yielding analytical and policy insights globally, in a variety of country settings. The second is to consider how the concept of social exclusion can contribute to the analysis of socio-economic change in Africa, particularly processes of impoverishment.

Throughout the discussion, social exclusion will be treated as an analytical concept, rather than a description of an outcome of processes and practices; and the thrust of a social exclusion approach will be broadly defined as seeking to increase understanding of the factors causing individuals and groups to be excluded from the goods, services, rights and activities which, in any given society, form the basis of citizenship. The literature review on which the argument is based includes material from anglophone and francophone Africa, but is strongly biased towards the former. The extensive literature on apartheid South Africa is not covered.

I. Social exclusion in the African literature

In the North American and European literature, interest in social exclusion has grown along with rising rates of unemployment, the dismantling of welfare states, and increasing international migration. In that context, social exclusion refers, in broad terms, to a situation and a process which arises when individuals and groups are unable to achieve full membership in national society, in the sense that they cannot participate in the relationships and practices considered by that society to be customary and constitutive of membership. Social exclusion is seen to be the result of

---

[1] This paper is based on Gore [1994].

poverty and long-term unemployment and, in turn, to reinforce those problems, as social membership provides access to resources to counter those problems. Social exclusion is said to affect, in particular, those subject to the multiple deprivations of gender, ethnicity and age, as well as immigrants. A weak and non-universal system of social rights, and the linkage of those rights to employment, is identified as contributing to social exclusion and, conversely, policy against social exclusion is said to require the provision of social rights for the marginalized.

This perspective has not been incorporated in the literature on current socio-economic trends in Africa.[2] There are scattered references to the emergence of an "underclass". But in a situation where it is estimated that on average in the late 1980s, in good years and bad, one quarter of sub-Saharan Africa's population (about 100 million people) received less than 80 per cent of recommended requirements of daily calorie supply, and where indicative and optimistic scenarios project that between 1985 and 2020, only 22 million new jobs are likely to be created in the modern wage sector, whilst, even with a slow-down in population growth to 2.75 per cent a year, 380 million jobs must be created if unemployment is to stay below 10 per cent [World Bank, 1989, pp. 41 and 72], the value of this concept is unclear. There are also passing references to African States as "an under class of States in the global economic and political system", and to the continent as a globally excluded "underworld". But these labels have more rhetorical force than analytical purchase.

In practice, the dominant analytical concepts which have been used to understand what is happening in Africa have been diametrically opposed to the notion of exclusion from national society and economy. In the immediate post-colonial period, key concepts were national integration and commercial (capitalist) penetration. Some dualist models posited the existence of an excluded sector (traditional, subsistence). But historical research challenged this view effectively and the conventional wisdom which had emerged by the first half of the 1970s was that individuals and communities had been incorporated into the broader economy and society and that what was problematical was their *terms of incorporation*. Since the late 1970s, with spiralling crises, key concepts have been "disengagement" and "withdrawal". People are not suffering from poverty owing to exclusion. Rather they are excluding themselves from the wider economy and society, and from the burdensome and unequal obligations of citizenship, in order to survive.

[2] An exception is Gaidzwana [1993].

Yet, if the notion of citizenship is broadly defined as "social membership" and "participation in public life", rather than simply as a strictly legal relationship between an individual and the national State, it is possible to find a range of literature which is concerned with exclusion from the goods, services, rights and activities which form the basis of citizenship.

Some of this literature focuses on exclusion in relation to national citizenship. Predating the recent interest in social exclusion, there is a small literature which focuses on the "stranger" in pre-colonial, colonial, and post-colonial African society and which examines, in particular, how this concept changed with the creation of the status of "national citizen" at independence. This literature developed in the immediate post-colonial period, and a central concern was to understand the dynamics behind the expulsion of "aliens", African and Asian non-nationals, from a number of newly-independent countries. Also, at about the same time, there developed a literature on the dynamics of incorporation of different ethnic groups, which had been arbitrarily joined together in the territories of colonial States, into nation States. An important analytical concept in this literature was "structural pluralism", which referred to a situation in which individuals were incorporated into a common political structure not on universalist and identical terms as citizens, but in particularistic terms, as members of corporate sections (basically ethnic and racial categories), and unequally. Such analysis posited a society in which an in-group assumed the right to exclude other groups, but the literature did not develop deeply because it did not correspond to the situation of most independent African States, describing more accurately multi-ethnic colonial States, apartheid South Africa, and the very few African States in which State power is in the hands of specific ethnic or ethno-regional communities, notably Burundi and Rwanda.

The main part of the literature focuses not on national citizenship, but rather on the ways in which access to resources is affected by membership of, and status within, groups and networks of various kinds. This literature examines a range of group memberships and social identities in terms of the ways they affect entitlements to a range of resources and social goods. The identities include: ethnicity, gender, livelihood, religion, age, language, place of origin, region, and nation. The resources and social goods examined include: land, labour, wage employment, informal sector employment, credit, inputs, education, health, social security, development projects, administrative positions, political representation, and political power.

The key motors in the literature, in terms of social identities, have been analyses of ethnicity, particularly in relation to the State, and analyses of gender relations and the position of women, particularly in relation to access to land and the control of labour resources. Less important, though significant, foci of attention have been on: pastoralists, hunter-gatherers, migrant workers, "strangers", refugees, internally displaced people, and (of emerging interest) officially designated target groups.

The main thrust of the literature, in terms of resources and social goods, has been on access to, and control of, land resources; and access to State power. The literature on labour markets includes material on ethnic segmentation but in general the literature on rural labour markets is thin and dispersed, whilst that on urban labour markets has been over-focused on the formal-informal dichotomy, though recent work is overcoming this strait-jacket.

II. The value of the African literature for conceptualizing social exclusion

The African literature is very valuable for thinking about social exclusion as a process in a way which is both analytically sophisticated and applicable to a variety of country settings in the world. Four major types of insights can be obtained.

1. The nationality of social exclusion

First, the African literature raises questions about the nationality of social exclusion, that is to say, the significance of the nation State in the institutionalization of exclusionary practices. In Western Europe and North America, the nation State is a primary frame for analysing exclusion, but part of the recent interest in this phenomenon arises because of increasing global interdependence, which is rendering the social contract based on national citizenship rights problematical in various ways. The same global forces are at work in African society, but they are occurring in societies in which rights and obligations defining access to resources and other social goods have not been fully "nationalized", in the sense that the enforcement of legal rights is not fully effective, and a national culture of expectations and norms has not been in existence for a long time.

For example, if one examines access to land resources, customary law is still important and notions of local citizenship affect how social identities regulate access. The nationalization of land has served as a basis for localized appropriation of land and its allocation to a select few. If one examines access to employment, it is apparent that indigenization decrees and alien expulsion orders affect opportunities in labour markets, but the main source of employment outside agriculture is not subject to legal regulation or even surveillance. If one considers the position of women it is apparent that, although statutory law does not formally discriminate against women, customary law, operating in tandem with statutory law, subordinates a woman within the extended traditional family placing her under the permanent guardianship of a male relative and severely restricting her ownership and inheritance of property. With regard to basic social rights, to take education, whose provision is closely related to national socialization, the gross enrolment ratio at the primary school level decreased from 80 to 75 per cent from 1980-87. A major mode of political representation is access to persons in State offices through clientelistic networks. These networks are quite extensive. But, according to one analyst, in the late 1980s, as access to patronage resources increasingly depended on relationships with external agencies and as patronage incentives in the countryside were reduced, rural areas "in such countries as Zaire, Uganda, and Chad" have been subject to "a kind of free-for-all system in which local officials, military men and security spoofs are given a blank check to use their prerogatives (and weapons) as they deem fit" [Lemarchand, 1988, p. 155].

Defining precisely the structure of exclusion in post-colonial Africa is difficult. It must be emphasized strongly that in no sense can it be regarded as "primitive" or "backward". African societies seem to be developing into post-national societies without going through a long period in which a national community has developed. Ethnicity is also important — but not in the way suggested by the dominant media image of Africa as a continent riven by ethnic strife and violence. Ethnic affiliation intertwines with national citizenship in complex ways in Africa, with the former acting as a realm of citizenship in which the morality of new forms of social inequality are tested.[3]

In a situation where rights and obligations are not "nationalized", there are multiple sites of exclusion and inclusion based on membership of a variety of shifting groups, categories and networks. The institutions in which the rules governing exclusionary and inclusionary practices are negotiated include: international regimes (for example, on food aid, refugees, and all aspects of public policy affected by structural adjustment policies); various corporate groups (such as villages) and networks of patron-client relations; and households — as well as national and local states.

---

[3] This view is elaborated in Lonsdale [1992]; Ekeh [1975; 1990].

An important feature of the way these institutions interact in processes of exclusion in Africa is that hegemony has not been achieved in the national framework fixed by the colonizers and maintained after independence. Exclusionary practices are apparent in situations where civil order is maintained but relations between dominant groups are unstable, and also in situations where hegemonic vacancy is manifested in violent civil disorder ("warlordism").

2. *Social identity and rules of entitlement*

The African literature provides various insights into the ways in which social identity is implicated in the rules of entitlement (both legal and non-legal) which govern access to, and exclusion from, resources and other social goods. The most basic insight concerns the two faces of processes of exclusion: access to "goods" (broadly understood), and affiliation to groups. The literature shows how rules of access to resources and social goods depends on rules of admission to groups and networks (rules governing social affiliation, social membership). Moreover, it goes further to examine: (i) ways in which membership and status within various social groups and networks is related to social identity; and (ii) ways in which changes in the economy and polity (including increasing resource scarcity and increasing market relations) affect the content of the rules of membership and rules of resource allocation within groups and networks, and the ways in which identities and rules are negotiated. The literature also indicates the changing significance of poverty and social identity in regulating access to resources and social goods.

These points can be most clearly illustrated through the literature on access to land resources. Analysts have observed, for example, how personal identities are defined and redefined at times when disputes occur to stress various kinds of social affiliation to groups (bounded units whose members are aware of common membership and may act collectively, notably households and villages), networks (based in kinship, friendship, and patron-client ties, which may or may not be local), and categories (persons with a common characteristic, such as gender, age and stage in the life cycle). Power and influence over landholding mean "power to define types of land, types of persons, and the bonds between them" [Shipton & Goheen, 1992, p. 311]. Access to agricultural land is also articulated in a system of tiered access, with different categories of people defined as "primary" and "secondary" claimants. Primary claimants have direct rights to land resources, whilst secondary claimants only have rights to land resources indirectly through primary claimants. With increasing scarcity of land and as farming becomes more profitable, there is a tendency for land to be reserved for primary claimants. There is increasing pressure to buy and sell land, and poverty begins to become more important in determining access to land.

Women are in a particularly bad position. In indigenous systems of land tenure they only gain access to land through household heads. Access is not completely associated with control over resources as the land which they are allocated is supposed to be used to grow food to support the family. Moreover, they are particularly vulnerable when people's access to land becomes more restricted as farming commercializes and populations grow.

With regard to access to labour markets, poverty is more important in affecting patterns of insertion, with educational qualifications permitting access to more remunerative sections of formal employment, and access to finance capital determining access to informal sector opportunities. However, ethnic identities are implicated in processes of exclusion and inclusion. Some analysts have observed how ethnic identities are mobilized as a weapon to ensure dominance in lucrative sections of informal trading, a process in which "who people are" is defined in a mutual relationship with "what they can get". Others have suggested that in the general conditions of extreme poverty, scarcity, insecurity and political uncertainty which prevail in Africa, everyone is engaged in a life-and-death struggle, to survive and if possible accumulate wealth and power, and in this situation the main strategy of the rich and the poor is to "wire" themselves into networks based on family, alliance and friendship. These networks are fluid and very variable. Family bonds and ethnic identity sometimes appear to correlate with these networks. But these ties are "above all instrumental arguments at th service of actors" [Bayart, 1993, p. 217], and part of a wider repertoire of politically legitimate discursive genres.

3. The relationship between exclusionary and inclusionary practices

An important insight in the African literature is the understanding that exclusionary practices are linked to the terms on which people are integrated into an economy and society. A classic example of this is the analysis of the relationships between the exclusion from the land resources by white settlers in colonial Rhodesia, and the increasing supply of labour as options and opportunities for making a reasonable livelihood within peasant agriculture were increasingly narrowed [Arrighi, 1970]. But, more generally, this underpins all analyses of clientelist networks.

Clientelist systems consist of chains and networks of patron-client relations, which typically split into factions as patrons compete for clients in the struggle to control key resources and offices. These systems are paradoxical with regard to their inclusionary/exclusionary nature. They integrate all participants in the network of exchange relations, but this form of inclusion of lower status groups is founded on, and reproduces, their exclusion. Clientelism is rational for the lower status groups in conditions where: (i) key resources, such as land or employment, are controlled by one group; (ii) the organization and cooperative mobilization of the client group to gain access to resources controlled by the patron group is inhibited; and (iii) universalistic criteria for allocating and exchanging resources are replaced by personalistic criteria [Clapham, 1982, p. 8]. The vulnerability and insecurity of individuals consequent on these exclusions creates the desire on the part of clients to seek patrons.

These relationships change over time, as suggested in the discussion of the relationship between social identity and rules of entitlement, and an interesting question is how they have changed with adjustment programmes. One thesis suggests economic stagnation and recession have, by increasing insecurity, strengthened the possibility of regulating clientelistic exchanges, and that the dismantling of public sectors associated with structural adjustment programmes have not condemned regimes in power by drying up patronage resources, but rather restored the position of presidents as "the principal distributor of sinecures" [Bayart, 1993, p. 225].

4. Social exclusion and economic crisis

The literature includes analyses of ways in which practices of exclusion and inclusion have contributed to the economic crisis in Africa, as well as the ways in which the crisis has affected these practices. Three important theses have been made with regard to the former relationship, and the last two are particularly interesting as they posit a link between *inclusionary* practices and economic crisis.

The first, which has been most influential, is Bates' analysis of the politics of agricultural policy, which argued that the immediate interests of the majority of farmers were not properly represented in the era before the structural adjustment programmes [Bates, 1981]. This contributed to economic crisis for, although farmers were politically excluded, they could accentuate or precipitate a fiscal crisis by reducing their marketed outputs of food and cash crops.

The second is based on the observation that many States have sought to govern through a "rule of inclusiveness", building multi-ethnic coalitions which include spokespersons from all major ethnic interests in key decision-making institutions.[4] Whilst these coalitions have served to reduce ethnic conflict they have had negative economic consequence as they have involved the wide distribution of resources. The macro-economic costs, and the loss of micro-economic efficiency associated with the politics of inclusive coalitions, is seen as integral to the genesis of the economic crisis and the legacy of the colonial construction of multi-ethnic States.

The most interesting thesis is that of Berry who argues that agrarian crisis in Africa may have its roots in the fact that surpluses from agricultural production are invested in access rather than increasing production. As she puts it, "Where access to land and other productive resources depends partly on non-market criteria, accumulation of cash and of the fungible assets may not be a sufficient condition for securing access to the means of production. If access depends on social identity, producers will use resources to establish or reaffirm advantageous identities and connections for themselves" [Berry, 1988]. Drawing on data from Nigeria, she suggests that access to productive resources is regulated by a number of social identities based on multiple and overlapping criteria. In these circumstances, "people invest in meanings as well as the means of production — and struggles over meaning are as much part of the process of resource allocation as are struggles over the labour process" [ibid., p.66]. She suggests that labour management and recruitment tends to be inclusive, in the sense that "exploitation operates through the subordination of some people within access-defining groups" [ibid., p.63]. But the inclusive mode of labour management and recruitment tends to promote unproductive patterns of resource use — overemployment, overgrazing, inefficiency, inefficient labour effort, accumulation of claims and clients rather than fixed capital.

In summary, according to Berry, a key current problem is that "many Africans have become locked into multiple channels of access and strategies of resource management which perpetuate low productivity" [Berry, 1989].

This thesis is important in than it affirms the value of a multiple sites perspective on social exclusion in Africa; it points to another aspect of the interplay between social identity, rules of entitlement, and wider economic change; and it cautions against the reflex policy conclusion that inclusion is the solution to the problem of exclusion. In this thesis, the inclusivity of

---

[4] Rothchild and Foley [1988]. For the basis of this in African nationalist thought, see Mazrui [1967].

African society is, on economic grounds, identified as problematical.

Whether the "nationalization" of rights and obligations (through more effective national citizenship) would rectify this situation, by redirecting energies away from investment in channels of access to production itself, is a critical issue. One of the vicious circles in the situation is that the crisis itself has undermined the capacity of the State to deliver civil, political and social rights. But important policy debates are going on, particularly with regard to democracy and land reform (the introduction of individual titles to land).

III. Social exclusion and the analysis of poverty

Whilst the African literature can usefully support the elaboration of an analytically sophisticated and non-Eurocentric concept of social exclusion, a more explicit social exclusion approach can also usefully inform analyses of socio-economic change in Africa, in particular processes of impoverishment. It does so, first, through directing more attention to the relationships between poverty and agency; and second, by providing a framework to draw together separate literatures on access to land, employment, organization and representation, and social services, and to inter-relate them in a way which illuminates trajectories of social change.

1. Poverty and agency

The African literature on access to resources and other social goods is characterized by a major divide. Some authors have focused on the practices by which privileged/powerful groups seek to maximize economic advantages by excluding others from resources and opportunities. Other authors have focused on the situation of marginalized/weak groups, indicating the negative consequences for them of exclusion from resources. In the literature on the informal sector, for example, most analyses are concerned with poverty, survival strategies and ways of increasing productivity and remuneration in marginal jobs. But since the 1980s, another strand of literature has emerged which focuses on informal activities such as smuggling, bribery, theft and speculation which offer major possibilities for capital accumulation for well-connected people.

An important conception of processes of exclusion which is used in the literature on the practices of rich groups is the Weberian notion of social closure, which may be defined as "the process by which social collectivities seek to maximize rewards by restricting access to a limited circle of eligibles" [Parkin, 1979, p. 44]. Model examples of this type of work are the studies of Abner Cohen [1969, 1981]. The literature on marginalized/weak groups tends to see processes of exclusion in terms of constraints on access to key assets, resources, and other social goods. In analyses with an historical perspective, a pattern of social differentiation at a particular point in time may be analysed in terms of paths of upward mobility. Excluded groups are those "left behind", as others improve their position.

An explicit concern with exclusion might serve as a way of bridging this divide and thus linking poverty and agency. Exclusion is not something which "just happens". It is a practice of the more powerful. Moreover, being denied access to particular resources does not completely block any possibility of agency on the part of excluded groups. Rather, exclusion structures their field of action. From this perspective, social exclusion is precisely a practice of the more powerful which structures the possible field of action of the less powerful.[5]

2. *Understanding the poverty transition*

One of the most important analyses of poverty in Africa is the historical analysis of Iliffe [1987]. He argues that "two levels of want have existed in Africa for several centuries" — the poor ("the very large numbers — perhaps most Africans at most times — obliged to struggle continuously to preserve themselves and their dependents from physical want" [ibid., p. 2]), and the very poor or destitute ("smaller numbers who have permanently or temporarily failed in that struggle and have fallen into physical want"). Focusing on the latter group, he notes that with regard to "long-term poverty of individuals due to personal and social circumstances" (structural poverty), the continent is going through a transition. That transition, which has already taken place in Europe and many parts of Asia, is from "land-rich poverty to land-scarce poverty". These are distinguished as follows: "In land-rich societies the very poor are characteristically those who lack access to labour needed to exploit land — both their own labour (perhaps because they are incapacitated, elderly or young) and the labour of others (because they are bereft of family or other support). In land-scarce societies the very poor continue to include such people, but also include those among the able-bodied who lack access to land (or other resources) and are unable to sell their labour-power at a price sufficient to meet their needs [ibid., p. 4].

---

[5] An example of the possibilities of such a synthesis in the African literature can be found in Elliott [1975].

According to Iliffe, southern Africa has, in the second half of the twentieth century, been making the transition from a land-rich to a land-scarce society, and the rest of Africa is likely to do so in the near future.

This notion of a poverty transition is useful from both an analytical and a policy point of view. A social exclusion perspective could elaborate it by providing a framework for synthesizing and inter-relating disparate debates on access to productive land and agricultural inputs, access to remunerative and secure urban jobs, and patterns of organization and political representation.

By putting Iliffe's notion of a poverty transition into a social exclusion framework, it is possible to analyse not simply changes in salience of different dimensions of exclusion (broadly from access and control over land to access to remunerative and secure positions in the labour market), but also: (i) changing inter-relationships between dimensions of exclusion from livelihood; (ii) changes in the relative importance of institutions (such as households, nation States, and international regimes) in regulating patterns of exclusion/inclusion; (iii) changes in the way in which social identities affect exclusion (such as increasing importance of national identities in the working of labour markets); and (iv) changes in the relative importance of, and relationship between, poverty and social identity in regulating access to resources and other social goods. Changes in civil, political, and social rights would be included in the frame of analysis as well, building policy implications directly into the analysis.

The adoption of such a framework is urgent. Although the literature on agricultural land, urban labour markets, political representation, and social rights is disarticulated, increasing interconnections between dimensions of exclusion are apparent, particularly in strategies of making a livelihood which involve "straddling", finding earning opportunities which bridge rural and urban locations, formal and informal activity, and the public and private sector. Access to remunerative off-farm income is a critical factor in determining agricultural incomes. Exclusion from livelihood based on direct agricultural production is a critical factor in determining the supply of labour, and the terms on which people enter labour markets, and access to remunerative positions in labour markets provides a basis for securing access to productive land and the inputs to maintain and increase its productivity.

By refining the thesis of a poverty transition from a social exclusion perspective, it may also be possible to gain a better view of the nature of the current economic crisis in Africa. Broadly, that crisis is defined by a temporal conjunction between a long-term structural trend in which access to remunerative livelihood through direct agricultural production is becoming more and more restricted, and a downturn since the mid-1970s in which access to remunerative livelihood through formal and informal employment is *also* restricted. The downturn is related to trends in the global economy, and may be cyclical in nature. But the politics of scarcity are fostering actions which may exacerbate scarcity. These actions include the adoption of structural adjustment programmes based on misconceptions of the situation.

IV. Conclusion

The African literature offers an important source for elaborating a concept of social exclusion which is analytically sophisticated, of policy relevance, and capable of application in a wide variety of country settings, including those outside the industrialized and post-industrial societies of Europe and North America. A social exclusion framework can also add new dimensions to discussions of socio-economic change in Africa, particularly enhancing understanding of processes of impoverishment. The concept of social exclusion can be advantageous if "social exclusion" is not reified as a new social problem, adding to the catalogue of woes besetting the continent, but rather treated as an analytical approach to understanding existing socio-economic trends and problems.

Bibliographical references

Arrighi, G. 1970. "Labour supplies in historical perspective: A study of the proletarianization of the African peasantry in Rhodesia", in *Journal of Development Studies*, No. 3.

Bates, R. 1981. *Markets and states in tropical Africa: The political basis of agricultural policies*. Berkeley, University of California Press.

Bayart, J. P. 1993. *The State in Africa: The politics of the belly*. London, Longman.

Berry, S. 1988. "Concentration without privatization? Some consequences of changing patterns of rural land control in Africa", in Downs, R. E.; Reyna, S. P.: *Land and society in contemporary society*. Hanover and London, University Press of New England.

—. 1989. "Social institutions and access to resources", in *Africa*, 59, No. 1.

Clapham, C. 1982. "Clientelism and the State", in Clapham, C.: *Private patronage and public power: Political clientalism in the modern State*. London, Frances Pinter.

Cohen, A. 1969. *Custom and politics in urban Africa – A study of Hausa migrants in Yoruba towns*. Berkeley, University of California Press

—. 1981. *The politics of elite culture: Explorations in the dramaturgy of power in a modern African society*. Berkeley, University of California Press.

Ekeh, P. P. 1975. "Colonialism and the two publics in Africa: A theoretical statement", in *Comparative Studies in Society and History*, No. 17.

—. 1990. "Social anthropology and two contrasting uses of tribalism in Africa", in *Comparative Studies in Society and History*, No. 32.

Elliott, C. M. 1975. *Patterns of poverty in the Third World*. New York, Praeger.

Gaidzwana, R. 1993. "Citizenship, nationality, gender and class in Southern Africa", in *Alternatives*, 18.

Gore, C. G. 1994. *Social exclusion in Africa south of the Sahara: A review of the literature* Discussion Paper Series No. 62. Geneva, IILS.

Iliffe, J. 1987. *The African poor: A history*. Cambridge, Cambridge University Press.

Lemarchand, R. 1988. "The State, the parallel economy and the changing structure of patronage systems", in Rothchild, D.; Chazan, N. (eds.): *The precarious balance: State and society in Africa*. Boulder, Westview Press.

Lonsdale, J. 1992. "The moral economy of Mau-Mau: Wealth, poverty and civic virtue in Kikuyu political thought", in Berman, B.; Londsdale, J. (eds.): *Unhappy valley: Conflict in Kenya and Africa. Book II: Violence and ethnicity*. London, James Currey.

Mazrui, A. 1967. *Towards a Pax Africana: A study of ideology and ambition*. London, Weidenfeld & Nicolson.

Parkin, F. 1979. *The Marxist theory of class: A bourgeois critique*. London, Tavistock.

Rothchild, D.; Foley, M. W. 1988. "African States and the politics of inclusive coalitions", in Rothchild, D.; Chazan, N. (eds.): *The precarious balance: State and society in Africa*. Boulder, Westview Press.

Shipton, P.; Goheen, M. 1992. "Understanding African land-holding: Power wealth and meaning", in *Africa*, 62, No. 3.

World Bank. 1989. *Sub-Saharan Africa: From crisis to sustainable growth*. Washington, DC.

6 Social exclusion and Latin American analyses of poverty and deprivation

Vilmar E. Faria[1]

The idea of social exclusion has not been widely used in discussions of Latin American economy and society except as a descriptive term. There is, however, a large literature which examines poverty, inequality, and deprivation. This paper examines the main dimensions of this material in relation to the concept of social exclusion, and considers the main insights which may be derived from the literature for conceptual understanding, theoretical explanation, and policy recommendations concerning social exclusion. It also assesses the usefulness of the concept of social exclusion for furthering understanding of the so-called "social question" in Latin America.

I. Dimensions of the Latin American literature

1. Conceptualization of social exclusion

There is an important literature in Latin American social science which provides a broad theoretical approach for conceptualizing and explaining the dynamics of poverty, deprivation, inequality and social exclusion. This literature grounds the structural processes generating poverty and deprivation upon the peripheral integration of Latin American economies into the world capitalist system. It also offers a critical assessment of the idea of exclusion as "lack of integration". It provides theoretical support to the idea that poverty, deprivation, and exclusion result from the pattern of integration of classes, social groups, families, individuals and regions into the prevailing division of labour. It also supports and contributes to an approach which emphasizes that "poverty

---

[1] This paper is based on a long bibliographic review [Faria, 1994]. Regina M. B. Faria and D. Graber did the research for the bibliography and provided the author with valuable intellectual contributions.

is not a marginal or incidental phenomenon, but is structurally related to the way economic and social systems function" [Infante, 1995].

2. Dimensions of social exclusion

The Latin American literature on poverty has always dealt with lack of access to goods, assets and services, and this work directly addresses the question of *who* is excluded from *what*. Poverty defined as deficiency of income has received far more attention than lack of access to other assets, services and goods. The two main ways of assessing deprivation regarding income have been, on one hand, the so-called "poverty line" approach and, on the other hand, the usual studies on income distribution.

The literature also has frequently estimated deprivation based on the basic needs frame of reference. Starting with the pioneering work by Oscar Altimir [1982], the measurement of deprivation based on the satisfaction of basic needs in conjunction with the poverty line studies have been useful in evaluating the impact of the recent crisis on the impoverishment of lower-middle and upper-lower income groups (sometimes called the "new poor" or the "recent poor"), particularly in some countries such as Argentina, Uruguay and Brazil. Deprivation in terms of lack of adequate access to food has also received some attention. It has been measured either directly, in terms of food intake, or indirectly, in terms of the estimated income necessary to purchase a socially defined minimum basket of food. Recent Brazilian studies coordinated by Peliano [1993] are a good example of the last approach.

3. Main determinants and processes of social exclusion

The literature which addresses the mechanisms and processes which produce, maintain, and reproduce poverty and deprivation includes a variety of viewpoints. Different mechanisms are emphasized by different authors and in different countries. However, four aspects have been strongly emphasized.

First, the existence of poverty and deprivation is related to the rural and agricultural structures prevailing throughout the region and on the transformations taking place in these structures over the decades. Lack of access to land, to technical assistance, to credits and to markets as well as the pattern of land tenure (the *latifundio-minifundio* complex) and labour-saving agricultural modernization have been stressed as causing not only rural poverty but also rural to urban migration and, as a consequence, urban poverty.

Second, poverty is causally connected to employment trends and the structure of urban labour markets, with key issues being employment scarcity, job productivity, lack of protection, instability and vulnerability. More recently, the problems of the growing precariousness of employment and the dualization of the urban labour market have also been discussed in connection with the economic crisis of the 1980s, the resulting adjustment policies and the ongoing process of economic restructuring. In this regard, a large amount of good research has been generated throughout Latin America, but ECLAC (Economic Commission for Latin America and the Caribbean), ILO and PREALC (Regional Employment Programme for Latin America and the Caribbean) should be mentioned as institutions playing a leading role in research as well as in policy recommendations on employment questions.

Third, the literature stresses the fragility of democratic institutions, authoritarianism, the lack of political participation, and the exclusion from the rights of citizenship as main determinants of poverty and exclusion. Finally, some work emphasizes the lack of adequate education as a main determinant of poverty and deprivation.

Analyses discussing the mechanisms behind discrimination against specific social categories and groups based on such factors as ethnicity, race, gender, and migratory status, has been growing recently, particularly regarding gender and race (in Brazil). But the literature is still insufficient.

4. Excluded groups: Size, characteristics and prospects

Particular attention has been paid to the problem of estimating the size, describing the main traits, and assessing the future prospects of specific groups who live in poverty and suffer from discrimination or deprivation. The three main groups studied are: the urban poor; children and adolescents; and urban migrants and squatters.

The urban poor — defined either in terms of income or basic needs — is, by far, the most studied group. The quantitative importance of this group, the availability of good quantitative information (from both censuses and household surveys), the existence of standard and well-tested technical procedures to measure and describe this group, are some of the factors accounting for the prevalence of such studies. There are several good such studies of urban poor households, particularly for the 1980s, when the economic crisis severely hit the Latin American economies. However, similar analyses of the rural poor are, unfortunately, more difficult to find.

The second group receiving close attention is the age group of children and adolescents, in part as a result of the influence of UNICEF.

The age group over 60, which will be growing rapidly in the next decades, has not received adequate attention.

As a consequence of rapid, concentrated urbanization and the resulting housing problems across the region, migrants and squatters are the third highly studied group. In fact, the term "urban marginality" was originally coined to refer to this group and several studies were conducted under this theoretical perspective, particularly during the 1970s and early 1980s.

What is certainly lacking in the literature are good studies of minority groups (such as blacks in Brazil), households headed by women, and the physically handicapped population.

5. Policies to combat social exclusion

The state-led import substitution industrialization model which characterized the growth regime of most Latin American economies from the 1950s until the 1970s entailed an active — even if not very efficient — role for the State in the provision of basic goods and services. In the late 1970s and early 1980s, most of the Latin American social protection welfare systems showed signs of deterioration and even collapse. In addition, the crisis of the 1980s put further pressure upon these faltering systems. As a consequence, the need for reform entered the public agenda.

There is by now a fairly large number of studies on the policies and public services aimed at providing basic goods and services. Topics covered by these studies include: the financing and functioning of existing systems; access to and coverage of health, education, and social security systems; and the distributive impact of these social welfare provisions. There are also several studies dealing with policy recommendations to change the system of social protection, particularly regarding better targeting, non-regressive financing, accountability, decentralization and cost-efficiency, as well as evaluations both of overall changes in the social protection system — as in Chile — and innovative emergency programmes — as in Bolivia and Mexico.

6. Social exclusion, land, and the agrarian question

There is a long tradition of literature dealing with the lack of access to land, but one feature of *recent* work on poverty and deprivation, particularly over the last 15 years, is that only a relatively small fraction of it deals with issues such as agrarian and land reform and rural poverty as a contemporary issue. This apparent neglect of rural poverty is noteworthy in that it is well known that the rural areas of Latin America contain a higher incidence of poverty than the urban centres.

Three reasons could help explain this shortcoming. First, Latin America is by now an urban continent and, in absolute terms, poverty is an increasingly urban phenomenon. Second, the information required to undertake the general estimation and characterization of poverty is more difficult to obtain for the rural area. Furthermore, the measurement strategies under more widespread use — the poverty line and the basic needs approach — are better suited to the estimation of poverty in the urban areas. And finally, for reasons that deserve adequate explanation, the agrarian reform question seems absent from the public agenda.

In any event, it is in the area of rural poverty that more studies should be conducted in the near future if we are to understand social exclusion better. For this reason, it has been identified as a separate dimension of the literature in this review.

II. Main contributions of the Latin American literature

The Latin American literature provides a number of important contributions to the study of poverty, deprivation and inequality which can usefully inform understanding of patterns and processes of social exclusion, and policies against it.

1. Import substitution industrialization, dependency, and economic restructuring with equity

The main and outstanding theoretical contribution of analyses of poverty, deprivation and inequality has been, first, to connect these phenomena to the way "social systems function" and, second, to insist that they are the result of specific *modes of integration*, both of the Latin American economies and societies into a changing world system and of social groups, families, individuals and regions into these national economies. In this regard, the basic concepts providing a theoretical ground for the analysis of poverty and inequality are related, in a variety of ways, to theories of the social division of labour [Faria, 1976].

It is for this reason that, even recently, the idea of exclusion — if interpreted as lack of integration — has not been used very often, except for descriptive purposes. Even those analysts working with the concept of marginality — an important theoretical contribution of the Latin American literature to this question — have criticized the idea of marginality as lack of integration, pointing precisely in the opposite direction and arguing that situations of "urban marginality" correspond to a specific mode of integration into the prevailing social division of labour.

The literature which analytically connects poverty and deprivation to the place of Latin American economies into the international division of labour is founded upon notions of centre-periphery relationships and revolves around the idea of "peripheral capitalism". But over the last 40 years, it is possible to see three distinct and important approaches within this general frame of analysis.

First and foremost, there were the empirical and analytical contributions articulated by and around the work of the Economic Commission for Latin America–ECLA (now also including the Caribbean–ECLAC) in the late 1950s and the 1960s. In a nutshell, widespread poverty in Latin America — mainly rural poverty at that time — was seen as the historical result of the pattern of integration of these economies into the world economy as exporters of primary goods (mining and agricultural goods), the nature of technical progress and its differential incorporation into production structures, the persistent deterioration of the so-called "terms of trade" and of the socio-economic structure stemming from this integration. The hopes for changing this situation of persistent and widespread poverty were put on import substitution industrialization and on the modernization of agriculture. This approach is represented by the work of its leading author, Raul Prebisch [1950]. It was, of course, modified by the course of events, but is still inspiring poverty analyses in some countries and in some research and policy institutions.

By the late 1960s and early 1970s, import substitution industrialization had already progressed far in some Latin American countries (for instance in Argentina, Brazil, and Mexico), whilst in others (for instance, Central America) the recommendations following from the so-called Prebisch-Singer-ECLA approach would have been difficult to apply. In both cases, although urbanization had gained momentum, poverty was still rampant and the political conflict over distribution had led to widespread authoritarianism. In this context, the Latin American social science literature offered a new theoretical approach to ground the analyses of poverty. Relying upon the previous intellectual tradition, different authors contributed to the so-called "dependency approach", which further elaborated on the implications (for growth, income inequality, job generation and the dynamics of the socio-political organization) of the different connections taking place among economic actors, old and new, on both sides of the centre-periphery relationship. The development of capitalism at the periphery of the world system, particularly if accompanied by the further erosion of the democratic tradition in the area, was seen as insufficient to overcome poverty and inequality. Hopes shifted from import substitution capitalist industrialization and modernization of agriculture to one form or another of socialism and democracy. This rather important contribution is represented by two of its leading authors, namely, Fernando H. Cardoso and Enzo Falleto [Cardoso & Faletto, 1970; Cardoso, 1973].

More recently, after the prolonged crisis of the 1980s and as an answer to the proposed hard-line neo-liberal adjustment policies, Latin American economists, social scientists and policy analysts have been generating still another general framework to deal with poverty and inequality questions, namely, the economic restructuring with equity approach. This approach provides a critical assessment of the state-led import substitution experience, analyses the impact of the recent crisis and the adjustment policies on Latin American societies, critically examines the transformations in the productive structures of the region necessary for a competitive integration into the international economy, and discusses a set of policies to face the perverse consequences of these transformations and to promote equity. This theoretical perspective is represented by recent ECLAC [1992] and PREALC [1992] works.

During the last 40 years, most of the contributions of the Latin American literature for the analysis of poverty and for policy recommendations have benefited from these comprehensive theoretical frameworks.

2. *Employment, occupational marginality and informal labour markets*

The second major contribution of the literature to the analysis of poverty which can potentially inform analyses of social exclusion is in the area of employment and labour market studies.

At the core of the comprehensive theoretical frameworks just outlined is the concern with how individuals, households, social groups, and regions participate in the prevailing social division of labour as a determinant of their life chances. Therefore, the employment question has been strategic to the understanding of poverty and thereby social exclusion over decades.

From the late 1950s until the early 1970s, with the population growing at very high rates, urbanization rates skyrocketing, and profound changes occurring in rural and urban productive structures, Latin American scholars turned their attention to the capacity of the modern urban industrial activities to provide adequate employment to the increasingly growing urban labour force. A large amount of work revolved around the concept of "urban marginality". The theoretical controversy over this issue within the Latin American intellectual tradition generated useful results for the understanding of urban labour markets at the periphery of world capitalism and for the discussion of social exclusion.

Two of these results deserve mention. First, critical evaluation pointed to the shortcomings of the approach which stressed a supposed *dualism* of Latin American labour markets by showing how the expansion of informal, service occupations with low productivity were connected to the expansion of the "modern" sector. Second, the idea that "marginality" should be understood as lack of integration of traditional migrants into the value orientations and behaviour patterns of the modern, urban society (which is found in the so-called culture of poverty approach) has also been severely criticized and undermined.

During the 1980s, under the intellectual influence of PREALC, attention turned again to the employment generation problem resulting, first, from the economic crisis, then from the adjustment policies implemented to face the crisis and, finally, from the economic restructuring taking place in the region as a result of new patterns of dynamic integration into the world economy. One of the main contributions of these studies has been to point out the growing *vulnerability* of several segments of the labour market (even some modern urban-industrial segments), the growing *precariousness* of work, and the increasing *dualization* of urban labour markets. Another contribution has been the discussion of the need to improve the qualifications and the skills of the labour force as a necessary step to overcome the crisis. Last but not least, this literature strongly supports the idea that, in the next two decades, the generation of productive jobs will continue to be one of the crucial issues regarding poverty and exclusion in the region.

3. The lost decade: Economic crisis and adjustment policies

Another important and more recent contribution found in the Latin American literature dealing with poverty and deprivation is related to the discussion of the impact of the world economic crisis upon the region and to a sharp critique of the neo-liberal policies that have been proposed by institutions such as the World Bank and the International Monetary Fund to deal with the crisis.

Such analyses recognize that the state-led import substitution growth regime is exhausted, and that to maintain it has entailed the perverse combination of inflation and stagnation, lack of competitiveness, inadequate incorporation of technical progress, growing public deficits and the presence of the state in productive endeavours marked by lack of dynamism and where corporativism prevails over the public interest. It is therefore imperative, according to these analyses, to eliminate the public deficit, to control inflation and to find a new growth regime for the economies of the area by promoting a deep restructuring of their productive sectors.

However, the same literature has stressed that the neo-liberal policies adopted to deal with the crisis have had a strongly negative impact on the social situation throughout the region. Very low or even negative rates of growth, growing open unemployment, declining government social expenditures and disorganization of the public sector have been some of the consequences of this adjustment, entailing increasing impoverishment and the growth of the social debt. It is no wonder that the 1980s are described in this literature as the "lost decade".

Against this background, the most recent publications have discussed alternatives to this dilemma and a set of policy recommendations has emerged, known in the literature as "economic restructuring with equity". This growth strategy recommends a careful and planned opening of the economies of the region, an increase in their systemic competitive capacities, a planned and sustained development of the region's scientific and technological resources, adequate environment protection and a major effort to enhance the quality of the human resources in the area. All these efforts require an increase in the steering capacity of the government and therefore imply a deep reform in the State structures of Latin America.

Even a cursory overview of the material on "restructuring" and an examination of the controversial issues involved will show that there are no reasons for optimism: the prospects for a rapid and significant improvement in the social situation are discouraging. Nevertheless, it is necessary to strengthen the public space and the democratic mechanisms and institutions to negotiate long-term solutions.

4. *Social protection and welfare policies: A renewed challenge*

Finally, there is the contribution that the literature offers regarding the past performance, the present crisis and the challenges facing the provision of social protection and welfare services in the region.

A distinctive system of social protection developed in most Latin American countries, associated with the state-led import substitution growth regime. Although varying from country to country, these social protection systems differed markedly from the welfare systems typical of the Scandinavian countries and from those prevailing in the USA.

In the last decade, a growing amount of research has been conducted leading to a better understanding of the functioning of these social protection systems, their financing, and their distributive impact. These analyses, associated with the impact of the economic crisis and with the processes of redemocratization occurring in the area, have also played a role — first, in the better understanding of the shortcomings of most of these social protection systems, particularly regarding their low or even regressive distributive impact and their low cost efficiency and, second, in the intense discussion around divergent policy recommendations for the urgent reform of these systems then taking place. The literature, contains evaluations of different initiatives taken to reform these systems, ranging from such deep reforms as the one taking place in Chile, to such cosmetic ones as those taking place so far in Brazil, and including new innovative emergency programmes such as the ones implemented in Bolivia and Mexico.

Except for the positive role that careful decentralization can play and for the need to improve cost efficiency, there is no widespread consensus on most questions such as targeting versus universalizing, privatizing versus increasing public control over services, or means-tested provisions versus universal citizenship entitlement to benefits. However, the literature is unanimous on two main conclusions. First, the region badly needs an efficient, publicly accountable social welfare safety net. Second, these systems, however efficient, universal or better targeted they may be, cannot carry all the burden of the fight against poverty. A higher per capita income, more and more productive jobs and a better primary income distribution are still necessary preconditions for the adequate functioning of welfare systems.

III. Conclusion: How useful is the notion of social exclusion for the analysis of poverty and deprivation in Latin America?

This paper has examined the main trends in the Latin American literature concerning questions of poverty and deprivation. It is apparent that the notion of social exclusion — except as a descriptive term lacking any major theoretical implication — has not been widely used. But at the same time, this literature could potentially be used to understand processes of social exclusion, and to inform policies designed to combat exclusion. It is worthwhile, therefore, as a conclusion, to say a word about the usefulness of the concept of exclusion for furthering the understanding of poverty and deprivation and as a more adequate basis upon which to ground policy recommendations.

In Western Europe, the concept of social exclusion refers, in its most recent version, to "the most characteristic mechanism of poverty in the industrialized countries and of the emergence of the new poor" [Gaudier, 1993; Yépez, 1994]. Gaudier, for example, writes:

> The concept implies that societies with a market economy have become *incapable of integrating a growing number of their members*. An extreme form of inequality, exclusion — described by the French sociologist Alain Touraine as the new social division, which set those on the outside against those in the inside, *in contrast to the older division, which set those above against those below* — would appear *to sanction the "dualization"* of society, the divorce between social demands and the organization, the rift between the actors and the system. Interpretations of this concept may differ, but they have one point in common. They [...] attribute [exclusion] primarily to socio-economic causes — exclusion is the direct consequence of the employment crisis — and *to political and cultural* causes — here *it is the result of the failure of institutions, the State, the education system, the trade unions*. Recently adopted into everyday language, the term embraces the sinister reality of a world of have-not: the homeless, jobless, powerless, penniless (p. 64; emphases added).

So understood, the notion of social exclusion seems to be rather context-specific, and of limited relevance to the Latin American context. It conveys ideas such as lack of integration, dualization, cultural distinctiveness, lack of formal civil and political rights and it refers to institutional determinants — as my emphasis in the quotation seeks to stress — that are not typical of the Latin American situation of poverty and deprivation. In fact, as we have seen in the previous section, one of the main contributions of the Latin American literature has been precisely a critique of these ideas. It may be that the term is useful to refer to situations either where international immigrants form a strong component of the poor population, or where there are strong ethnic, religious and cultural differences. But in contexts which are both politically and culturally homogeneous, the thesis that poverty and deprivation is the result of *a specific pattern of integration into the social division of labour*, which the Latin American literature argues, seems more adequate.

However, the usefulness of the concept of social exclusion can perhaps be claimed on other grounds. In brief, it offers a way of integrating loosely connected notions such as poverty, deprivation, lack of access to goods, services and assets, precariousness of social rights, and of providing a general framework.

If it is to be useful as such an integrating framework, the concept of social exclusion will have to have a far more strategic importance for articulating social theory then it seems to have thus far. The Latin American literature has up to now relied on concepts articulated around the notion of social division of labour to provide this grounding framework.

Most of the material included in this review provide examples of the usefulness of this approach. It will only be on the basis of fresh knowledge inspired by the notion of social exclusion that the usefulness of this alternative approach can be evaluated.

Bibliographical references

Altimir, O. 1982. *The extent of poverty in Latin America.* World Bank Staff Working Papers No. 522. Washington, DC, World Bank.

Cardoso, F. H. 1973. *Dependency revisited.* Institute of Latin American Studies, The University of Texas at Austin.

—; Faletto, E. 1970. *Depedência e desenvolvimento na América Latina.* São Paulo, Zahar Editores.

ECLAC. 1992. *Equidad y transformación productiva: un enfoque integrado.* Santiago.

Faria, V. E. 1976. *Occupational marginality, employment and poverty in urban Brazil.* Cambridge, Harvard University. PhD. Dissertation.

—. 1994. *Social exclusion in Latin America: An annotated bibliography.* Discussion Paper Series No. 70. Geneva, IILS.

Gaudier, M. 1993. *Poverty, inequality, exclusion: New approaches to theory and practice — Pauvretés, inégalités, exclusions: renouveau des approches théoriques et des pratiques sociales.* Bibliography Series No. 17. Geneva, IILS.

Infante, R. 1995. "Labour market, urban poverty and adjustment: New challenges and policy options", in Rodgers, G.; van der Hoeven, R. (eds.): *The poverty agenda: Trends and policy options.* Geneva, IILS.

Peliano, A. M. T. M. (Coord.). 1993. *O mapa da fome: Subsídios a formulação de uma política de seguranca alimentar.* Brasília, IPEA - Documento de Política No. 14.

PREALC. 1992. *Empleo y transformación productiva en América Latina y el Caribe.* Santiago, Working Paper Series No. 369.

Prebish, R. 1950. *The economic development of Latin America and its principal problems.* New York, United Nations.

Yépez, I. 1994. *Review of the French and Belgian literature on social exclusion: A Latin American perspective.* Discussion Paper Series No. 71. Geneva, IILS.

Part II: Country studies

7 Patterns and processes of social exclusion in Russia

Natalia Tchernina

I. The macro-economic context of social exclusion

1. The process of transition

Over the past three years of reforms, Russian society has experienced several massive shocks. First, there has been a process of mass impoverishment following the Gaidar Cabinet "shock treatment" for the economy. The share of the population in Russia which has an aggregate per capita income below the officially set subsistence minimum is about 30 per cent on average, and about 5 per cent of the population is starving.

Second, the threat of mass unemployment has become more and more real. With the sudden and almost unlimited opening of the national market to leading world companies, national manufacturers, and primarily the industrial giants, producing poor quality and ill-assorted goods, and having to cope with the effects of the break-up of former economic ties and a sharp rise in energy and transport prices, have lost markets and have had to cease production. Masses of industrial workers and professionals are undergoing financial difficulties and the moral discomfort associated with a feeling of uselessness, as they think that their skills are no longer necessary to anybody.

Third, the society is rapidly stratifying into the rich and the poor. The ratio of the average income of the richest 10 per cent of the population to the average income of the poorest 10 per cent is growing constantly: from 5:1 in 1989 to 11:1 in 1993. Within a large country involved in an economic crisis, the outline of a "country of the new rich", with a population of some 10-16 million people at most, is thus appearing.

Finally, there has been a devaluation of the former Russian ideology and national mentality as ideas and values of Western culture spread. These ideas and values are not the result of the inner positive development of Soviet society but have accompanied rapid importation of the Western model of development, with an emphasis on the values of the consumer society rather than the cultural and ecological components of the model. Most of the ideals and values persistently installed by the mass media are in conflict with old values (for example, the ideology of service to the people and the State is forced out by an egocentric ideology — selfish enrichment at any cost). The old values are maintained and reproduced by the growing poor strata of the intelligentsia. But they have become passive participants of the reform, not benefiting from the reform process but bearing the full burden of its social costs. Ironically, the active importation of ideas for transition to a market economy has taken place in conjunction with an obvious lack of social actors (managers, lawyers, economists specializing in market economy, etc.) who can realize them.

The concurrent influence of these types of shock reveals the state of Russian society. In brief, it is characterized by the break-up of old forms of social organization without their replacement with appropriate new forms. For example, the State system of public health has been destroyed while the system of medical insurance is still to be established; or private pension funds are set up without appropriate legal rules.

In general, there has been an evident and steady loss in the decision-making capacity of the nation State over the last three years. This is manifested in two main ways. First, the range of functions and activities under State control has been constantly and intentionally reduced. Second, there has been a transition from a unitary State, with a super-centralized system of planning and management, to a federal State in which the role of regional elites has been strengthened, with a corresponding loss of control by the centre and weakening of the ability for vertical and horizontal coordination. Regional elites pursuing their own political interests sharpen the conflict between executive and legislative power, and between the federal and regional authorities. The quest for "regionalization" and independence from the Federal Government is realized through the establishment of large regional associations (such as the Siberian Agreement, comprising the regions of Western and Eastern Siberia, or the Far-Eastern Association of Economic Cooperation), or even in the declaration of republics (e.g. the Ural Republic, 1993).

The federal and regional authorities are now bargaining over the distribution of tax burdens and government expenditure. Instead of rendering regular subsidy assistance to some needy regions and making more or less equal conditions of life for the poor strata of the population in all regions, the Government pursues a policy of allocating subsidies and tax privileges to those regions which support it. Such a policy of "region-splitting" undermines confidence in the exercise of State power and decreases the level of execution of government decrees. There is a constant struggle for the redistribution of the burdens and benefits of the budget at federal and regional levels, which not only adds to the economic instability paralyzing decision-making, particularly in the crucial area of investment policy, but also alienates foreign capital.

2. Economic trends

The transition to a market economy is posing great problems for Russia. It is estimated that in 1993, the gross domestic product was 38-40 per cent lower than in 1989 and that the volume of industrial output was half that of 1990. Available statistics also suggest that during the first half of 1994, output fell by a further 27 per cent, an even steeper decrease than the 16 per cent drop recorded over the same period in 1993. The general reduction of the level of business has been accompanied by a hollowing-out of the economic structure. By the end of 1994, there is a real threat of irreversible destruction of many branches of mechanical engineering, chemical and light industries, which constituted the backbone of the national economy. It is estimated that, in the first half of 1994, the fall in their production amounted to 40-50 per cent. High technology industries, where the most skilled personnel are concentrated, are in a particularly difficult situation. Orders from the defence establishment, including orders for research and development work, have decreased alarmingly. This has brought about a sharp decrease in capacity utilization, large arrears of wages of the Ministry of Defence, and the delayed payment of wages to workers. It is estimated that 80 per cent of enterprises in the military-industrial complex will become bankrupt in the very near future, and there will be a mass reduction of the most skilled workers, approximately 1.5 million people. This number is almost one-and-a-half times larger than the total number officially registered as unemployed at the beginning of 1994.

Conversion of military production presupposes technological change, which is impossible without large investment. But State economic programmes have no investment policy, and a deep and protracted fall in the level of investment has taken place. Almost all productive capacities are out of date in the technological, physical, ecological and social senses.

Russian agriculture is also in a disastrous state. The area under crops, particularly grains, decreased dramatically in 1993 and the yield per hectare has also decreased. Experts foresee a complete destruction of home cattle-breeding and other problems include: a sharp decrease in soil fertility; a worn-out fleet of agricultural machines; and severe social problems in rural areas.

There is a high probability that at the close of 1994 the Russian economy may assume a qualitatively new structure which will differ from the former structure. This transition is apparent in a sharp increase in the share of raw materials industries in total output and the disappearance of the greater part of high technology engineering industries. The new structure is typical of many low-income countries. The government policy of passive adaptation to the spontaneous processes hollowing out the economic structure has resulted in the country's entry into a regime of deindustrialization, though Russia still retains the greater part of its educational, scientific, cultural and industrial potential which had accumulated by the early 1990s. There is thus still the potential for overcoming the crisis and structural regress.

3. Unemployment, poverty and inequality[1]

One curious feature of the transition period is the apparently low unemployment rate. An ILO official, G. Standing, points out that "no economy in the world had ever gone through such a serious recession as that in Russia without mass unemployment". But in the first half of 1994 the registered unemployment rate was at a level of 1 to 1.5 per cent of the total labour force (1.1 million people in April 1994).

The conjunction of serious recession and a low official rate of unemployment arises because there is widespread latent unemployment. Estimates for the early 1990s suggest that 25 per cent of the workforce were surplus to requirements and, with production falling by 40 per cent since then, one may estimate that one-half of all those employed in the economy are now superfluous. The low registered unemployment rate also reflects Russian employers' practice of not making surplus labour redundant at the present moment. There are grounds for believing that privatization of large and middle-size enterprises has blocked the mass release of workers, as managers have pursued a policy of maintaining "worker collectives", thus forming an alliance with workers against external shareholders during privatization.

This management strategy is a peculiar pay-off to workers for the opportunity for "managerial" privatization. It involves inherited stereotypes

---

[1] For a fuller discussion, see Natalia Tchernina: *Employment deprivation and poverty: The ways in which poverty is emerging in the course of economic reform in Russia.* Discussion Paper Series No. 60 (Geneva, IILS, 1993).

and also structures of social relations between workers and the management, formed over the course of decades, which are characterized by the "semi-feudal" dependence of workers upon the distribution system on the one hand, and by a certain paternalism of managers with regard to workers, on the other. Once a joint-stock company is registered, stocks — and hence control over an enterprise — will be gradually transferred to either a small group of managers, or to new owners "from the outside". This process may take from three to five years. But the transfer of production to private capital is incompatible with the keeping surplus workers in employment. In the long run it will be found that one-half of all those employed at present-day enterprises cannot be provided with a job. To put it another way, it will be necessary to double the number of effective workplaces in order to turn the bulk of able-bodied people into wage workers rather than lumpen-proletarians.

An inevitable process of rejection of unprofitable production and surplus workers calls for a consistent State policy of social security to be put into effect. The establishment of a reliable social security system is in fact on the agenda. It includes at least the following elements: (i) an acceptable level of unemployment benefits; (ii) organization of public works; (iii) development of a broad system of occupational retraining; and (iv) real possibilities for substantial migration of the workforce throughout the country. However, the current state of each of these elements of the social security system is unsatisfactory.

Of these elements the first is most easily quantified. Only the registered unemployed receive benefits, but it is well known that open unemployment is only one-fifth of the total number of unemployed. For most of those who receive a benefit, this is set at the level of a minimum wage, which was 14,620 roubles during the first half of 1994. This is much less than the official minimum subsistence level which, in the first quarter of 1994, averaged 53,945 roubles. Thus, in the first quarter of 1994, the minimum wage represented 27 per cent of the subsistence level. This ratio still persists.

Not only does a large proportion of the population have a per capita income below the official subsistence level, but many have lived in this situation for the last two or three years. This suggests that a poverty trap is appearing. The phenomenon of "irreversible poverty" reveals the Government's inability to exercise control over the social consequences of the reform. Provision of citizens, especially the least prosperous strata of the population, with major social guarantees for the stabilization of their standard of living, was declared the top priority orientation of social policy (7 July 1994). But the President's Decree "On preparation of the plan of stabilization of living standards of the Russian Federation population" was issued too late.

During 1994, living standards of the population were decreasing, large enterprises were closed down one by one, the State delayed payments for its orders, and the tariff agreement was not fulfilled. In these circumstances, a number of leading trade unions decided to withdraw from the "Agreement of Civil Concord in Russia", signed in spring 1994. In so doing, they absolved themselves of the responsibility not to oppose the Government.

Social peace cannot be achieved in a society which is splitting into the poor and the rich. A stratum of new rich is emerging as some people derive profit from the transition. Defined as those with over 500,000 rubles per month, the size of this stratum is about 16 million people (9-10 per cent of the population), including, according to official statistics for the first four months of 1994, about 1.1 million people (less than one per cent of the total population) who had a per capita monthly income of 50 million roubles (US$25,000). The fragile social concord is likely to break in a situation where a minority enriches itself whilst the greater part of the population experiences rapid pauperization.

There are clear indications that Russia is exhibiting features of the Latin-American model of development, in which a middle class is absent and society is starkly polarized between a rich minority and a very poor majority. The former middle class in Russia is degenerating, while a "new" one is being formed only slowly. This is because the quasi-market Russian economy has no need of the mass intelligentsia which was the heart of the old middle class.

At present a considerable part of the old middle class is in a state of latent unemployment, suffering material and moral losses. In this state, labour relations are maintained with employers who cannot provide their employees with the means of subsistence, whilst the latter search for gainful employment in the informal economy. All this is a certain form of adaptation to the new situation, or — more accurately — a pseudo-adaptation, combining outward adaptation to the situation with inner negative estimation of its rules and requirements. The egalitarianism of the former society has also contributed to the demise of the old middle class because skilled labour still receives low pay compared to many types of relatively unskilled labour. Representatives of the mass intelligentsia experience financial deprivation and strong psychological stress associated with the impossibility of being masters of their own lives, with a growing sense of hopelessness, and with the uncertainty about the very near future. They are prisoners of unpredictable circumstances. A distrust of the socio-economic policy pursued by the State intensifies still further the obvious tendency for individuals to withdraw into their own problems and failures, and their own narrow social space.

II. Sociological investigation of social exclusion in Siberia

The micro-dynamics of social exclusion were examined through three in-depth case studies and surveys of social groups in Siberia: rural residents; the salaried middle strata (the mass intellectuals) now in a state of latent unemployment; and the long-term unemployed. The degree of social exclusion was assessed in terms of the exploitation, insecurity, and impoverishment of people in these categories.

1. Overall patterns and processes

The *rural residents* are the group worst affected in terms of exploitation, insecurity, and impoverishment. Their exploitation is realized in two ways. First, the non-equivalent urban-rural exchange, in favour of industrial products, has been taking place in both the Soviet and post-Soviet period. Secondly, *kolkhozniks* (people who used to work on State farms) working in the public sector of agriculture continue to be exploited by heavy work, long working hours and extremely low rewards. The situation of rural residents has been, and still is, made insecure by changing weather conditions, procurement prices, and State subsidies. In 1993-1994, insecurity was intensified by the deepening economic depression and the crisis of State social policy, which resulted in long delays in payments for agricultural products and therefore wage delays; and then delays in the payment of social benefits.

The overwhelming majority of rural residents has always been needy. They have become resigned to this condition and have developed their own survival strategies. But in the period of transition to a market economy, these minimal survival strategies have proved insufficient to keep great numbers of the rural population from "sliding down" to extreme deprivation. The signs of impoverishment are especially vivid among those categories of persons whose social conditions render them non-competitive: first and foremost, single mothers, and then families with a number of dependents, families with children of pre-school and younger school age.

The second excluded group are *workers of the military industrial complex and academic and research workers*, who were previously in a better position than other groups of the employed. They had a high social status, but are now in a state of latent unemployment. Losing their privileged status, and feeling they are victimized by changed priorities in the State structural policy, these workers are more acutely affected by perceived exclusion than the groups which previously had fewer rights and privileges. Their lifestyle still retains the imprint of their former relative prosperity; and most of them keep to their accustomed culturally defined standards (CDS). But the salaried middle strata are beginning to feel an increasing sense of superfluity and they are becoming convinced that commercial, intermediary and financial activities are decisive in a market economy, rather than the production of material and intellectual values. The mass of intellectuals are thus newly excluded, mainly as a result of the reform process itself, particularly the very slow conversion of military production and the sharp decline of State expenditures on research and development.

The culturally-defined standards to which most people in this group continue to adhere reflect their fidelity to the values of the former socialist system. They are accustomed to, and continue to aspire to: free professional education and health services; housing subsidies; and the possibility of sustaining or exceeding their parents' social status. Strangely enough, abnormal working conditions (which are now becoming more common) are not viewed as conflicting with their right to work, i.e. this right is somewhere on the periphery of CDS. But the right to be regularly paid is somewhere near the centre of CDS. The level of remuneration for work, which is low in comparison to Europe, also seems to be included in CDS. With high inflation, however, it is becoming ever more difficult to subsist on low pay, and it is becoming almost impossible to do this when payments come late.

Latent unemployed workers seem to be less affected by exclusion than the open unemployed. The reason is that the former retain the illusion that they are still under the protection of their old organizations and they continue to benefit from some of their social privileges (which are denied to the open unemployed). Amongst the open unemployed, the *long-term unemployed*, who cannot integrate into the local labour market, are in the worst situation. Those who fail to find a job for a long period (over one year in the case studies) accumulate a "negative potential": poor health, loss of skills, dejection, self-isolation, etc. After many vain attempts to find a job, their social vigour declines and, as their family's situation worsens, even fewer efforts are made to improve the quality of their skills (by retraining, mastering new skills, undertaking a business activity), and more and more time is focused on a primitive survival strategy in the household economy.

A common feature discovered in all the three groups under study was their active improvising of minimal survival strategies, mostly in the sphere of household economy, and a lack of long-term strategies to deal with the setting which has excluded them. The case studies revealed no integrative processes through group action, either in the real life of these people, or in their intentions. Their survival strategies are focused on self-provisioning, and mainly on self-provisioning of food, usually in their place of residence, urban or rural, as the case may be. Whereas previously the middle class preferred to spend free time on intellectual activities, tourism and health improvement, at present the cultivation of an individual plot associated with manual labour is becoming a new culturally-defined standard. People are also becoming accustomed to the state of being unprotected, as expectations of the State social security system change and paternalistic illusions evaporate. A side-effect of the State shouldering its responsibility for the citizens in the past is their self-isolation, as they keep away from social settings and withdraw into private life.

The period of these transformations has as yet been too short to make any definite conclusions about the emergence of a new culturally-defined standard of living, and thus we can only ascertain the appearance of certain changes. But people are gradually beginning to realize that the former ways of earning a living will no longer provide them with their accustomed level of consumption and way of life. In the case studies, signs of this awareness were apparent in increased potential mobility of rural workers and the separation from agriculture of the economically most productive labour, i.e. men aged 30-40 with comparatively high skills. The side-effect of this separation is the influx of labour to the city, even stiffer competition on a labour market which is characterized by limited demand, and the expansion of the informal employment sector where the employer can use unlimited flexibility to economize on direct labour costs and social benefits.

2. *The marginality of rural residents*

The genesis of the objective exclusion of a population can be described as a chain of events in which people move from a state of vulnerability, to dependence and, finally, to marginality. Of the three groups studied, rural residents as a social group are at present marginal.

The exclusion of the rural population has a long history and is of a mass character. It is well-known that it was not until the early 1960s that Russian rural residents received passports, without which they could not freely move about the country, nor take up residence and get employment in a city. The system of residence permits still exists in Russia. Most of the rural population are excluded from a modern way of life both in the sphere of domestic amenities and in the sphere of work. This is seen in the general absence of practically all modern facilities, except for electricity in homes; the scarcity of consumer establishments in the rural centres; excess working hours and lack of leisure; heavy and abnormal working conditions; and the burden of a double workload embracing both the public and household farming sector. Women bear most of the burden of this double load, and the more children there are in a family, the more important is the household economy in the survival strategy.

The pattern of exclusion described above was constantly reproduced through non-market factors, particularly because of the notion that peasants, as a class of small proprietors, were of second-rate quality (compared to the industrial proletariat), and the idea that the agrarian sector played an inferior role to industry and other urban branches of the economy. Primitive production techniques in agriculture, a narrow job choice and poor transport and communications in the vast spaces of Russia (which rendered commuting impractical in most rural settings), also contributed to the situation. But exclusion has intensified in the transition period.

Both agricultural production and the rural community were not prepared for the transition to a market economy. The former *kolkhozes* have been converted into peasant farm associations (PFA), joint stock companies and other new economic forms. But they are now in a deep crisis, having lost support from the State in the form of subsidies and rigid control over consumption of resources.

Before the transition, the rigid control of all activity in the village was exercised by the party-State system. It could not create economic efficiency, mainly due to the absence of relevant incentives for investment and for labour productivity. But it did manage to keep social distances between people within limits, not letting great differences in consumption and the living standards of different social groups emerge and keeping to the principle of equality. No new democratic institutions, which could regulate the social life in the village, have been created as substitutes for the dismantled party-State system so far. Moreover, new economic mechanisms which now regulate PFA activity have failed thus far to produce the relevant forms of control over the actions of the administration because the PFA members have no experience in using democratic and legal procedures to defend their interests.

These deficiencies, peculiar to the period of transition to a market economy, arouse in rural residents a sense of nostalgia for the old party's methods of management. Some of the respondents expressed regret about the dismantling of party committees in the early 1990s, because they had been the only place to which they could turn with complaints against their managers if their rights were infringed. These committees were a kind of counterbalance to the often "omnipotent" power of the *kolkhoz* chairman. The residents, however, forget that party committees would not often take the side of rank-and-file *kolkhozniks*. At present the only agency that is left to defend them is the court. But there are very few people who bring their cases to court in situations of severe conflict (because of general legal illiteracy, lack of skills in normal forms of defending one's interests, and a tradition of enduring suffering). As a result, the rural population has accumulated sentiments of exclusion.

The low legal experience of rural residents makes them helpless against the power of local chiefs who have sought, in particular, to keep people in low-paid public agriculture and prevent them from taking more attractive and higher-paid jobs. The curtailment of public expenditure on social infrastructure in rural areas worsens the living conditions, has a negative impact on the raising of children, and narrows the sphere of female labour, leaving women with only two or three kinds of jobs on farms, all of which have heavy and harmful working conditions. Males often have illegal earnings on the side. As a result, the improvisation of survival strategies by rural residents is limited to a choice between household production and a heavy additional workload. The proportion of wages of agricultural workers in the total incomes of a typical rural family is less than 40 per cent. The absence of any means of mechanization in the individualized economy and the absence of money savings for the use of paid services make household production economically dependent on support from the collective farm, and more specifically on its Board, which is the only manager of the resources (allocation of fodder, garden ploughing, repair of buildings, etc.). The consumption cooperative society cannot integrate individual farm producers; and the State, in spite of its declarations, has left the private farming movement almost without support.

The State system of social security would be a great help for rural residents, especially because many families have more than two children. But the condition of the system is unsatisfactory at present. There are only cash benefits, and payments are small and paid irregularly.

Finally, common to all respondents in the surveys — rural and urban — is a feeling of poor protection against crime. But criminality is growing in society: an increasing number of acts of terrorism against successful businessmen, bankers and managers arouse in ordinary workers a sense of defencelessness. They have no confidence in the bodies responsible for keeping public order and fear for the safety of their families in the districts where they live, particularly in the city.

In this situation, people hope only for the support of their relatives and sometimes their friends. However, according to the data of the mass polls, these primary social relationships are being broken, as valuable human relations between kin and friends become weaker.

III. Regional and local agencies combating poverty and social exclusion

In Russia at the *oblast* and city level a number of social actors and institutions are concerned with eradicating poverty and social exclusion as part of the realization of a regional social policy. These include: social security bodies; employment centres; and trade unions. The functions of these agencies are mostly dictated by laws, President's decrees, and agreements at the federal level. Moreover, regional social policy is in a stage of formation. But the nature of the present efforts of these agencies indicates how little is being done to counteract the strong exclusionary tendencies which are apparent in the transitional period.

In Russia *social security bodies* give priority to rendering assistance to disabled people, primarily those receiving old-age and disability pensions. This is the only category of the population which receives support from the State in the form of pensions. Other categories of poverty-stricken people depend on local budget receipts, and the resolutions of the local administration concerned with the distribution of expenditures in different spheres.

The shortage of financial resources has restricted the identification of people among the low-income segment of population in need of support from Social Security Department (SSD). The data bank of people in need is obviously incomplete because it includes only those who apply to SSD on their own initiative. As a consequence, the targeting of social aid is limited in scope and many people in need have been left without any support. For example, amongst all members of large families (with three and more children), who as a rule are low-income families, only 13 per cent were registered by the SSD in the Novosibirsk *oblast*, and only 6.8 per cent received aid in one form or another.

The case study of the workers in the military-industrial complex and academic and research workers highlights people's expectations concerning the functioning of the social security system. The sample of respondents distinguished seven main forms of social support:

(a) *Guarantees for work*: guarantees of the right to work as the source of subsistence; regular professional work; guaranteed employment up to pensionable age.

(b) *Guarantees for pay*: a level of pay which guarantees normal living standards; pay which appreciates the true value of intellectual's work; stable pay; well-timed pay for work.

(c) *Provision of housing*: improvement of family housing conditions; provision of housing for young professionals.

(d) *Provision of medical services*: free or privileged medical service; spa treatment.

(e) *Guarantees for education*: free education.

(f) *Prevention of crime*: freedom from worry about the life and health of the family and safety of property.

(g) *State financial support for other aspects of family life*: improvement of the financial position of large families; pay for holidays and journeys; defence against social cataclysms (inflation, unemployment, etc.).

It is clear from these answers that culturally-defined standards, which originated in the socialist period, have partly survived the first years of transition in the sample population. At the same time, the respondents, who are representative of the mass intelligentsia, were including a new standard. That is: guarantees of citizen rights and the provision of access to social services for all members of the society irrespective of the ability to earn, or of sources of income. Thus, the respondents formulated intuitively and exactly the essence of a new model which corresponds to the model of social security which used to exist in western welfare states.

Answers of the respondents also indicate their wish to use State support in the social security system to provide a guaranteed subsistence minimum.

The second social actor at the regional level — the *Employment Centre* — has existed in today's form since 1991. According to the data of the State Statistical Committee of the Russian Federation, 4.6 million people (6 per cent of the labour force) were out of work and counted as unemployed in August 1994. At the same time, the number of those officially registered as unemployed was 1.4 million people (1.9 per cent of the labour force). The functions of Employment Centres listed in the Employment Law include: manpower redistribution; workers' retraining for the purpose of widening their professional potential; support for the entrepreneurship of the unemployed; and business loans. But in practice the Centres adopt a passive, rather than active, policy in the labour market. Most managers regard the Centre only as a body for manpower redistribution and they try to avoid the execution of the other functions listed above. The leaders of the Employment Centre also aim to economize on financial means, using the vagueness of criteria for allocation of the status of unemployed and relying on the fact that the unemployed are poorly informed about their rights.

By reducing retraining activity, the Centres can offer only manpower for which there is no demand and, being aware of this, the employers avoid reporting to the Employment Centres their good vacancies, preferring to resort to other mediators.

In the records of the Employment Centres, certain people with special needs are identified, namely: the disabled; job-seekers who are of pre-retirement age; and young job seekers (16-29 years of age). At the end of 1993 in Novosibirsk *oblast*, these categories made up 39 per cent of all persons registered at the employment offices. The latter seem to limit their activity to the registration function.

Trade unions exist in all State plants where the respondents to our surveys work. But in situations of violation of the labour law and collective agreements (delays in the payment of wages, the absence of payment for part-time employment, unpaid leave, etc.), not one of the respondents in the surveys appealed to the trade union to obtain justice, protection of rights, or for exerting influence on the management. As before, trade union committees are perceived as bodies which act together with the management and not as independent guardians of working people's interests. In the course of 1993-94, trade unions pursued a policy aimed at reducing conflicts both in the internal and external labour markets. They tried to avoid strikes; they persuaded people to take unpaid leave; they tried to prevent the mass release of workers in order to avoid an increase in the number of the unemployed. This activity of trade union committees contributed to the growth of latent unemployment and shifted the burdens of the economic crisis to working people. Working conditions deteriorated greatly and the rights of workers, primarily the right to receive pay for one's work, are now infringed on a massive scale. But, as before, trade unions render assistance in meeting workers' needs outside the sphere of labour: distribution of vouchers for sanatoriums, plots of land, housing, etc.

As for the social protection given by the trade unions, a national survey (1993) found that this role was negligible: 52 per cent of respondents said it was insignificant and only 18 per cent assessed it as perceptible. Those employed in private firms also often report the absence of unionization.

Such things as strike committees, regional compliance committees and government-union agreements are absolutely new in Russia, and were unknown before the early 1990s. At present, the main way in which unions negotiate for workers' interests is through their participation in three-party meetings, commissions which also include regional officials and employers (who, as a rule, are directors of large State-owned enterprises). At the beginning of the year, such commissions try to agree upon decisions of a long-term nature in three basic spheres: employment and prevention of mass unemployment; social security; and property privatization. These efforts are mostly limited to the development of regional programmes, e.g. the employment programme. The system of social partnership for the purposes of social security obviously requires the development of mechanisms for the execution of the programmes adopted. In the absence of such mechanisms, the only vehicle which the unions can use in dealing with employers is, conventionally, collective bargaining.

According to the data of the All-Russian Poll of Workers (1993), trade unions, as institutions of collective management, have lost even the small influence on making important decisions which they formerly had. Only 23 per cent of those polled were of the opinion that unions at their plants are able to solve problems which arise under market conditions.

IV. Conclusion

A number of fundamental causes of exclusion are arising from the new system of socio-economic relations. New socio-economic processes have in general led to the intensification of preceding forms of exclusion rooted in the Soviet period, and to the appearance of new forms. The situation of economic crisis could be remedied by the restructuring of the economy, but this is progressing too slowly. The strategic course of action in the fight against exclusion is to prevent the formation of an underclass and "ghetto-ization" of cities.

8 Patterns and processes of social exclusion in Thailand

Pasuk Phongpaichit, Sungsidh Piriyarangsan and Nualnoi Treerat

I. Macro-economic change, poverty and social exclusion

Economic growth rates have been consistently high in Thailand for many years. From 1986 to 1994, the economy grew at a rate of around 8 per cent per annum and the same rate is expected to prevail for the next five years. This growth is founded on a process of industrialization which initially was oriented to import substitution but, since 1977, has been export oriented. The share of the GDP from industry rose from a mere 15 per cent in 1960 to 30 per cent in 1990, and now manufacturing goods, notably transport equipment, leather goods, electric and electronic appliances, garments, precious stones and jewels, comprise over 70 per cent of total exports.

Despite the achievement of rapid economic growth rates, Thai society still faces many problems. As a fast growing-economy there is little open unemployment. Indeed, the official unemployment rates were only around 4-5 per cent per annum for the early 1990s. However, there are various other forms of social exclusion and a sizeable number of people live below the poverty line. Income inequality is also increasing. In 1975-76 the richest 20 per cent of the total population received 49 per cent of the country's total income, whilst the poorest 20 per cent received only 6 per cent. By 1987-88, the difference in the income between these groups had increased from 8 to 12 times, and the richest 20 per cent increased their share of the national income to 54.9 per cent whilst the share of the poorest 20 per cent fell to 4.5 per cent.

The total number of people living below the poverty line in 1988 was 11.5 million. The majority of the poor, some 95 per cent, live in rural areas. The rural poor have inadequate public provision of basic amenities.

For instance in mid-1984, 55 per cent of rural households did not have toilets, and in 1989 one-fifth of rural households did not have access to safe drinking water. Poor rural households have to send their children to work as child labour in cities so that the households have fewer mouths to feed and receive additional cash from remittances from their children. This often happens after the completion of compulsory elementary education (six years), but many drop out earlier. In 1988, according to official statistics, the total number of working children between the ages of 11 and 14 was 1,230,000, representing 24.8 per cent of all children in the age group. Most worked in agriculture. Half of the total were female and studies of child labour show that most of the working children come from poor rural households. The poor rural sector is also the major source of migrant female labour, who each year enter low-paid wage employment, or informal employment opportunities, particularly the risky prostitution trade in the service sector of provincial towns or Bangkok.

The urban poor, who in 1988 were estimated to number 600,000, also face problems of inadequate public provisions. This is particularly evident in the slum areas of Bangkok and other towns, whose population comprises mainly rural migrants. While many studies show that slum-dwellers can usually get jobs and earn reasonably, their living conditions are often substandard. More importantly, their children do not receive adequate care and education and are thus among those who are subject to exclusion from good jobs. Further slum environmental conditions which are marked by gambling, prostitution, drug trafficking and crimes, complicate the upbringing of youngsters.

In recent years, rising urban land prices in the core city centre of Bangkok has caused owners of land occupied by squatters to evict them. Many densely-populated slum areas have been subject to disputes and many slum residents have been moved to the outskirts of the city. So the trend is for the population in traditional slum areas in the core city to remain stagnant or decline as space for new settlement becomes limited and as some slums are being moved out. Meanwhile, the city core remains the hub of labour demand for all kinds of lucrative service and vending jobs for poor people. Smaller slum areas continue to persist and new types of urban poor have emerged, such as street children and the homeless living under bridges in the city centres. Elsewhere, in other towns outside Bangkok, such as in the north-east and the north, the slum population has increased. The slum residents are increasingly subject to eviction as urban land prices soar.

Whether living in urban or rural areas, a particular feature of the poor population is their low level of education. In 1988, 80 per cent of the poor had only elementary education and 16 per cent had no formal education whatsoever. Poorly educated people have to work in low-paid jobs because of lack of suitable skills and the higher educational levels required for better-paid jobs. Young women from rural areas with little education, if they get work as unskilled labour in factories, can receive at the most a minimum wage of 132 baht (US$5) a day.

The pattern of poverty and processes of social exclusion reflect the bases of national economic growth and also Thailand's specific development path. Up to now, the macro-economic success of Thailand's industrialization has been predicated upon two major factors. First, Thailand has a surplus supply of labour. From the mid-1970s to the mid-1980s the agricultural sector has faced declining commodity prices in the world market. Rural incomes have consequently declined and the agricultural sector has had a large supply of underemployed labour. As the industrialization process picked up momentum in the second half of the 1980s (due to a large influx of direct foreign investment from Japan and Asian NIEs and successful export promotion measures), employers faced a "buyer's labour market". They have been able to employ rural migrant labour needing employment to supplement their farm income at relatively cheap wages. Second, low labour costs have been maintained through government policies towards labour which have resulted in fragmentation of industrial labour, weak trade unionism and casualization of labour. Thus, whilst the industrialization efforts so far record high growth rates and low open unemployment, employed workers face the problems of sweat shops, low wages, insecurity of employment, unequal pay between the sexes, inadequate recognition of rights to unionization and collective bargaining and lack of rights to settle redundancy payments and training.

Processes of social exclusion in Thailand take various forms, ranging from the active expulsion of people from the productive resources upon which their livelihood depends, to exclusion from rights based on subtle institutional arrangements.

In rural areas, processes of exclusion reflect a major change in the relationship between State and peasantry. Until the 1970s, agriculture provided the mainstay of the economy and the State played an active role in promoting peasant expansion. But with export-oriented industrialization, agricultural produce now plays a minor role in overall exports and in the supply of inputs to urban industry. The utility of the countryside for the city is now as a source of labour and the State has adopted an attitude to the peasantry which is indifferent or positively antagonistic. The share of public expenditure in rural investment has consistently declined over the years to the extent that the share of the country's tax revenue remaining in, or being allocated to, the rural sector has become less than 10 per cent.

The changed relationship between the State and the peasantry affects government policies to the countryside in many ways, but it is most evident at the point where the old momentum of peasant expansion clashes with the new forces of expansive urban capitalism, which geographically is the forest fringe. Here there are peasant communities which were at the forefront of the century-long process of agricultural expansion at the time when State and city decreed the process should cease. Here, too, there are various city-based interests keen to gain access to land, including plantation businesses, real estate developers, State electricity generating authorities and many others.

For peasant farmers, land and forest resource entitlements are important as a means of livelihood, as a subsistence guarantee, and as a safety valve in times of economic and political difficulty. But recently, urban business has had the political leverage to push the government to make changes in land policy which benefit capital at the expense of the peasants. Peasants are thus being actively excluded from access to resources. The agents of exclusion include forest authorities, the military, and other officials, backed strongly by big conglomerates. The result has been increasing problems of displacement, rural poverty, and worsening income disparities between city and countryside. The process of economic exclusion from the natural resources on which peasants depend results in cultural exclusion from their traditional practices and communities, and also sometimes in political exclusion as they come to be labelled dissidents.

If industrialization in cities were to provide ample remunerative and secure employment for the rural people who become displaced, their plight would be somewhat improved. But industrial employment is growing relatively slowly due to the increasingly capital-intensive nature of present-day industrialization. In 1990, Thailand still had over 50 per cent of its total labour force employed in agriculture, and the manufacturing sector absorbed only about 12 per cent of the total labour force. About 60 per cent of those working in non-agricultural activities are in the informal sector.

Because of the limited absorptive capacity of the manufacturing sector, many poorly-educated young men and women from the countryside seek jobs in the service sector, including working as female/male prostitutes in towns. Those wanting to earn higher cash income seek work overseas — in Japan, Taiwan and elsewhere — and they tend to face a high risk of being under the control of labour agents and Mafia groups.

Official social security schemes (covered by the Social Security Act) are available only to formal sector workers in the civil service and those working in enterprises employing ten workers and more. Those working in the informal sector do not receive protection under the labour law, nor are they covered by social security provisions. Thus, while open unemployment is not a serious problem, the problems of low quality of work and insecurity in work are still serious.

Even for those in formal employment, there are subtle institutional arrangements with respect to the particular framework of labour relations which make it difficult for workers to realize their basic workers' right provided by the legal framework. Unionization is weak and there is inadequate enforcement of labour laws.

The existing law permits workers in the private sector to form enterprise unions. However, only a segment of workers in the big establishments have already achieved their rights of association and negotiation. The majority enjoys a lesser degree of workers' rights and most of the workers in small and medium-sized establishments are still not unionized. Union membership in the whole of the private sector in 1991 was such that only 1.64 per cent of total employees in the non-agricultural sector were unionized. In the public sector, unionization has been banned since 1991.

One of the major concerns of workers in Thailand has been the annual minimum wage negotiation at the national level, which has been set by tripartite bodies including five representatives each from government, national labour centres, and Employer's Councils of Thailand. Most unionized workers receive (at least) the official minimum wage, but this is insufficient to cover the whole of the necessary expenses of an individual or a family. Moreover, there is limited enforcement of labour law and a large number of employers do not pay the minimum wage. According to a surveys of the Office of the National Wage Committee, the percentage of workers not receiving minimum wage was estimated to be 44 per cent for the whole country in 1990, and 55 per cent in 1992.

With the present trend of globalization, Thailand has also been receiving illegal migrant workers from abroad, estimated to be around 700,000 in 1993. Most were unskilled workers willing to receive wages lower than the official minimum wage in Thailand. The inflow of illegal immigrants acts to offset the outflow of Thai workers going abroad, and the decline in the number of new entrants to the labour force resulting from the decline in natural population growth rate in the past two decades, thus sustaining, for employers, a "buyers' labour market".

II. Specific excluded groups

1. Women

One of the major issues in Thailand has been the widespread exploitation and trading of women in sex services and inadequate government action to prevent young girls with little education in poor families from being sold by their parents, or being lured into the trade by agents and *mamasans*. Although in Thai society there is no discrimination against women receiving education, working outside the home, entering professional work or running a business, the widespread exploitation of poor women in sex services runs counter to this general picture. Apart from the lucrative returns which provide economic incentives for the proliferation of the sex trade, closer analysis reveals the existence of deep-rooted cultural factors which provide legitimacy for trading in sex and for the exploitation of the female sex in particular.

There are built-in mechanisms in Thai society which exclude poor women from their entitlements as human beings. In short, there are unequal gender relations. There are cultural and religious factors which influence beliefs and attitudes, leading to formation of unequal gender relations and insensitivity to poor young women's rights as human beings.

Buddhism and male-dominated culture in *sakdina* ideology[1] are deeply implicated in the problems of exclusion of women. Several Buddhist practices, as adopted in Thailand, exclude women in various ways. First, while female monks were permitted in Buddha's time, in modern Thailand this is prohibited. Instead, Buddhist nuns, who are considered inferior to monks in all respects, function in practice as servants for monks in Buddhist temples. Second, women's presence is not allowed in certain Buddhist rites, such as in the ordination chamber. While this in fact reflects men's fear of women — novices may be tempted by the presence of women and obstruct the ordination — the practice leads to women being discriminated against. Instead of explaining the reasons for not allowing women's presence in a rational way, women are portrayed as inferior or as having an evil influence on men seeking higher goals in life.

Third, in Thai practice, men can save their parents from entering hell after death by being ordained, even if the parents have accumulated sin and no merits in their lifetime. Sermons in up-country areas concerning the power of ordination to elevate parents' life after death are living witness

---

[1] *Sakdina* refers to the social system in nineteenth-century Thailand, equivalent to the feudal system in Europe, but different in detail.

to this. The implication of this belief on attitudes towards gender and on gender relations is enormous. Young girls are inferior to men: to the parents, a male child is enough to save them. In Thailand, demonstrating gratitude to parents is one of the duties and virtues to follow. For males, gratitude towards parents can be achieved by being ordained as a monk for a short period of time. Sons do not have to do anything else. Being female is not valued in the same way, so the daughter must be prepared to do anything in the name of gratitude to parents, including selling herself as a prostitute and sacrificing her life. This culture, which has been developed through religious teachings, has the effect of making the people insensitive to women's rights.

Fourth, while in *Jataka* tales women's roles are portrayed as varied — as mother of Buddha, as monks, as mistresses, as prostitutes but appreciating Buddhist teachings, as patron of Buddhism, as saviour of Buddha against Mara *(Mae Thoranee bib muoy phom*, subduing Mara) — the emphasis in sermons in Buddhism as practised in Thailand is on portraying women as mother, as young wives with a duty to look after an older husband, and as temptresses. The sermons are all given by males and male monks play down the role of women as patrons of Buddhism, as mother of Buddha, as monks, or as equal partners in society.

Fifth, up-country Buddhism is intertwined with Hindu beliefs about pollution and it positions women as part of the pollution, especially with respect to menstruation. Lack of rational understanding on this biological aspect of motherhood makes people, even females and nuns, become prejudiced against menstruation and see it as pollution. This prejudice is manifested in attitudes that view women as inferior and polluted. They must be treated differently and may be excluded. Over time, this breeds an attitude of contempt and insensitivity towards women and has become part of the culture.

Central to the culture of old *sakdina* is the military culture, which emphasizes dominance and superiority of maleness. The power and privileges of the king, the prevalence of *droit de seigneur*, the power of the male king to demand complete subordination and obedience from women, become adopted and reinforced by the rest of men and are accepted by society. In gender relations, this means inequality and exclusion of women's participation and rights.

Thai Buddhism and the military culture of male dominance and superiority are two cultural belief systems which lead, as a matter of course, to unequal gender relations, insensitivity of males — especially male government officials — and to the denial of the rights of poor women as human beings. This raises complex issues of policy. Apart from trying to enforce the law concerning child prostitutes and to encourage NGOs to help track down abuses, there is the wider question of how to change the attitudes of males, of civil servants and of society at large. This is a difficult task which must be done at different levels, starting from households, with education of teachers, and at school from elementary education onwards. There must also be campaigns at the national level to soften and change the attitude of people, civil servants and politicians.

2. Ethnic minorities

The problems of ethnic minorities and their exclusion are not so serious in Thailand compared to some other countries in the region, but they do exist. In the South, in the past, the leaders of the Muslim minority (5.8 million in 1993, out of the total population of about 60 million) resented the central government's attempt to incorporate and assimilate them into the "Thai national culture" and the Thai kingdom. The conflict resulted in a separatist movement which received assistance from abroad. At present, the movement has been contained and the conflicts reduced, as the central government has tried to bridge the gap between officials and people. The democratic political system has eased the situation, as members of the Muslim elites have been able to enter parliament as MPs and as cabinet members.

Other minority groups in the north and central regions include the hill people and the Karen (500,000-700,000 in 1993) who live in the hill and forest areas and are jealous of their remoteness and their traditional ways of living and culture. They increasingly face the problems of outside investors encroaching upon them, taking away their forests and land. Many of the hill people, including the Karen, live in areas now designated as national forest reserves or natural watershed areas. They are facing eviction as the government wants to conserve these places and move them out. Hill people have been accused of deforestation. Opium growing and drug trafficking are cited as additional problems caused by some hill people in the north to justify moving them out of their traditional homes. Researchers have argued that such accusations are inaccurate and unfair. Research studies have also shown that hill people are well aware of the environmental impact of swidden agriculture and, as their livelihood depends on balanced local ecology, their agricultural practice is sustainable. It is the outside loggers and corrupt officials who are to blame for destroying the forests. As for the question of opium growing and drug trafficking, it has been pointed out that problems on the demand side and the complicated network of illicit trade, ridden with corruption within the high circles, must also be taken into account.

Many of these hill people are fighting against the government to defend their natural rights over their land and means of livelihood. Whilst the government does not believe that man and forest can coexist, the hill tribes are arguing that man and forests can live together in harmony, without destroying the forests and the environment. They also argue that they can protect the forest better than government officials whom past experience has shown to be more susceptible to offers of bribes from investors, resulting in rapid destruction of forest cover. The struggle of these hill tribes to protect their land continues. Without assistance from NGOs and the enlightened middle classes at home and abroad, it is very likely that many of these hill people will be on the losing side.

III. In-depth case studies

In the framework of the IILS/UNDP project, in-depth case studies were carried out to examine the micro-dynamics of exclusion in three different situations, namely: hill people and poorly educated farmers who have been displaced from their land by government policy; informal sector workers excluded from social security provisions; and the homeless living under bridges in Bangkok.

1. Displaced rural population

The first case study is an example of active exclusion measures carried out by the Government, or with government departments playing a role. It concerns some hill people and poorly educated farmers who have been moved away from their homes to distant resettlement sites which are less suitable for farming. These people were occupying land designated as "forest" by the authorities. Some were working the land before it was thus designated, whilst others moved into these areas. Because of the availability of land in the past, the Government wanted to encourage peasants to expand cultivation for export which, in turn, increased government revenue and the country's wealth. There thus emerged a traditional custom of allowing a new farm family to clear forest land of up to 4 hectares for their own use. The Government collected land taxes but refused to recognize legal ownership of the occupants. From the government point of view, farmers were given occupancy rights only, while the land still belonged to the State. From the point of view of the poor peasants, the land they occupied became theirs by natural right, especially after they had paid the taxes on it.

The fact that the government has been reluctant to give legal land title deeds to poor peasants, occupying forest land according to the traditional custom, has become a major source of problems. With pressure from businessmen to make use of the land for lucrative investment in recent years, the government has proceeded with measures to evict poor peasants from degraded forest areas and allow businessmen to exploit the land on concession. The Government justified its policies in the name of forest conservation and protection of watershed areas. But this hides the real reason which was that "big business" and influential individuals in government aimed to make money from using the land to grow eucalyptus trees to supply the pulp and paper industry, or from turning the hill lands into resort and golf courses and other real-estate investment. This is really a case of active exclusion, with policy measures driven by the economic motives of the powerful which, as a consequence, further impoverishes poor farmers. The policy runs counter to the declarations in all of Thailand's Economic and Social Development Plans, which profess to reduce poverty.

The case study focuses in particular on villagers subject to the *Kho Jo Ko* programme, initiated in 1991, which aimed to move up to 5.8 million people under resettlement schemes. The programme was initiated by the National Security Council and its implementation was entrusted to military personnel. The study documents the escalating disputes between villagers and the forestry department granting concessions to companies to grow eucalyptus on peasants' land which preceded the programme, and also villagers' resistance to resettlement during implementation, before the final abandonment of the programme in 1992. Villages which successfully resisted exclusion from their traditional lands were characterized by effective leadership, strong kinship and cultural ties and strong village solidarity founded on common customs and a culture of mutual assistance. NGOs played an important role in supporting peasant resistance. Villages which were unable to resist tended to be poorer and were either forced out by soldiers or police or succumbed to financial promises. Contrasting these two experiences may lead to relevant policy considerations, as it highlights the importance of and the need for associational and solidarity processes and the skills necessary to activate and sustain them in an effective way.

2. Social security of informal sector workers

The Social Security Law for workers was enacted in 1990. In the beginning, the law covered only people working in establishments with over 20 workers. By the beginning of 1994, the scheme was extended to cover workers in establishments with ten workers and more. The provisions are applicable only to individual workers and cover the following branches: health insurance, maternity, invalidity and death benefits. The provisions do not cover family members of the worker (wife/husband and children) and the existing law does not yet cover unemployment benefits and pension schemes, which are at present being elaborated.

The case study was based on a sample survey of 100 workers in the informal sector who are not covered by social security. It shows that most workers receive less than the official minimum wage. Most are rural migrants. Half the sample were male and half female and 87 per cent were less than 40 years old. Most had received only elementary education or none at all (88 per cent). They worked as daily workers or on piece rates. Fifty-two per cent received no welfare from their employers, 23 per cent received some medical care, 9 per cent received annual bonuses during the Chinese New Year, 7 per cent received food free of charge, 4 per cent received shelter and only 2 per cent were entitled to sick leave. About a third of the workers in the sample had work accidents in 1993. They paid for medical care themselves. Sixty-nine per cent were not members of any group or association, while the remainder were members of various cooperatives. None joined any formal groups or associations other than cooperatives. The majority of them had heard of the government social security scheme, but they were not covered in the scheme. When they had problems, most of them relied on relatives and neighbours for assistance. Twenty-two per cent said they had received help from no-one and only 1 per cent had help from the Government.

Other studies of informal sector workers have highlighted other problems faced by workers, such as: bad working conditions; low pay; long working hours; vulnerability to health hazards due to bad lighting; bad posture due to unsuitable chairs and tables; ignorance about the negative effects of chemicals in the materials used; lack of access to training for further skills; and lack of bargaining strength with buyers or contractors because of lack of association among themselves.

In Thailand and elsewhere in South-east Asia, informal work arrangements are widespread, as part of firms' strategies to reduce costs of production in the face of intense competition. Any attempt to solve the problems of labour exclusion cannot stop at labour protection and provisions of security for the formal sector alone. Informal sector workers must also receive protection and the Government must design policies for them, especially in areas of education, training, credit, technical and marketing assistance.

3. The homeless in Bangkok

The homeless in urban areas are also growing. The case study which was carried out to examine the situation of the homeless in Bangkok has concentrated on the families living under the bridges in the core areas of Bangkok. They are dispersed under 65 bridges in 21 districts. Settlement under bridges is part of the slum problem but the characteristics of these homeless are different from those of traditional slum dwellers. The size of the community settled under each bridge is small (the biggest being 66 households and the smallest being one household), leading to powerlessness in negotiation with the authority. Housing facilities and living conditions in the settlements under bridges are much worse than those in slums because, among other things, they have no direct access to electricity and water supply.

Unlike the slum dwellers, most of whom tend to be rural migrants from the north-east and the north of the country, more than half (54 per cent) of those settled under the bridges in Bangkok are people from the central region of the country, including Bangkok and neighbouring provinces, such as Prathumthani and Ayutthaya. The remainder came from the north-east, the north and other regions. Most have migrated at least once from another slum in Bangkok. They have lived under the bridges for five to ten years, and the longest time of settlement is about 40 years!

These people have poor education. Around 67 per cent finished only primary education and 23 per cent never registered in or attended school. Since they cannot read and write properly, the chance of entering the labour market with a reasonable job is low. Most of them earn income from hired labour, hawking and collecting garbage for resale. Their average income is 3000 baht (US$ 150) per household per month, which is far below the poverty line in Bangkok.

Apart from trying to live on this low income, the facilities available to the communities are also poor: they rely on the electricity and water supply of neighbours; they use public toilets if they can. Some bathe in the dirty rivers or canal and they live on what they can find in the dustbin. Thirteen per cent of the households have no birth certificates; 11 per cent have no identity cards. This means they will have difficulties in registering in public schools or availing themselves of government facilities, such as hospitals and public welfare offices.

In March 1993, the Government adopted a plan to improve the environment of Bangkok and Metropolitan areas. This project has threatened the people living under the bridges because the Government wants to move them out and settle them somewhere else. The Government also has plans to prevent new settlements, but the National Housing Authority, which is assigned the task of relocating and finding new homes for these people, still does not have a proper plan for their relocation. The families who settle under the bridges, with help from some NGOs, are negotiating for a solution.

One of their major problems is that they have very low educational levels and few skills. Therefore their chance of finding jobs, other than collecting garbage for sale, is remote. Their present jobs are possible because they live near densely-populated areas. If they are moved away to the outskirts of the city, the government will have to find them new jobs, but no clear policy and measures have been decided.

IV. Conclusion

Because of its fast-growing economy, social exclusion due to high rates and long duration of open unemployment is not as prevalent in Thailand as in the West at present. But Thailand does have problems of social exclusion due to uneven development and unfair institutional arrangements, such as inadequate provision of basic social goods — safe drinking water, toilets, basic education for poor and disadvantaged people in rural areas and in urban slums, lack of provision of at least minimum social security mechanisms for workers in the informal sector and inadequate respect of workers' right to unionization. The right to form labour associations is a basic worker's right whether in the formal or the informal sector. Labour association is considered necessary not as a business unionism or as a basis for political parties, but as a means to enable workers to cooperate or work in partnership with employers and government in enhancing productivity and building up a social market economy with quality employment and social justice.

As far as exclusion by gender is concerned, Thai women are still very much subject to male domination and the society's double standards, as seen in the prevalence of the exploitation of women in sex services. While economic factors are important in explaining the problems of women in Thailand, cultural factors which influence the attitudes of males and the public in general, and in particular government officials, are also important in degrading women.

In addition, there are incidents of active exclusion due to government measures and policies, especially with respect to poor rural families living in degraded forests and minorities living in the hills in the north. These have occurred because the government itself is subject to pressure from businessmen to pursue policies which benefit their lucrative investments, but which result in excluding poor people from their means of livelihood. The solution is not only to focus on planning for social secury, but also to change the attitudes of government officials. They must be persuaded to refrain from pursuing policies which exclude poor people and women in the process of rapid economic change.

Effective measures for reform of the bureaucracy in the face of the present-day globalization trends should be considered a part of the policy to combat exclusion. Exclusion problems result not only from the working of the markets but also from action of governments and cultural expectations. With respect to gender and exclusion, society as a whole must be re-educated in their attitudes towards gender so that they appreciate the equality of the sexes and so that poor rural women's right to education and good jobs in the labour markets is respected.

On the question of minorities, the problem really stems from insensitivity, lack of respect for cultural diversity and, more importantly, lack of respect for rights of minority communities over their natural resources and means of livelihood based on sustainable agriculture (which can be supported and promoted). The basic problem remains the political will of the central government to prevent businessmen and individuals both inside and outside the government from taking undue advantage of vulnerable ethnic minorities in the name of economic growth, but with no respect for human dignity.

9 Patterns and processes of social exclusion in Tunisia

Mongi Bédoui and Ridha Gouia

This paper focuses on three issues: the conceptualization of social exclusion in the specific situation of Tunisia; the structural and conjunctural causes of social exclusion; and policies to prevent social exclusion. The Tunisian case is particularly important because of the experience acquired in policies to fight exclusion, especially in the design and implementation of a social development policy as an integral, rather than supplementary, element of economic reform programmes.

I. The concept of social exclusion

The concept of social exclusion is broadly synonymous with the concept of marginalization and is related to a number of other concepts, notably poverty, unemployment and deprivation. It is a multidimensional concept, covering social, economic, cultural and political situations. Analyses of exclusion are concerned with the possibilities of participation in development in all its various aspects and with mechanisms of exclusion from active life and social action in general.

The importance of the concept lies in its depth, comprehensiveness and its ability to stimulate remedial action. The concept has depth because it encompasses both description of the actual conditions of life of marginalized people and analysis of the causes of these outcomes. It is comprehensive in that the analysis of causes can cover international relations; participation in development, deprivation and the distribution of gains from production within countries; the relationship between communities and national society; and even individuals' subjective sense of their isolation from society. And it stimulates counter-measures by directing attention both to policies of integration and to the seeds of marginalization and exclusion which can, paradoxically, be inherent within those policies. For example, the integration of women in economic life, with all their family responsibilities and without providing the necessary social institutions to help cater for children, can lead to their marginalization and exclusion from social, cultural, and political life.

The concept of exclusion appeared in Western Europe in the 1970s and generally refers to the rupture of social cohesion caused by unemployment which has reached proportions never seen in contemporary history. The inability of societies to integrate a growing part of their labour force in productive activities is seen to set in train a process at the individual level in which: loss of employment leads to a loss of income, rights associated with employment, and the ability to satisfy basic needs with regard to housing, health, etc.; and a developing sense of hopelessness and need for assistance leads to the breakdown of relationships with family, friends and, in the end, with the community and society.

In Tunisia, the concept of exclusion was used incidentally as early as the 1940s with reference to the slums of Saida El Manoubia and Jebel Lahmar, which were pockets of poverty, deprivation and disease within Tunis. These slums were growing through the drift of population from rural areas to the capital, and only a limited number of their inhabitants were able to find a job. A social study carried out in 1956, which warned about the situation in these slums, defined a situation which came to be known as exclusion in the 1970s. Later, this concept was used explicitly in an analytical study on social marginalization in Arab countries published by the Social Studies Centre in Tunis in 1992.

In order to advance the conceptualization of social exclusion in the specific situation of Tunisia, the country study examined the perceptions of exclusion held by certain groups of people who, to outside observers, might in some sense be considered excluded. This is important in that the way in which exclusion is defined depends on who is defining it.

A survey of a sample of unemployed persons, housewives and working women showed that the concept of exclusion is defined in different ways by these groups. For the housewives, particularly those in urban centres, employment was considered the basic factor of integration into society. "Excluded persons" were also secondarily defined as those who do not fit into the society's laws and codes and who are, as a consequence, irremediably isolated from the community for a reason for which they are not responsible. The working women in the sample tended to define exclusion in terms which go beyond employment. They gave particular consideration to literacy as one of the elements of integration, as literacy enables the person to be up-to-date with events and to develop the feeling of belonging and indirect participation through following events. "Excluded persons" were primarily defined in relation to the factors of illness, perversion and disability. For the unemployed in the sample, exclusion is defined as lack of income and unemployment but, interestingly enough, a significant proportion of the unemployed did *not* think that to be unemployed is to be excluded. The sense of marginalization amongst the unemployed was stronger for those who had been unemployed for a longer period, and also for those who felt poorly prepared for work due to limited instruction and training levels as well as the loss of family support. In general over two-thirds of the unemployed and housewives expressed a feeling of exclusion and isolation.

Three important findings can be deduced from this survey which can usefully inform the theoretical analysis of exclusion. First, it is necessary to use diversified indicators to identify exclusion. Second, exclusion is defined differently by different people according to their social status and living conditions. A person tends to feel excluded with regard to things he or she does not have. Thirdly, both employment and the guarantee of a source of income are important indicators of integration, and unemployment, poverty, and lack of resources play an important role in inducing a sense of exclusion.

Unemployment, in itself, is not exclusion. But it bears a relationship to exclusion in the sense that there is a process of exclusion associated with: (i) the increasing length of the unemployment period; (ii) the limited personal capabilities of the unemployed which hinder his/her easy integration; (iii) the loss of family support which may help a person to face his/her unemployment situation; and (iv) the growth of a feeling of isolation from public life. All these factors combine to make an unemployed person into an excluded and marginalized person. The key policy issue is how to prevent this shift from unemployment and poverty to exclusion.

II. The causes of the unemployment situation, poverty and social exclusion

Analysing the causes of social exclusion requires, as a first step, understanding of the situation of the unemployed and people with limited income, because it is through poverty and unemployment that the process of exclusion occurs. In Tunisia, contrasting trends are found. There have been very significant achievements in the fields of education, health and population growth, to the extent that the country is amongst the five most successful countries in the world in terms of the improvement of indicators of human resource development over the period 1962-92. Poverty is also diminishing, according to available statistics. In 1967, the proportion of the population living below the poverty line was 33 per cent whilst in 1990 it was 6.7 per cent, according to the National Institute of Statistics. This consisted of 83,000 families and, of these, only 18 per cent had some qualifications which could enable their economic integration. But unemployment is rising. Between 1984 and 1989 the unemployment rate rose from 12.9 per cent to 15.3 per cent. At the latter date, the number of unemployed persons was 316,000, of whom 66 per cent are in a state of structural unemployment, having been unemployed for more than one year. Most of the unemployed do not have the necessary educational level to get jobs, nor vocational training, and 43 per cent of the unemployed (135,000) are young people looking for their first job.

The causes of the unemployment situation and pattern of poverty, which can lead to exclusion processes, can be classified into two types: first, the long-term structural framework of development in Tunisia, which is characterized by some disequilibria at the social and economic levels; and second, temporary and transitory causes, the most significant of which at the present moment is the social impact of the Structural Adjustment Programme implemented since 1986.

1. Lack of structural equilibria

There are four imbalances in the development path of Tunisia which underlie processes of social exclusion. The first is the lack of equilibrium between the modern economic sector and the traditional economic sector. This imbalance exists as a legacy of the colonial period (1881-1956) when a dual economy, consisting of two separate modes of production, emerged. The "modernizing" operations of the colonial power established activities such as modern mechanized agriculture and heavy industry but these were integrated with the economy of the metropole. They had no links with the local development fabric and they existed alongside a traditional mode of production based on peasant farming, handicrafts and some production of goods and services for the local market. Rural people lost land as a result of the expansion of the colonizers and the opposition between the two modes decreased income levels and precipitated the breakdown of the local economy, leading to an increase in the drift of the rural population to big towns and the formation of slums. Available statistics show that in the marginalized shanty towns around the capital, Tunis, more than 55 per cent of the population was living in poverty and the unemployment rate was about 40 per cent during the years 1945-47.

Second, there is a disequilibrium between the rate of population growth and the rate at which new jobs are being created. Despite the important success of Tunisia in reducing annual population growth rates from 2.5 per cent for the period 1975-84 to 2.3 per cent for 1984-94 — this being the lowest rate in the Arab countries — the number of newcomers to the labour market remains higher than new jobs created. This means that unemployment primarily affects young people who, because of their lack of knowledge of practical life, are more prone to marginalization.

Third, there is a disequilibrium between development poles and their regional surroundings. After independence, the Tunisian government, like many other developing countries, adopted a development model which involved the promotion of heavy industries and the establishment of development poles in the south, centre and north of the country.[1] These poles were meant to be linked to each other and to integrate with their respective regional settings in a mutually stimulating, interactive growth dynamic. However, these development poles failed to promote significant subcontracting activities or to achieve significant inter-industry linkages. As a result, the development poles have become isolated from their environment. They clash with the traditional economy and thus bring into operation a new dynamic of exclusion.

Fourth, there is a disequilibrium between the limited qualifications of the unemployed in relation to the needs of economy. Despite the rapid spread of education, to the extent that the rate of school attendance for children at the age of schooling is currently situated at 98 per cent, a large proportion of the unemployed are illiterate or untrained. Recent figures suggest that about 70 per cent of the unemployed in Tunisia are either totally illiterate or their level of formal instruction does not go beyond primary education. This plays an extremely important role in the process through which unemployment leads to exclusion. Those people with poor qualifications tend to be unemployed for longer periods. Their situation tends to worsen from one year to the next as the number of educated and trained people increases on the labour market. The deterioration of their standard of living may further disqualify them from getting a job, magnifying their feeling of despair. The utter poverty experienced by the unemployed and the structure of the family may prevent them from moving to other places to look for employment. Active search for a job requires a minimum level of income and a situation of sheer poverty prevents this.

---

[1] The chemical industries in Gabes in the south-east of Tunisia; the phosphates industry in Gafsa in the south-west; the cellulose and paper compound in Kasserine in the western centre; the steel plant in the north, in addition to the textile compounds in the Sahel and various manufacturing industries in Tunis.

2. Impact of structural adjustment programmes on the labour market

The way that the long-term structural framework of development in Tunisia entrains processes of exclusion varies over time with transitory conjunctural changes. It also depends on the prevailing culture and the implementation of remedial measures. Currently, the most important conjunctural determinant of exclusion is the Structural Adjustment Programme (SAP) which has been implemented since August 1986. This programme has a significant social impact mainly on and through the labour market.

The main aims of Tunisia's SAP are: (i) to re-establish the country's financial equilibrium through public spending cuts, limiting imports, wage freezing, trimming subsidies and going back to market-based pricing; (ii) to redistribute the roles of the public and private sectors and to promote the private sector to enable it to play its full role in production and distribution on the basis of market forces; and (iii) to ensure the openness and the integration of the Tunisian economy in the international economy and to increase its ability to face the challenges of international competition through reducing costs, enhancing the quality of products and raising the productivity of capital, labour and equipment. This liberal economic policy has succeeded in bringing about a new dynamic to the Tunisian economy. In spite of adverse climatic conditions, economic growth rates averaged 4.5 per cent per annum from 1987 to 1993 and more than 50,000 jobs were created annually from 1991 to 1993. The current account balance has also experienced a noticeable improvement. But the negative social effects of the SAP have been considerable, particularly for vulnerable groups.

The liberalization of the economy and the spread of regulation of economic activity by the laws of supply and demand has led to a new structure of the labour market. New labour laws began to take shape. Programmes aimed at reforming and privatizing State enterprises came into existence and often led to redundancies for some workers and changing work routines for others. New types of unemployment appeared for those who lost their jobs, differing from the traditional unemployment which arises when young people first try to enter the labour market. Micro-enterprises and the family economy have also become increasingly important parts of the labour market.

The economic reforms in Tunisia have been accompanied by the curtailment of labour migration to Europe and Arab countries. In the 1970s, international migration played an important role as a regulator of the labour market and contributed to decreasing the negative social effects resulting from capital-intensive industrialization and the mechanization and modernization of the agricultural sector. Nowadays, the country has to balance economic and social considerations without this form of support from the international economy.

The SAP has had three important social effects which are related to present processes of exclusion and marginalization. First, although the economic reforms have not adversely affected the *quantity* of jobs created, as the new jobs created actually increased from an average of 40,000 per year in 1980-87 to 47,000 per year in 1987-93, some deterioration in the *quality* of employment has occurred since the implementation of the economic reforms. This is best demonstrated by classifying types of jobs according to levels of skills needed, levels and continuity of income and levels of social security, rather than with a simple dichotomy between "good" formal sector employment and "bad" informal sector employment. Breaking the structure of employment into five groups, namely: (i) protected wage employment; (ii) first-class wage employment, non-protected and open to competition on the labour market; (iii) second-class (temporary) wage employment, non-protected; (iv) self-employment and employment in small production units; and (v) "marginal" activities,[2] it is apparent that the biggest share of newly created jobs in Tunisia during the period of the reforms has been in categories (iii) and (iv), and growth of activities of the marginal sector has also occurred. Employment in the textiles and food processing sectors has grown significantly, though this employment does not require high skills. And there has also been a significant growth in the number of micro-enterprises, particularly because of assistance provided by regional development programmes.

Second, although real wages have begun to rise since 1990, after the stabilization of the financial situation of the economy, real incomes fell during the 1983-90 period, particularly amongst the poorest workers. Research carried out by Hassine Dimassi[3] shows that, between 1983 and 1990, the purchasing power of workers earning the minimum wage fell by 23.5 per cent for industrial workers and 18.5 per cent for agricultural labourers.

Third, the restructuring of the sectors which are big employers of women, notably textiles and food processing industries, has exacerbated the difficulties facing women in the labour market. Between 1984 and 1992,

---

[2] This classification follows J.-P. Lachaud: "Urban labour market analysis in Africa", in *Labour and Society* (Geneva, IILS), Vol. 14, No. 4, pp. 333-362, October 1989.

[3] Dimassi, H. *Séminaire National sur les politiques de promotion sociale des catégories de population les plus défavorisées*. Ministry of Social Affairs, Kairouan, 1991.

the unemployment rate amongst women rose more quickly than amongst men, reaching a rate of 20.5 per cent for women as against 11 per cent for men at the latter date.

As far as the decrease in real incomes and the increase of women's unemployment are concerned, the sample survey of the unemployed shows that several members of the family are found to be looking for jobs on the labour market at the same time so that they can cope with the fall in the household income. Of the 31 married persons in the sample of unemployed, there are 22 cases looking for a job at the same time as their spouses. Moreover, two-thirds of the unemployed have one or more brothers looking for a job at the same time as them and 29 per cent have one or more sisters also looking for a job. In addition to the effect of the fall in income on the increase in the family search for jobs, unemployment is found to be closely related to the general situation of the family and its vulnerability. The survey shows that two-thirds of the unemployed belong to poor families.

III. Policies to prevent exclusion

The social effects of the SAP have prompted a response to meet the needs of various adversely affected groups, particularly young people entering the labour market for the first time, unskilled workers and women. From 1986-89, the measures adopted were meant to reduce the negative social effects of economic decisions and they were agreed through a tripartite dialogue between trade union representatives, the State and enterprise owners. Since 1989, the social element was included as an integral, rather than supplementary, part of development policy. The rate of social transfer payments has gone up, and they represent 18 per cent of the GDP despite the application of the economic reforms. Three-year pay rises, covering the periods 1990-92 and 1993-95, have also been agreed through collective bargaining.

The social development policies adopted in Tunisia along with the economic reform programmes are daring, innovative and original. They offer a policy experience for the design of measures to prevent exclusion which is instructive both in terms of principles and practices.

1. Principles

Amongst the principles which underlie the formulation of Tunisia's social development policy, there are four which are particularly important for overcoming exclusion. First, social policies are based on participation, with important roles being played by trade associations such as the employers' board, trade unions, farmers' associations and NGOs. Regional development councils and local councils, which have been given a large number of prerogatives to run and manage programmes to prevent marginalization, have also adopted a participatory approach. The importance of improving local structures is emphasized by the survey results and is particularly important where people have limited ability to leave their geographical environment.

Second, the process of social inclusion is seen in combination with the integration of the individual into the economy (i.e. economic integration). This is apparent, for example, in a new approach to the various records concerned with categories of people who are marginalized or vulnerable to marginalization. In the past, attention used to be devoted to their social conditions and family situation. Today personal capabilities (such as qualifications and aptitudes) are also recorded in order to identify the possibilities of their integration and adopt a socio-economic approach.

Third, a gender approach is adopted giving attention to the specific problems facing women. There is a Ministry devoted to women and family affairs and various special programmes and specific institutions have been set up to deal with them.

Fourth, a geographical approach is adopted paying specific attention to marginal regions (which are known as "shadow areas").

2. Policies

The policy mechanisms which serve to prevent exclusion include:

(a) measures to alleviate poverty, either directly or through improving the economic environment of "shadow areas";

(b) measures to assist and integrate the unemployed;

(c) income generation schemes and the promotion of micro-enterprises;

(d) adjustment of job creation through enterprises;

(e) structural reforms of the employment services.

A. *Measures to alleviate poverty*

The two main programmes to alleviate poverty are: the National Programme of Assistance to Poor Families, and the National Solidarity Fund. The *National Programme of Assistance to Poor Families* provides continuous cash grants and free medical and social security services to families identified as "poor". The programme is evolving, in terms of its organization and the families who have access to its services. Thus far, more than 100,000 families have access to the grant which increased from 40 dinars in 1986 to 310 dinars per quarter in August 1994. The programme has played an important role in alleviating the negative impact of the SAP on the purchasing power of poor families. In managing the programme, important issues have been: first, the problem of integrating the family dimension of poverty with the individual dimension; and second, the differentiation of poor people into those in a temporary state of poverty and those in a permanent state. The former have some capabilities which permit inclusion and they need temporary assistance accompanied by mechanisms for training and for potential economic integration. The latter need permanent assistance, and their integration must be treated as a social issue. Mechanisms for identifying, assisting and following these different groups amongst the poor are important.

The *National Solidarity Fund*, to which all economic actors contribute, is in charge of elaborating a programme to eradicate "shadow areas", which suffer from poverty, a lack of facilities and no growth dynamic. This programme seeks to reduce poverty through intervention aimed at the economic environment in a whole geographical area. Interventions are focused on infrastructure investment to link the area to the rest of the country and the promotion of income sources for citizens. Intervention is decentralized and all enterprises and organizations contribute to the Fund. The Fund's activities have drawn great enthusiasm from citizens, as they rely not only on the vitality of a sense of solidarity, but also organize new channels for the practice of solidarity. But the programme has not been in operation long and therefore it is too early to evaluate its effectiveness and costs. In its preparation, design and implementation, it has, nevertheless, been original and innovative. Within the framework of this programme, there is a strategy aiming at integrating, by the year 2000, 850 zones which have been identified as being critical by the various surveys.

B. Measures to assist and integrate the unemployed

Assistance to the unemployed includes special programmes for young people who are entering the labour market for the first time and for illiterate job applicants. Youth employment promotion programmes have played an important role in providing young people with the opportunity to get to know the work environment and to increase their potential for integration into it. Through employment and training contracts, 18,671 young people had access to training between 1981 and 1993, and 88 per cent were subsequently integrated into the work environment. From 1987 to August 1994, 16,501 university graduates received "Initiation for Professional Life" training and 73 per cent of these were integrated after finishing their training. From 1991 to 1993, 2,730 secondary school leavers completed preparatory vocational training and 50 per cent were subsequently integrated.

Illiterate job applicants or those whose level of instruction does not go beyond third-year secondary education, have access to the programmes of regional working sites. These sites, which generally involve public works, are meant to enable poor people to earn a minimum income and meet their living requirements, particularly during droughts and crises in the agricultural sector. They provide 50,000 jobs, repeated each year.

Evaluation of these programmes of assistance to the unemployed suggests that the youth employment programmes really promote the integration of young people into the workforce and they should be reinforced and their mechanisms diversified. But the regional working sites programme, which was first created in 1956, has unclear goals; over 70 per cent of those who have access to the services of the programme are over 50 years old; 20 per cent are working with public enterprises as a replacement for recruitment; and the costs of the programme are continuously rising, from 42.1 million dinars in 1987 to 75.5 million in 1991. This programme needs to be reviewed, to consolidate its role in providing a source of income for people but enhancing its ability to promote economic integration of the individuals who seek its services.

C. Income generation schemes

Programmes aiming at promoting income sources are one of the most important methods of integrating individuals into the economy. They have evolved particularly during the implementation of the economic reforms as the possibilities of securing wage employment diminished. The Regional Development Programmes and Integrated Rural Development Programmes include special funds for income generation, through creating micro-enterprises and supporting self-employment and the family economy. The funds allocated for this purpose increased in both of these programmes over the period 1987 to 1991: from 26.8 million to 28 million dinars in the former, and from 31 million to 70 million dinars in the latter. Special regulations have been developed to support the informal sector and to promote a transition of informal sector activities to the formal sector. The Handicraft and Small Trades Promotion Fund, created in 1981, provides a specific mechanism for financing persons promoting small projects. It has created 64,000 jobs in 16,000 small projects since 1981. The capital of the Fund increased from 5 million dinars in 1987 to 8 million in 1991. Financial management is undertaken by banks, and this has reinforced the reimbursement of loans and helped to secure the cost-effectiveness of the projects. All evaluations recognize the importance of this Fund.

These income generation schemes have paid particular attention to the needs of women. Projects promoted by women with the help of the Handicraft and Small Trades Promotion Fund rose from 11 per cent in 1985 to 21 per cent in 1991. Women's participation in the regional development programmes amounts to more than 50 per cent.

D. *Adjustment of job creation through enterprises*

An important initiative affecting the working of the labour market, which has been adopted as part of the SAP, is the Insertion and Professional Training Fund. It includes five mechanisms: insertion training; training for persons promoting micro-enterprises; facilitation of geographical mobility; implementation of comprehensive in-service training to preserve jobs; and training through specialized organizations. This Fund is jointly financed by the Tunisian Government and the World Bank. Funds amount to 22 million dinars for three years. Evaluation of this programme shows that up to 31 August 1994, 33,812 people benefited from the Fund's services. Sixty-six per cent of the beneficiaries are female; 82 per cent are unemployed; 50 per cent have education at the primary school level and only 16 per cent have an education beyond the second year of secondary school. It is therefore apparent that, although the Fund's mechanisms are directed at enterprises, its interventions have served to meet the needs of categories of people who are prone to marginalization and exclusion, particularly women and the unemployed with limited education. This is a pioneering experience conducted jointly by the Tunisian Government and the World Bank with a view to enhancing the structural reform.

E. *Structural reform of the employment services*

A programme to reform employment services has also been initiated for the period 1994-96. This programme, called "Services", has the following functions: (i) improvement of professional guidance and information to provide equal opportunities for young people to take advantage of the State's programmes in training and employment; (ii) the extension of professional guidance to all regions to enable young people to have access to the available vocational training opportunities throughout the country; (iii) the reinforcement of the active processing of labour supply and demand and improving services provided to enterprises and job applicants through specific intervention mechanisms; (iv) the improvement of employment services to help the creation of micro-enterprises and the promotion of family production and self-employment; and (v) the reinforcement of follow-up mechanisms in the labour market, monitoring, in particular, long-term unemployment and unemployment by sex, in order to break the exclusion process. This programme is characterized by the fact that it enhances partnership between the public and the private sectors. This makes it possible to assist the unemployed and liberalize the processing of job supply, offering an approach which is neither a completely private alternative nor a totally public one.

IV. Conclusions and suggestions

Five major lessons can be drawn from Tunisia's policy experience. First, a country's specific social, cultural and political conditions have to be taken into account in the implementation of structural adjustment programmes, and the room for manœuvre in these programmes is strongly related to the long-term trends in development within a country (such as education, health, population, growth). Second, social policies which are accompanying appendages to economic reforms do not provide a basis for successful social development, and instead social development policies need to be at the core of development policy. Third, participation is a fundamental factor in the success of social programmes. The elaboration of programmes without participation does not promote responsibility, discourages self-reliance, and does not enable the discovery of personal abilities which can help in the inclusion process. Fourth, women need to be involved in all programmes on an equal footing with men in order to ensure the wider participation of women. The key to integration is the economic contribution which individuals make. Fifth, in the elaboration and evaluation of programmes, both economic efficiency and social goals should be considered.

These lessons provide a basis for making various prospective suggestions in elaborating policies to fight against exclusion:

(a) Programmes to assist job applicants need to be carried out in conjunction with programmes rooted in the economic fabric which, for example, improve the working of labour markets.

(b) Specific programmes aimed at the unemployed should take more account of the length of the unemployment period, the qualifications

of the unemployed and their living conditions, in order to break the process leading to exclusion.

(c) Employment services should be preserved, though they may be usefully implemented through a combination of privatization and an administrative approach.

(d) Participation should be emphasized in the elaboration and implementation of inclusion programmes.

(e) The fight against exclusion requires measures at the family level, but these need to be supplemented by a policy of integrating the "shadow areas" and measures at the individual level which encourage self-reliance.

(f) Policies to promote the creation of income sources through financing micro-enterprises, integrating this operation into the normal financial market and making funds available to promote the transition of enterprises from the informal to the formal sector. Employment services can play a role in this respect.

(g) More attention needs to be paid to the most poverty-stricken categories of people and to those who have been in unemployment longest in order to draw a red line which must not be crossed if exclusion mechanisms in society are to be kept in check.

(h) Specific programmes aimed at integrating women have a high value-added, though it is necessary to avoid women-only programmes which convey the impression that the remaining programmes are intended only for men.

(i) It is important to introduce procedures for evaluating the various programmes and their impact on the surrounding environment.

(j) It is important to elaborate a system of unemployment benefits which provides, on the one hand, financial support for short-term unemployment, based on an insurance scheme to which employees contribute, compulsorily up to a specific level of income and then voluntarily; and, on the other hand, the active processing of job applications through specific programmes, explicitly introducing the factors of sex and length of unemployment period in order to prevent further exclusion. The greater the threat of marginalization, the more developed should be the intervention mechanisms for integration and against exclusion.

10 Patterns and processes of social exclusion in the Republic of Yemen

Mouna Hashem[1]

This paper examines the nature of exclusion in Yemen at the macro and the micro levels. At the macro level, it seeks to define the concept of social exclusion in a way which relates to the historical, social, political and economic context of Yemen. At the micro level, it identifies the dimensions of exclusion, the groups most vulnerable to exclusion, and existing mechanisms that promote the processes of exclusion. Throughout the discussion, the concept of exclusion is related to poverty, unemployment, and social integration.

The analysis has two main objectives. The first is to illustrate that, although poverty and exclusion are interdependent, they are not the same. Poverty involves deprivations from goods and services. Exclusion encompasses these deprivations but also raises broader issues of citizens' rights in economic, social, and political participation. The second objective is to draw the attention of policy-makers and other social actors to the urgent need to design policies that prevent exclusion and emphasize integration in the development process.

The analysis is founded on the view that the application of ideas about social exclusion formulated in Western Europe and North America, on the basis of economic and social experiences in a post-industrial society, to the question of exclusion in developing countries has many pitfalls. There is a need to develop an approach to analysing exclusion which is appropriate to the experiences of the political, social and economic changes in the "pre-industrial" and newly-industrializing societies of developing countries.

This is particularly so in a country like Yemen. It has a dual economy rather than a market economy. The institutions that mediate moral norms for a "collective consciousness" are not the market and the economy.

[1] Dr. Hashem worked in close collaboration with the Education Development and Research Centre in Sana'a, and in particular with Dr. I. Al-Houthy.

Structural differentiation is not as high as in industrialized societies. It continues to be based on cultural identities. A process of differentiation based on the division of labour and individualism is not well-developed. The economy remains strongly embedded in forms of cultural integration that limit the full development of private property rights and market individualism. People perceive the problem of their exclusion as a problem that involves the family and the community and not as a problem that is limited to the individual.

I. The concept of social exclusion in Yemen

Social exclusion in Yemen is associated with the marginalization of certain groups from social and economic development. As the process of development occurs, those that are left behind become trapped in a cycle of poverty and exclusion. Political history, geographic dispersion, cultural norms, and social and economic development are important factors in understanding the concept of social exclusion in Yemen. The dual nature of Yemen society gives rise to dual mechanisms of exclusion. On the one hand, exclusionary practices arise in social relationships based on traditional cultural values, i.e. structural norms which continue to influence social relationships. On the other hand, there are mechanisms based on national development policies that have not succeeded in distributing development benefits equally. Structural norms and development policies overlap in the exclusion process.

Yemen consists of a heterogenous agrarian society. Social divisions have been defined by geography, tribal affiliations and religion. Social identity, solidarity and social order are largely based on these cultural structures. Genealogy defines social stratification and economic and political power. This process represents an important structural norm. These social structures represent closures which reflect an inclusion-exclusion process. A consequence of this type of exclusion is that individuals whose genealogy is not traceable are marginalized in social and economic participation. Access to land and employment are strongly influenced by social identities and networks based on kinship and friendship between equals. Consequently, those who lack these modes of access encounter barriers to the labour market. Although these perceptions are slowly changing in urban centres, they continue to be dominant among the rural population. The Government's objective of social integration entails challenging these structural norms to assert its role as the sole legitimate authority. This aim of replacing solidarities from the cultural level to the national level has been a major challenge.

Social exclusion that results from social and economic development policies is more complex. Yemen is considered to be among the least developed countries of the world. It ranked 130 in the UNDP human development index. Although the government tries to provide all citizens with equal access to development benefits, this task is impeded by many obstacles. The major obstacles include political crises, a high rate of inflation, unemployment, a highly centralized bureaucratic system, high rate of population growth, and limited financial resources.

The ability to identify mechanisms of exclusion in the development process, and to reverse them to promote integration, are critical for the country's ability to achieve its objectives relating to economic development. Until this is achieved, the country will continue to be pulled apart by the two opposing dynamic forces: the efforts to transform the country into a modern market economy, and the acute problems of poverty and poor mobilization of human and natural resources.

II. Political and macro-economic change and exclusion

Yemen's economy is characterized by a weak domestic industrial sector, a strong dependency on imports for virtually all essential needs, and a large trade deficit. The GDP is $5.3 billion and the per capita income is $545 (1991). Although terms such as "economic growth" and "economic development" are used interchangeably, there is a significant difference between them, especially in relation to the study of social exclusion in developing countries. Economic growth is a function of a market economy, occupational diversity and institutional transactions. In this situation, as is the case in industrialized societies, social exclusion may result from the rapid economic changes and the breakdown of social ties. In developing countries, and Yemen is no exception, there is a preponderance of unskilled labour, a dual economy, inefficient infrastructure, and a lack of market and labour information systems. Social exclusion in this setting is related to the poor mobilization of human resources.

Unlike other developing countries, Yemen has been relatively spared from the effects of economic policies such as "structural adjustment" that have been imposed on many developing countries. The economy of Yemen, however, has been adversely affected by numerous political crises that have occurred since the beginning of the decade.

In May 1990, the Yemen Arab Republic (YAR), also known as North

Yemen, and the People's Democratic Republic of Yemen (PDRY), also known as South Yemen, united to become the Republic of Yemen (ROY). Sana'a was designated the capital of the new nation State (Sana'a was originally the capital of the YAR). The population of the new ROY was estimated at 12.4 million in 1992.[2] This consisted of 9.9 million from the YAR and 2.5 million from the PDRY.

Before the unification of North and South Yemen, the two countries had very different political and economic ideologies. The North was a free market-oriented State, while the South was socialist. Social services such as education, training and health care were provided free of charge in both countries. Both North and South Yemen suffered from a serious lack of resources. In spite of the different political ideologies, poverty was equally prevalent in the South and North. Both had been largely unsuccessful in integrating their populations in their development policies.

The unification of the two Yemens resulted in the unification of the problems of poverty and social exclusion. During this period of political transition, problems of poverty and exclusion were compounded by other internal and external political and economic factors. Internally, the expenses of unification resulted in a big financial burden on the country. South Yemen, which was the poorest of the two, made very little financial contributions to the unification process. North Yemen's limited resources had to be further stretched to accommodate another three million people. As a result, the satisfaction of basic needs became more difficult for some and totally unattainable for others. Following the unification and the economic and political changes that followed, the number of individuals and groups in the new Republic that are unable to participate in economic development increased markedly.

The outbreak of hostilities in 1994 between the Government and a faction which aims to secede will undoubtedly have dramatic effects on the economy of Yemen. The full effect this will have on people's livelihood remains to be seen.

Externally, a few months after unification, the Gulf War broke out. The political stand taken by the ROY during the Gulf War was resented by many donor countries, especially the oil-rich Arab countries. The consequences have been devastating for Yemen's economy. First, over one million emigrant Yemeni workers in the Gulf were forced to return to their

---

[2] Ministry of Planning and Development (ed.): *Population and development in the Republic of Yemen*. Proceedings of the First National Population Policy Conference (Sana'a, Ministry of Planning and Development, 1992).

country at very short notice. The Government was not prepared to provide housing, health care, employment and other social services for the emigrants. Furthermore, their annual remittances that used to contribute approximately 400 million dollars to Yemen's GNP were also lost. In addition, all aid from the oil-rich Arab countries was halted. Shanty towns consisting of emigrant families spread in and around the cities, schools became overloaded, and unemployment rates increased.

III. Patterns of social exclusion

Three types of exclusion appear to be particularly prevalent in Yemen: exclusion from basic needs, exclusion from livelihood, and exclusion from social participation and representation. These non-mutually exclusive processes interact in a dynamic cycle of poverty and downward mobility.

1. Exclusion from basic needs

The unfavourable ranking of Yemen on the human development index is a result of high illiteracy (62 per cent), a staggering population growth rate (3.8 per cent), high mortality of infants and children under five (109/1000 live births), a high fertility rate (7.5), and high maternal mortality. In addition, this ranking reflects the poor standards of health services, electrification, housing, tapped water and sewerage facilities, low skill levels and an undiversified labour force structure (Ministry of Planning and Development, op. cit.). These indicators underscore the urgent need for the provision of basic needs to provide an acceptable standard of living.

The exclusion of some groups from basic needs can be explained by a simple supply and demand equation. Although the equitable provision of social services to all citizens is a governmental priority, efforts to provide these basic services have been compromised by technical and financial limitations. As a result, many groups continue to be deprived from access to basic social services.

2. Exclusion from livelihood

This type of exclusion is reflected in unemployment and underemployment, insecure jobs, lack of wage protection, and lack of social insurance. This is compounded by a slow-growing economy and a large share of unskilled labour, lack of investment in industrial and modern sector activities, and conventional development planning which has also contributed to a maldistribution of employment opportunities. That is, industries, services and utilities are concentrated in the major cities and their outskirts. Furthermore, the use of capital-intensive techniques has led to an increase in productivity with no additional employment opportunities.

The size of the labour force in Yemen has increased from approximately 2.6 million in the year 1988 to 3.5 million in 1991. This translates into an average annual growth rate of 9.9 per cent which is threefold higher than the growth rate of the population (Ministry of Planning and Development, op. cit. p. 103). This rapid increase in the size of the labour force has been a direct consequence of the Gulf War and the influx of large numbers of Yemeni workers who returned from neighbouring Gulf countries.

3. Exclusion from social participation and representation

Social participation and representation are influenced by social networks and social awareness. The lack of strong social networks inhibits the ability of the poor to organize. Their economic dependence makes them socially and politically passive. The constitution guarantees the right of people to politically organize. However, there is a general lack of confidence in the political system and in what the system can do. This has been compounded by political representatives at the community level who often fail to represent effectively the people's needs. Eventually, some people start believing that they have no rights and they isolate themselves from the mainstream of society.

IV. Excluded groups and mechanisms of exclusion

For the purpose of the IILS/UNDP project, the study on Yemen identified four groups as the most vulnerable to the dimensions of exclusion discussed above. These four groups are: the *akhdam*, the returnee emigrants, day labourers, and inhabitants of remote rural villages.

1. The akhdam

The *akhdam* provide a perfect example of a group caught in a vicious cycle of poverty and social exclusion. This is particularly evident in the northern governorate. Their social exclusion is a result of embedded cultural norms that define them as an out-group. Their poverty is due to marginal participation in the labour market. The dynamic process of poverty and exclusion has pushed them to the fringes of society. The exclusion of the *akhdam* has been multidimensional: from livelihood, from social participation and from basic needs.

The physical features of the *akhdam* are close to those of Africans. There have been numerous studies that unsuccessfully attempted to establish a link between the *akhdam* and the Africans. The language of the *akhdam* and their religious practices, however, are the same as the rest of the Yemeni society. Their exclusion is reinforced by embedded cultural social norms that define them as outsiders due to their untraceable genealogy.

The continuing use of the term *akhdam*, the plural for *Khadem* which means servant, is clearly discriminatory. The *akhdam* tend to keep to themselves since they know they would not be welcomed if they try to mix with others in society. They live in closed ghettos of tin huts with no piped water, sanitation facilities or sewage systems. Although, demographic data on the *akhdam* is scarce, it is widely believed that the majority are illiterate. Their children are frequently not sent to school since their parents cannot afford school expenses. In addition, children may be called upon to participate in work that will add to the family's income. Those that go to school drop out in some cases as a result of discriminatory practices. The racial and emotional uneasiness and uncertainty in dealing with the *akhdam* is best characterized as "aversive racism". This is a more hidden form of racism which is expressed in simple avoidance. Social distance is maintained separating this minority group from the rest of society in relation to work, neighbourhood, and friendships and marriage.

Economically, the *akhdam* are employed in jobs that are considered "degrading" in Yemeni society. They make up the majority of the city street cleaners and waste collectors. In rural villages, the *akhdam* are hired to work on the farms but are not always paid in cash nor do they have a say in how they get paid. Instead, they may be given crops, food or temporary housing.

Politically, they are weak and subservient. Although they have community representatives, these representatives merely serve as arbitrators in their internal community disputes.

2. Day labourers

Day labourers in Yemen are referred to as *al-mouhamashine*, or the marginalized. In general, the term *mouhamashine* could refer to any under class group in Yemeni society. Recently, this term has been widely used to describe poor casual labourers who seek work on a daily basis and gather in several locations in the major cities. They are primarily landless workers and marginal landowners who migrate to the cities with expectations of improving their economic status. Instead, they arrive in urban centres that are unable to absorb them. In addition, they have no existing social networks or skills that could help them. The day labourers primarily encounter exclusion from livelihood. Their exclusion represents a temporary type of exclusion, i.e. one that is dependent on the state of the economy.

Their migration to a new city and their marginalized participation in the labour market contributes to their exclusion. The problem is compounded by their weak social interactions that result from the lack of housing and the lack of permanent employment. Thus, besides being poor and living in urban zones deprived of both residential security and other basic services, their livelihood is always at risk. At present, there is no labour legislation (such as a minimum wage) or social insurance to protect such marginalized groups in the labour market.[3] There is also a domino effect that is set in motion when poor men emigrate and leave their families behind in the rural villages. In addition to breaking up the family, the elder sons are often taken out of school to take over the responsibilities of the family in the absence of the father. This includes looking for additional work to supplement the family's income. Consequently, the sons, like their fathers, grow up with minimal qualifications and skills. This deprives the younger generation of the chance to improve their own quality of life. Plans have just been completed for major investment in vocational centres. These centres, however, are primarily targeted for high school students. The high percentage of unskilled labourers also raises the issue of gender exclusion. Poor landless men have been overlooked in many development projects. There are few or no rehabilitation programmes linked to the needs of the labour market that would train men in income-generating skills. Many foreign government donors and international organizations have designed projects for poor women relating to literacy, health and training in income-generating skills. Poor men have largely been overlooked in these efforts.

3. The returnee emigrants of the Gulf War

Six months after Yemen's unification, the Gulf War started with the Iraqi invasion of Kuwait. As a result of Yemen's stand in the war, over one million Yemeni emigrants in Kuwait, Bahrain, Saudi Arabia, the United Arab Emirates and Iraq were forced to go back home. According

---

[3] Ministry of Planning and Development, op. cit., p. 110.

to estimates of the Central Statistical Organization (CSO) in 1991, this represented an 8 per cent increase in the population of Yemen.

Four years after the Gulf War, about 75,000 families of returnee emigrants continue to live in camps in pathetic conditions on the outskirts of major cities. The difficulties of camp life include lack of electricity, uncertain water delivery, lack of privacy and unpredictable food supply. Malaria and other diseases are widespread in these camps. Although most of these emigrants had previously been able to establish themselves elsewhere, the consequences of their unexpected return have been devastating to them and their families. The adverse combination of their return to Yemen during an economic crisis and the lack of belonging to a village or patronage have made it very difficult for them to integrate back into their own country.

A recent CSO survey provides some information on the characteristics of these returnees.[4] The largest group of returnees (92 per cent) came from Saudi Arabia. The majority of returnees (65 per cent) have been out of the country for more than ten years. Seventy four per cent of them are between the ages of 15 and 45 years. Almost half are illiterate and only 18 per cent have some formal education. Fifty one per cent were employed as skilled labourers. Only 13 per cent had found employment when the survey was conducted. The CSO survey shows that 10 per cent of the returnees were born outside Yemen and 74 per cent did not own land or houses in Yemen.

The unexpected return of these emigrants became a nationwide crisis. Unemployment in Yemen increased from 7 to 25 per cent. Shortages and inflation pushed food prices up by more than 200 per cent between 1990 and 1992 (*Yemen Times*, 11 March 1992, p. 6). Demonstrations erupted frequently in different parts of the country protesting about lack of jobs, inflation and increasing poverty.

The exclusion of the returnees has been multidimensional. They have been excluded from basic needs since basic services have not been extended to them. They have been marginalized from the labour market due to the glut of manual labourers and lack of economic growth. They have been deprived of effective social representation because of their weak social networks.

The Government and several international organizations have attempted to develop relief programmes for these returnee emigrants of the Gulf

---

[4] Central Statistical Organization: *Al-Mongtaribonn* [The emigrants] (Sana'a, Ministry of Planning and Development, 1990).

War but these efforts have been largely insufficient. As a result of the ongoing political and economic crises in the country, their situation is no longer considered an urgent priority. Thus, their exclusion may eventually be transformed from a temporary situation to one of a more permanent nature.

4. *Inhabitants of remote rural villages*

Rural villages in Yemen are dispersed in areas ranging from rocky mountains to semi-desert plains. The exclusion of these villages is primarily territorial exclusion. This exclusion is also multifaceted, i.e. geographic, social, economic and political. The people in these villages live in impoverished conditions. They are under the impression that the Government is not interested in including them in the overall social and economic development of the country. The Government, on the other hand, has always considered the social integration of these inhabitants a vital objective. The provision of basic services to the inhabitants of these villages that are geographically distant and where traditional social structures are dominant has been a complex and costly endeavour.

Although agriculture is the predominant employment sector (77 per cent),[5] cultivable land makes up only 9.5 per cent of the total area of Yemen. In the past few years, the Ministry of Planning and Development reported a progressive reduction in the land that is cultivated annually. This has been attributed to meagre water supply, deteriorating production levels as a result of migration to urban areas or abroad, the limited availability of production inputs, and rising production costs. The efforts to promote economic development in remote rural villages have been hampered by shortages of capital investment, meagre private sector investment, low level of technology, labour shortages, lack of basic infrastructure (e.g. roads, storage facilities, energy) and land ownership.

Growing traditional crops, especially grains, is no longer profitable since the market value is frequently less than the cost of its production. The transformation of agricultural production to meet the needs of a market economy is evident only in rural villages that are closer to major cities. While some of the rural villages in marginal areas are being abandoned, the rich lands which have access to water and whose owners are capable of investing in modern agricultural machinery such as tractors are heavily farmed. This intense exploitation of the good land has only been possible for farmers who have liquid assets available to them.

The marginalization of some rural communities from social and

---

[5] Ministry of Planning and Development, op. cit., p.107.

economic development reflects institutional development strategies that fail to provide all citizens with equal access to these resources. Disparities between the rural and urban areas, and also within rural populations, are increasing. The consequences of the exclusion of remote rural areas has compounded the problem of rural-urban migration and impeded the transformation of the economy from a subsistence to a market economy.

V. Policy issues and the role of social actors

Development policies should emphasize social integration and should be sensitive to problems of exclusion. In order to fight social exclusion in Yemen, it is important to overcome traditional structural norms and to implement development strategies which overcome mechanisms of exclusion. This task should ideally be undertaken jointly by international and national (government and non-government) agencies with the participation of the communities involved.

Society itself is predominantly responsible for social exclusion based on structural norms. None the less, this process of exclusion could be combated by affirmative social policies. The success of such a strategy has been demonstrated by the experience of the *akhdam* in South Yemen. The Government developed specific policies to prevent social discrimination against the *akhdam*. For example, the use of the term *khadem/akhdam* was forbidden since it referred to a social status. The *akhdam* were encouraged to seek education and training. Most importantly, in both rural and urban areas, they were given equal employment opportunities. As a result, in the 1980s, the *akhdam* of the Southern governorate were able to find employment in different administrative positions such as civil servants, teachers, policemen and soldiers. These policies proved to be successful in promoting the upward mobility of the *akhdam* and freeing them from the social stigma that was previously attached to them. Currently, there are no active policies to integrate the *akhdam* into society.

Future development programmes should make it a priority to attack mechanisms of exclusion. Such policies should be incorporated in the overall framework of development. There are several development policies that should be reconsidered in the light of the ongoing problems of exclusion. Privatization of social services such as health care and education is currently being considered as a potential new strategy. Although this may alleviate some of the Government's financial burdens that result from the provision of social services to the population, it represents a major threat to vulnerable groups that may find more barriers to such social services. This is already taking place in the education sector. The registration fees in public schools have recently been increased. Although this increase was modest, many lower-income families had to withdraw their children from the schools. To them, even such a modest increase made schooling not affordable. A risk of privatization of the health system is that the cost of medicine may increase. This is particularly serious since medicine is already beyond the reach of the poor. Promoters of privatization argue that safety-nets will be instituted to ensure the access of all citizens to these services. It is still not clear, however, how these safety-nets are going to be designed and implemented.

Other development strategies that should be reviewed in the light of the existing mechanisms of exclusion include those that relate to the involvement of inhabitants of remote rural villages in social and economic development. For example, the current policies for rural areas are designed to increase agriculture production.[6] In a list of strategies for the implementation of this objective, the only one that relates to improving the livelihood of small farmers is improving small farmers' standard of living through increased production. There do not appear to be any specific plans for human resources development. Instead, the emphasis is primarily on the industrialization of agricultural production.

The international community plays an important role in the exclusion-inclusion process. Yemen depends heavily on multilateral and bilateral aid in its programmes of social and economic development. Foreign-sponsored development projects can alleviate the marginalization of certain groups from basic services and catalyze the development process. Unfortunately, the international community has recently compounded the problem of poverty and exclusion in Yemen by decreasing financial assistance in the wake of the Gulf War. These measures were primarily directed against the Government but they exerted their heaviest toll on the poor and vulnerable.

Non-governmental organizations (NGOs) can also play an important role in eliminating social exclusion. Many of their projects provide deprived groups with social services such as literacy programmes, primary health care and training in income-generating skills. In the last few years, the number of local NGOs increased significantly. The Ministry of Insurance and Social Affairs has supported local NGOs by making yearly financial contributions to them. International and bilateral donors have also provided them with financial and technical support. NGOs should be used to help identify exclusionary process. They should also be encouraged to function as effective representatives of the excluded groups.

---

[6] Ministry of Planning and Development, op. cit., p. 7.

11 Patterns and processes of social exclusion in Tanzania

Anna Tibaijuka and Frederick Kaijage

I. Introduction

Social exclusion is so far not part of political language or of the conceptual baggage of social science discourse in Tanzania. The related concepts which enjoy currency in Tanzanian social science literature and political discourse are national unity, equality, popular participation, basic needs and poverty. The pressures on the social programmes instituted during the Nyerere era, and the growing problem of urban and rural poverty in the present period have engendered a certain disquiet about the welfare of the nation as a whole.

Since independence, a national ethos has evolved according to which a quest for minimum standards of material welfare and social rights for every citizen in the context of a "united" nation is taken for granted. In current political discourse these issues are linked to the question of democratization. Social exclusion as a concept is therefore relevant for the current political and scholarly concerns in Tanzania.

In our study we have isolated critical economic and social processes which have an important bearing on the concept. We analyse acutely disadvantaged social groups in rural and urban areas, and discuss the question of exclusion from land and the plight of AIDS orphans. Discussion of the macro-economic and social policies provide a setting for the study.

II. The macro-economic and social policy framework

In Tanzania, the State has played such a conspicuous role in determining the fate of the general populace that we think a grasp of government economic and social policies is essential for understanding the process of social exclusion. Needless to say, such policies need to be examined in the context of their interactive relationship with other historical, cultural and social forces which are at play in Tanzanian society.

Three distinct phases in the evolution of post-independence Tanzania's economic and social policies are easily discernible. The first begins from independence in 1961 to the adoption of the policy of "socialism and self-reliance" in 1967. The second is the "socialist" phase from 1967 to the end of Julius Nyerere's presidency in 1985. The third is the "structural adjustment" era which dates from 1986 to the present. The latter period is marked by Tanzania's adoption and implementation of economic stabilization measures under the tutelage of the International Monetary Fund (IMF) and the World Bank (IBRD).

Economic development and growth was the paramount consideration during the first phase. In industry, the strategy was to encourage private foreign investment mainly in import substitution industries. In agriculture, government pursued a dual policy signified by the "improvement" and "transformation" approaches. The improvement approach was a frontal policy aimed at raising the quality of peasant farming through cooperative marketing and promotion of community development activities in ways that would inculcate in the majority of the peasantry attitudes conducive to "modern" living. The transformation approach was a crash programme of "modernization" which sought to resettle select groups in "modern" villages in which production was based on capital-intensive agriculture, with hopes of a demonstration effect on the larger rural population. Relatively little consideration was given to issues pertaining to equity and distribution during this phase.

During the socialist phase, the Government pursued both growth and equity, using State intervention as its main vehicle. In industry and trade, State enterprise played a conspicuous role following nationalizations of private companies. Resettling peasants in nucleated villages and encouraging collective farming constituted the central strategy of rural development. Villagization, as the policy is popularly referred to, aimed to enhance the productivity of agriculture and to make it possible for government to provide social services to the rural masses.

A serious attempt at addressing poverty and redistributing resources in favour of the popular masses is a notable feature of the socialist phase. A wages and incomes policy was pursued which sought to protect the underprivileged through price controls, imposed a minimum wage and restricted wage rises for the highly paid. A generous system of State-sponsored social services was instituted, leading to the introduction of universal primary education, provision of free secondary and tertiary education on the basis of merit, and improved access to free government-sponsored medical services and rural water supply.

Unfortunately, the foregoing measures of "inclusion" were progressively eroded by the poor performance of the economy, characterized by a balance of payments crisis, declines in agricultural and industrial production, and chronic shortages of essential goods. Educational standards declined for lack of basic facilities in the school system. Shortage of drugs and other essential supplies and equipment at government hospitals and other health facilities was proverbial. Rural water pumps fell into disrepair for lack of proper maintenance. Tanzania's economic misfortunes not only impaired the existing social services but also led to a decline in rural and urban incomes and therefore a general fall in living standards.

In the political sphere, an elaborate system of popular participation was put in place, especially after the introduction of "decentralization" in 1972. Although this system appears "inclusionary" on the surface, the doctrine of party supremacy which underlay its implementation engendered a top-down system of communication and power relations whereby the party oligarchy monopolized the decision-making process.

The advent of the structural adjustment era in 1986 was a result of a deepening economic crisis even as the government was pursuing home-grown stabilization measures between 1981 and 1985 in the wake of stalled negotiations between Tanzania and the IMF. Pressure from bilateral donors gave an extra impetus and the country accepted an IMF/IBRD-imposed stabilization package whose essential features were: restrictive monetary and fiscal policies, government decontrol of the economy and exchange rate adjustments. Although there were positive indicators, especially in the initial period, in terms of GDP growth, production of agricultural staples, availability of consumer goods, and a modest drop in the rate of inflation, the programme has had differential effects on the various social groups, creating conditions for intensification of the process of exclusion.

Agricultural output has been adversely affected by rising production and marketing costs due mainly to the effects of devaluation. Manufactured goods imported in response to the liberalization of trade have out-competed the products of local industries, leading to declines in industrial employment. The restructuring of the civil service and the privatization of the public enterprises have compounded the unemployment problems in the short term, if not in the medium, or even long, term. The intractable problem of inflation has continued to erode living standards, especially for the more vulnerable social groups. And the cuts in government budgetary allocations to the social sector have served to limit access to social services and led to further deterioration in the standards of these services.

The "Priority Social Action Programme" (PSAP) launched in 1989 and incorporated into the second and third phases of the stabilization measures was meant to avert a further deterioration of the social sector, steer the country towards a sustainable social service delivery system, ensure greater food security and increase levels of employment. The central concern was the welfare of the low-income groups: those either already, or in danger of becoming, socially excluded. But because, in its design, the PSAP envisaged dependence on donor support in these times of donor fatigue, the programme was apparently still-born. As a result, the social sector is in danger of falling into atrophy. The programme's only achievement so far is the introduction of cost-sharing in education and health which has further disadvantaged the poor.

Other issues bearing on social exclusion have hardly been addressed in government policy-making. The most troubling ones include inequitable allocation of development resources to the different geographical regions, and discrimination on the basis of gender, age and ethnic or cultural affiliation. Our analysis in the next section on marginalized groups in one rural and two urban locations indicates that these issues, among others, are manifestly at work in the process of social exclusion.

III. Study of marginalized groups

Six urban and three rural categories of marginalized people were identified and studied between March and July 1994. The urban-based groups consisted of beggars, stone-crushers, peddlers and street traders, open-air food vendors, casual labourers and fresh fish dressers. The rural groups were the landless, the near-landless and those without access to fertilizer, an important agricultural input in the respective study area.

The study started with a listing exercise, or reconnaissance survey, followed by a detailed survey. The reconnaissance survey was the basis of our sampling frame. A total of 300 individuals (100 from each location) were studied in groups of about 20 from each cluster. The three study locations were Dar-es-Salaam city, Mwanza municipality and three villages in Arumeru district. Dar-es-Salaam, the national political, commercial and industrial capital, has a population of about 1.8 million. Mwanza, with a population of 250,000, is the second largest town after Dar-es-Salaam and is the commercial and industrial centre of the lake zone. Arumeru district is a relatively well-watered area in an otherwise dry part of Arusha region. It is densely populated and has a history of land alienation related to colonial white settler farming. Land scarcity in the district is therefore proverbial.

Central to the process of marginalization among the groups studied is the plight of peasant agriculture. Always prone to the vagaries of weather, peasant production is now also beset with diminishing access to good land, ecological stress and declining soil fertility, rising costs of agricultural implements and farm inputs, poor producer prices, and marketing problems due to the endemic difficulties of the marketing cooperatives and to a lack of dependable rural roads. These problems constitute the major push factor that have engendered the current phenomenal rural-urban migrations. The situation would not be so bad if the urban economies could gainfully absorb the rural migrants. The best option for most rural migrants is to seek entry into the already glutted urban informal sector or simply to join the ranks of the unemployed. The failure of social provisioning only serves to aggravate a hopelessly bad situation of social exclusion.

A number of common features characterize the different marginalized groups. Basing itself on Peter Townsend's[1] indices of material and social deprivation, the study was able to highlight a number of areas in the process of exclusion. Education comes out as a major factor in social exclusion. In general, individuals among the studied groups either have no education at all or, in the majority of cases, have only a primary education. It is certain that lack of education limits their chances of employment and other opportunities.

The predominant majority of the marginalized live on very low incomes. On the basis of expenditure data, 64 per cent of the respondents in Dar-es-Salaam are below the poverty line. The corresponding percentages for Mwanza and Arumeru are 74 per cent and 82 per cent, respectively. Inadequacy, or in some cases a total lack, of income limited access to such important items as diet, housing and medical care.

A high degree of dietary deprivation in both quantitative and qualitative terms was noted. Such deprivation affected between 57 and 70 per cent of the respondents in the three study locations. Housing was also a major problem. Of the entire surveyed sample, 15 per cent had no access to living accommodation. In Dar-es-Salaam, 21 per cent of the sample had nowhere to live and 38 per cent lived in shared overcrowded units which are deprived of the most basic of facilities, including water and sanitation. Homelessness is highest among the beggars, affecting all except two in

---

[1] P. Townsend: *The international analysis of poverty* (London, Harvester Wheatsheaf, 1993).

Mwanza town. Access to medical care among the studied groups is quite limited, especially after the introduction in 1993 of medical user fees. Some 20 per cent of the respondents failed to attend hospital for lack of money. Another 20 per cent who went to hospital had no money to purchase the prescribed medicines.

Different factors at play in the process of exclusion apply across the board to all the studied groups. Family circumstances is one such factor. A sizeable proportion in the sample, especially among the urban dwellers, was deprived of normal family life. Cases of broken marriages, single mothers or infirm and vulnerable people living on their own were considerable. Also, there were numerous complaints concerning denial of access to employment on grounds of race, gender and ethnic background. It is noteworthy that a significant proportion of those participating in the urban informal sector (UIF) do not regard themselves as employed. Some 59 per cent of the UIF respondents stated that they had "no work". More likely than not, this perception is a reflection of objective reality in terms of the precarious living of most participants in the sector.

A close scrutiny of the circumstances and personal histories of the marginalized people reveals the multifaceted nature of the process of social exclusion in Tanzania. Among the beggars of Dar-es-Salaam and Mwanza the most important factors underlying their social status are education, health status, age, geographical origin and, to a lesser extent, gender. In Dar-es-Salaam, only 2 per cent of the beggars had any formal education. In Mwanza the proportion of beggars with school education, though rather low, was better at 23 per cent. Poor health is a major determinant in begging. The most common disease was leprosy which affected 60 per cent and 90 per cent of the Dar-es-Salaam and Mwanza samples, respectively. Other fairly common disabilities among the beggars were blindness, epilepsy and mental illness. The mean age of the beggars was the highest among the studied groups, indicating the absence of social provisioning for the aged. Most of the Mwanza beggars originated from the contiguous rural districts, but in cosmopolitan Dar-es-Salaam they originated from different locations, especially areas where food security is precarious because of drought conditions.

Grinding rocks with a hand hammer to supply gravel to the buoyant urban construction industry has attracted many, mainly young, town dwellers on the margins of the urban economy. It is a physically strenuous and low paying activity which people engage in for lack of better alternatives. Most stone crushers are in their prime. A sizeable presence of females in what is otherwise a masculine occupation is a telling commentary on the process of social change. Here, there is a difference between Mwanza and Dar-es-Salaam. In the Mwanza sample the women constituted 20 per cent; in the Dar-es-Salaam sample, however, they accounted for 52 per cent. An overwhelming number of the women were single, divorced or widowed mothers with young children to support. As in the case of the beggars, ethnic groups from either geographically remote or arid and semi-arid areas were over-represented.

The self-employed open air vendors of cooked food (*mama Ntilie*) in Mwanza and Dar-es-Salaam were, in keeping with tradition in households, predominantly women. The proportion in the Dar-es-Salaam and Mwanza samples were 78 and 79 per cent, respectively. Age was less of a factor than education and geographical origin. Consistent with other marginal groups, the food vendors tended to be either uneducated (25 per cent) or had at best a primary education (74 per cent) and tended to come from economically disadvantaged rural areas.

Fish dressing in Mwanza and casual work at construction sites in both towns is work of the last resort for town dwellers. Their earnings very much depended on chance, especially for those at construction sites. Almost all of them were in their prime in the 18-40 age range. The Dar-es-Salaam cluster was dominated by people from the least developed part of southern Tanzania.

With the liberalization of trade, the bigger towns, including Dar-es-Salaam and Mwanza, have been inundated with street traders and peddlers. Most of them are acting as agents for Asian shopkeepers who, through them, are trying to outdo one another in their efforts to reach customers in an intensely competitive retail business environment. The street traders are paid a commission on the basis of sales results, and our findings indicate that their economic lives are characterized by extreme uncertainty. Nevertheless, peddling and street trading have become the refuge of many rural migrants in towns where industrial unemployment is hardly ever obtainable.

Street traders and peddlers were studied only in Dar-es-Salaam. In the sample none of them was above age 30 and all, except one, had a school (mostly primary) education. It seems that networking is important in enabling one to obtain the necessary wares. It is no wonder, therefore, that the group is dominated by specific ethnic groups, especially those from Mtwara region in the south.

In the rural study, age, gender and, to a lesser extent, education proved to be the main factors at play in determining access to productive resources: land and fertilizer. In the landless category, the mean age was 38, with 82 per cent of the sample falling below 40. In the near landless category (those with less than 0.5 ha.) the average age was 32 years. Most were either rural labourers or tenant farmers, waiting for their fathers to die before they could inherit land. Female-headed households constitute between 21 and 25 per cent of the households which are landless, near landless and have no access to fertilizer. Given the patriarchal set-up in Arumeru households, this means that women were relatively far more disadvantaged than men in terms of access to productive resources. The main factor here is customary laws relating to land inheritance which discriminate against the female gender. The low education of those studied (primary school or none), meant that they had no access to well-paid jobs which would have enabled them to buy land or fertilizer. In the next section we explore further the issue of exclusion from land in the country as a whole.

IV. Exclusion from land

In Tanzania, land is the most important productive resource as more than 80 per cent of the country's population derive their living from it. Although, at 29 people per sq. km., the country's population density is quite low, settlement patterns are skewed because of the fact that most of the country suffers from shortage of rainfall, surface drinking water and infestation with *tse-tse* flies. The population is therefore concentrated in no more than 20 per cent of the total land area, especially in well-watered elevated parts of the territory where pressure on land is critical. In some other parts, the nucleated villages created during the "socialist" phase, have added to the land problem. The question of access to land in Tanzania is therefore a subject of extreme importance.

The factors which govern exclusion from land are many and complex. The most critical are: State-civil society relations, differential tenurial regimes, gender discrimination, development of the land market, and competing demands between agriculture and other forms of land use.

Under the 1923 Land Ordinance, the principal land law, all land in Tanzania is "public land" whose control is vested in the State through the President who owns the radical title. The administrative agencies authorized by various subsidiary legislations to act on behalf of the Head of State in land matters include the Ministry responsible for lands, the district and urban councils, and the village governments.

The nationalization of land has served different purposes since the Land Ordinance was passed. In colonial times, it mainly served to sanction the alienation of native land to colonial settler farmers and planters. For a good part of the post-independence period, the State endeavoured to protect ordinary land users, subsistence farmers in particular, from the spectre of landlessness, especially as a result of land grabbing and speculation. In the more recent period, however, State intervention in land matters has sometimes constituted an accessory to exclusion from land, especially for those with neither money nor political connections.

During villagization, district and village authorities confiscated and allocated land plots with extreme arbitrariness. In the Mbulu, Hanang and Babati district of Arusha region, district leaders dispossessed hundreds of landowners and redistributed land on the basis of equal acreage, regardless of customary rights in land. More recently, numerous complaints were made before the 1991-92 Presidential Commission of Enquiry into Land Matters (hereafter the Shivji Commission) concerning corrupt practices on the part of village governments (especially the chairmen) in their allocation of village land. At Ifunda, for example, villagers complained that their leaders were corruptly allowing rich town dwellers in Iringa to buy village land. For quite some time now, the news media has been replete with complaints about alleged corrupt practices by land officers in the allocation of urban plots.

In Tanzania, land is held under either a "granted right of occupancy" or an "deemed right of occupancy". The former allows one to occupy and utilize land for a fixed term not exceeding 99 years, while the latter allows one access to land "in accordance with native law and custom". The first, because it involves payment of fees, is usually associated with the well-to-do, for example commercial farmers. The other is the usual mode of land ownership among the peasantry. In actual practice, granted rights of occupancy are superior to deemed rights of occupancy. From colonial times, customary land rights have been taken to be "permissive" and therefore subject to loss, especially in the absence of "effective occupation". As the Shivji Commission observed, peasants holding land under customary law live under "perpetual fear of alienation, expropriation and encroachment". There are innumerable cases of State-sanctioned loss of peasant land to commercial developers, tourist operators and even speculators.

Some people are excluded from land not so much by the State as by tradition and custom. Prominent among these are women who cannot inherit or own land according to most customary laws. In Kilimanjaro and Kegara regions, for example, such lucrative permanent crops as bananas and coffee are appropriated by husbands and fathers who own the land, despite the fact that it is the women and children who provide most of the labour for their production. The areas which grow annual crops are no different. In the testimonies to the Shivji Commission, many female witnesses in different regions complained of being denied access to land ownership on grounds of their gender. Such a situation renders the lives of widows and single mothers quite precarious.

Many of the land disputes in contemporary Tanzania represent a rising value of land due not only to its scarcity but also to the new prominence of the land markets. In areas with a long history of cash crop production, landlessness due to land sales dates back to the 1920s. The phenomenon has intensified due to the liberalization of crop marketing which has lent a new significance to commercial farming, especially production of maize, rice and beans for the urban market. More land is changing hands than used to be the case and in the process, some people, especially among the cash-strapped peasantry, are losing access to land for their own subsistence. Arumeru is a case in point.

Land pressure is probably worst among the pastoralists and hunter-gatherers, especially in the Arusha region. Both pastoralism and foraging are land-intensive economic activities owing to the need to move over large expanses of land in search of pasture, water or, in the case of hunter-gatherers, forest products in accordance with the seasons. Because land use is in the form of deferment rotational systems, pastoral and foraging land has frequently been grabbed by other users on the assumption that it is idle. What is more, government development policy has demonstrably given priority to agriculture, relegating pastoralism to the role of an appendage.

The net result is that pastoralists in Arusha region have lost much of their land to outsiders. Partly as a result of villagization, the Barbaig people of Hanang have been edged out of the plateau by agriculturalists and forced into valley land where access to water, schools and health facilities is extremely limited. Others fell victim of a State-owned large-scale wheat scheme. Agriculturalists from Kilimanjaro region or Arumeru district and other areas have taken over Masai pastoral land in Kiteto and Monduli districts. There are numerous allegations against local Masai leaders, who are accused of earning rent by facilitating transfers of Masai land to land speculators and commercial developers. Game conservation policy has also exacerbated the exclusion of the Masai from land. The Game Park Laws (Miscellaneous Amendments) Act of 1975 completely bans cultivation within the 8,292 sq. km. Ngorongoro Conservation Area. But the 23,000 inhabitants of the area can no longer survive on pastoralism alone as their herds have been afflicted by a number of diseases. Their plea to government to allow them to cultivate at least around their homesteads has so far fallen on deaf ears.

There is every indication that Tanzania's hunter-gatherer community, the Hadzabe (or "Tindiga") of Mbulu, Iramba and Meatu districts are being slowly but surely excluded from adequate access to their resources. It is estimated that in three decades (i.e. since independence) this group has lost about half its land to commercial developers and, especially, cultivators. Most of the encroachment has been gradual and therefore imperceptible.

Because the Hadzabe are constantly on the move in their food procurement endeavours, they are usually not there to defend their resources against external intruders. By the time they realize that their land has been colonized, it is usually too late. Their ecosystem has been seriously tampered with and their very survival is at risk. Government attempts to convert them to a sedentary way of life has failed because they have not been receptive to an externally imposed model of existence.

V. The crisis of AIDS orphans

Our survey of marginalized groups in Mwanza town indicated that a significant proportion of street children are orphans, a good number of them due to AIDS. An interview-based study of orphans in one urban and three rural locations in Mwanza region revealed that this is a rapidly increasing population whose plight epitomizes a process of social exclusion underlain, in part, by long-term, almost imperceptible, changes in the nature of the African family as a social safety net. The kinship or extended family system under which orphans have traditionally been absorbed into normal family life is under such stress that orphans are facing untold difficulties.

The study was conducted in Yitwimila and Kahangara villages in Magu district, Nakatunguru village in Ukerewe district, and in the urban district of Mwanza. The presence of AIDS in these locations was acknowledged, especially in Mwanza town. In 1992 it was estimated that about 10 per cent of the region's population was HIV positive. Hospital-based cumulative AIDS cases in the region by that time were 130.3 per 100,000. There are so far no reliable statistics on orphans but a headcount of orphans in the five primary schools visited indicated proportions ranging from 5 to 10 per cent of the school populations. Given the fact that the figures exclude orphans of pre-school age, the problem is certainly serious. A group of ten AIDS widows whom we met in a focus group discussion had between them a total of 55 paternal orphans.

All the communities in Mwanza region traditionally make arrangements for orphan care after the period of mourning in a meeting of clan elders. Bilateral orphans are entrusted to paternal uncles or, in their absence, any close male blood relative. Paternal orphans will essentially remain under the care of their mother who, in most traditions, will be inherited in marriage by one of the deceased's brothers. Maternal orphans will remain the responsibility of the father who will invariably remarry and bring them up with the assistance of the stepmother. Traditionally, orphans are supposed to be fully integrated into their foster families without any discrimination in relation to biological children. This is seldom the case.

The traditional system of orphan care functions quite imperfectly. Many relatives are refusing to take on care-giving responsibility. Others might accept do so in order to save face and, as we discovered, many orphans have consequently to endure numerous hardships inflicted by their care-giving relatives. It is mainly grandparents who readily accept responsibility, because they usually do not have young children of their own to take care of.

The most common forms of orphan mistreatment that we came across included denial of love and affection, verbal and physical abuse, exploitation of child labour, denial of food and clothing, denial of educational opportunities, and squandering of orphan's inherited property. The main reason underlying these problems is the pressures on the family budget. In the rural areas, these relate to drought-induced shortages of food and to a high cost of living. In the urban areas, economic hardships mainly relate to lack of employment opportunities, shortage of housing and inflationary pressures on household budgets. Now there is the question of user changes in health and education. Under such adverse circumstances, the concept of family has undergone a redefinition in which it is increasingly viewed in terms of the nuclear family.

Grandparents and widowed mothers, who readily accept care-giving responsibility, are in most cases either too infirm or too economically deprived to face up to the challenges of this task. The best they can offer the orphans is affection. Most of the widowed mothers surveyed in Mwanza town had been full-time housewives prior to being widowed. A number of them had even been dispossessed of family property or evicted from their marital homes by their husbands' male relatives because of customary inheritance laws which discriminate against women. The best that most of them could do was eke out an existence for themselves and their children from petty street trading.

Orphans have been sent away from school for lack of money for school fees and other compulsory contributions — uniforms, pens and notebooks. Others have withdrawn of their own volition or played truant in order to seek casual employment in an attempt to alleviate their suffering.

So far the Government is doing precious little about the plight of orphans apart from supervision of two orphanages in the region which are financed and run by religious organizations. There are orphan care programmes in education, income-generating projects, food relief and apprenticeship training conducted by non-governmental organizations. These are generally patchy and underfunded and so leave the majority of orphans without cover.

As children whose early lives are deprived of family affection, educational opportunities and minimal material satisfaction, orphans in our area of study are growing up without hope and their exclusion from mainstream society is almost total. The plight of AIDS orphans is an eloquent testimony to the dismal failure of the customary safety nets and government social provisioning in Tanzania.

VI. Policy implications

The evidence from the study has shown that current orthodox adjustment policies aimed at generating general economic growth have proved ineffective in promoting integration. Where growth has occurred, it has failed to trickle down to different layers of society. A profile of poverty, inequality and social exclusion in Tanzania has revealed that, in both rural and urban areas, some groups are being systematically marginalized and are entrapped in chronic deprivation.

The foregoing findings call for a five-pronged approach to promoting integration:

(a) Launching broad-based interventions to strengthen agricultural technical services and infrastructure, raise productivity and therefore rural incomes and living standards. This would go a long way in arresting current high rates of rural-urban migration.

(b) Creating off-farm employment opportunities in rural areas which would absorb surplus rural labour in the course of structural transformation.

(c) Improving urban employment opportunities by reviving industrial activity using appropriate technology. The priority is financing programmes for the redeployment of the retrenched and the unemployed, particularly the visibly excluded groups.

(d) Improving access to social services and basic welfare provisioning by allocating adequate resources and restructuring modes of delivery in

such a way that the socially disadvantaged who are unable to share the costs of such services are protected. As traditional safety nets become overloaded by both structural and contingent factors, vulnerable groups should be guaranteed social protection. AIDS victims, orphans and the elderly are a case in point.

(e) Creating a legal and institutional framework for the promotion of integration. Both statutory and customary laws as well as administrative practices, especially those relating to access to education and productive resources, need to be revisited with a view to empowering the socially disadvantaged. Women in particular, being the principal farmers in Tanzania, should be entitled to full land rights.

A successful implementation of the above, essentially inward looking, strategy requires the active participation of the Government, the local communities, including private economic agents, as well as the international community. Ability to break the currrent gridlock and get the country back on a sustainable development path will require both political will and accountability on the part of the Government, and commitment on the part of the donor community.

12 Social exclusion and social inequality in Peru

Adolfo Figueroa, Teofilo Altamirano, Denis Sulmont

Peru is one of the countries with the highest degree of economic and social inequality in the world. This paper examines factors which explain these inequalities. It develops a new theoretical approach, which focuses on social inequality and introduces the concept of social exclusion into the analysis. In so doing, it specifically addresses the question: is inequality a result of some peculiar form of social integration, or rather a result of some exclusions taking place in the social process?

Social inequality is conceived in this paper in broader terms than income inequality. The social process is, for analytical purposes, divided into three components: economic, political, and cultural. Social inequality refers to the aggregation of inequality on these components.

Social exclusion is also considered in a particular way. As a fact of life, we know that the same group of people who participate in some social relations may, at the same time, be excluded from others. Hence, to say that a person is excluded from something is a purely descriptive statement, with no analytical value. In analytical terms, the question is whether there are *some exclusions* that have important effects upon social inequality. Which are these exclusions in a particular society? *Who* is excluded and from *what*? *Why* do these exclusions take place?

Social exclusion is evident in each of the three components of the social process which contribute to social inequality, and the paper analyses each case independently. However, this separation has been made for purely analytical reasons. We understand that the overall exclusion of a social group may be more, or less, than the sum of these independent exclusions. Therefore, an integration of our independent results has also been attempted. In this sense, this study intends to be truly interdisciplinary.

I. The concept of social assets

Our study deals with a society which is organized as a capitalist democracy, and which is "over-populated" in the sense that there is significant surplus labour. In a capitalist democracy, individuals participate in economic and social exchange endowed with a given set of assets. We consider here three types of assets: economic assets, which refer to productive resources, such as land, physical capital, financial capital and human capital; political assets, which refer to the access of people to the rights established by the society; and cultural assets, which refer to a system of social evaluations of the personal characteristics of individuals, such as their language, race, sex, kinship, education, occupation, religion and geographical origin. The hierarchy of these values is established by the cultural values of the society, which we assume as given.

While economic assets indicate what the person *has*, political and cultural assets indicate who the person *is*. In these terms, citizenship is a political asset; and the individual's personal characteristics (identity) are his or her cultural assets, which give the individual either social prestige or social stigma, leading to discrimination and segregation. Clearly, an individual with the same set of personal characteristics would have a different mix of cultural assets if the system of cultural values changed. Political and cultural assets are intangible; they are not tradeable, so they do not have market values attached. However, as we argue below, they play a significant role in the social process.

At any given point in time, individuals are endowed with different amounts of these assets. Economic inequality is the inequality in economic assets, whilst social inequality is a combination of inequality in economic, political and cultural assets. In a capitalist democracy, political rights tend to create a homogenous society ("all men are equal"), cultural assets may also tend to be equalizing, but economic assets tend to be distributed unevenly among the members of a society.

A society where the only source of inequality is economic assets could be called a "liberal society." Political and cultural assets would be evenly distributed. In this society, "the only difference between the rich and the poor is that the rich have more money".

II. Social exclusion and social inequality: A theoretical framework

What is the role of social exclusion in the observed social inequality in Peru? In order to answer this question, we propose a theoretical framework for analysing the mechanics of inequality.

1. Dimensions of exclusion

This framework separates exclusion into three categories: (i) economic; (ii) political; and (iii) cultural.

Exclusion from the economic process means exclusion from market exchange. Conventionally, it is assumed that markets are "Walrasian", in the sense that individuals can buy or sell a good or a service as much as they want at the prevailing market price. In such markets, rationing operates through prices, and the amount to be exchanged is just a matter of money. In these markets no-one willing and capable of buying or selling could be excluded from exchange. People are excluded from exchange because their real income, or productive capacity, is too low.

However, some markets operate with quantitative rationing. These "non-Walrasian" markets share the property that the expected *quality* of a commodity or service demanded or supplied is a function of its price. In this type of markets, some people will be excluded from exchange in spite of having sufficient real income or productive capacity. The economic literature suggests that the labour, credit and insurance markets may be "non-Walrasian". This is significant in that these markets can be regarded as *basic markets*, in the sense that they are fundamental for livelihood and security.

Exchange in non-Walrasian markets is carried out under conditions of imperfect competition and uncertainty, and it is then based on *promises* (to repay a loan, to work hard). In this context, asset endowments play a role in providing signals for the rationing process. Exclusions from non-Walrasian markets are not random; they depend upon the social asset endowment of individuals. Individuals who are poorly endowed with assets will be more likely to be excluded from basic markets. Also the individual's asset endowment will determine in which of the segmented markets he or she can participate.

Exclusion from the political process, in the context of democratic capitalism, means exclusion from citizenship rights. Democratic capitalism functions with a system of rights which, amongst other things, acts to set limits to the inequalities generated by the market system, and thus makes society viable. The factors which determine the set of rights in a particular capitalist democracy are various, including: on the demand side — social pressure, tolerance to inequality, the culture of inequality, degree of democracy, and level of income amongst the poor; and on the supply side — the production capacity of the economy, the preference of the ruling classes to allocate scarce resources to the production of rights in the form of public goods, and international agreements. In the short run, State policy to manage aggregate demand is the most important variable explaining changes in the *effective delivery* of a given set of rights. Periods of economic growth will be favourable and periods of recession unfavourable.

All citizen rights are not universal, and even universal rights are not equally realized. When rights are non-universal, or when formally universal rights are not effective in practice, some people are excluded from some rights: participation in the administration of political power (the right to elect and be elected), the right to property, to justice, to social protection, and to basic services. Different categories of citizenship will then be created.

Exclusion from the cultural process has to do with the individual's exclusion from participation in particular social networks. Because of differences in cultural values, some people will be excluded from participating in some social relations.

2. Exclusion from basic markets

In the particular case of Peru, the basic hypothesis is that the labour market (a non-Walrasian market) operates as the primary mechanism of social exclusion. In this market, the following variables are determined: the quantity of wage employment, real wages, and profits. Given the labour supply, the total quantity of surplus labour is then determined. In an overpopulated economy, the amount of surplus labour takes the form of unemployment and self-employment.

In our view, the incomes of the self-employed must be lower than wages. This income difference among workers is necessary for the functioning of the system because it creates an incentive system by which workers prefer and seek wage employment. The logical consequence is that those excluded from the labour market become the poorest. Among the surplus labour we also find superfluous labour.

Who are those excluded from the labour market? For a given type of labour, workers with the lowest cultural assets will be the most likely to be excluded. Social groups that belong to different subcultures inside the society will be viewed by employers as the least reliable workers. Due to language and cultural barriers, employers may also expect that the cost of extracting economic surplus from this type of labour will be higher. Thus, through the workings of the labour market, people bearing a social stigma for the capitalist class will be placed at the bottom of the income pyramid.

Most of the surplus labour will also be excluded from the credit and insurance markets. Banks and insurance firms do not expect to make much profit by doing business with peasants or the urban self-employed. For the surplus workers, this is the secondary mechanism of market exclusion. They cannot escape becoming the poorest. Also, the surplus workers will be the most likely group to be excluded from political and cultural processes.

3. Exclusion from rights

Most universal rights are distributed through the fiscal budget. This is clearly the case with economic rights, which take the form of goods and services that are supplied free of charge by the State as public goods (schools, health service, food, shelter). But some non-economic rights, such as the right to vote, the right to justice, the right to protection, are also financed through the fiscal budget as public goods. These goods and services are taken out of the market and delivered to the population in the form of rights. The objective is that money should not buy everything in society. However, this objective is not always achieved because of the influence of money on the delivery of rights.

Are there theoretical reasons to believe that those excluded from some rights are the same social groups that are excluded from basic markets? Here the issue is the effective exclusion from a right, instead of the formal inclusion. We postulate that effective exclusion from rights depends on the set of State policies. Although the elites seek political legitimation through the establishment of some formal rights, we also postulate that political elites have an incentive to exclude people from rights. In the absence of universal rights, government expenditure will be used to gain political support, in a clientelistic relation.

The right to participate in the political process of elections is now universal in Peru. However, some groups are excluded from property rights, social protection rights and basic public services (health, education, justice). They tend to be the same groups as those excluded from basic markets.

Property rights are essential to the efficient functioning of the market system. Besides, property rights are also essential to the understanding of social inequality. If legal rights on private property are not guaranteed, exchange contracts cannot be legal. As a result, "informal contracts" and "informal markets" will arise. Market segmentation may be based in many cases on the lack of property rights. The credit market would be a case, as property cannot be used as collateral due to the lack of legal titles. We assume that the surplus labourers are the ones who mostly lack these rights because the relative cost of getting property rights legalized is larger for them.

Social protection or social security is another basic right in a capitalist system. People are granted some ways to insure risks associated with health and income streams in the form of access to health insurance, unemployment insurance and retirement pensions. However, these rights are not universal. The coverage is usually limited. Who is excluded from these rights? A common practice is to restrict these insurance programmes to wage-earners alone, so that employers can contribute to the financing of these rights. This has an economic logic: employers create an additional incentive system for workers to seek wage employment. Then, surplus labourers would also be excluded from these rights.

4. *Exclusion from social networks*

Exclusion from the cultural process has to do with discriminatory treatment in some social relations. In particular, it has to do with the membership of some social networks. Social networks can be thought of as "clubs." Rights and duties determine the rules of a club membership. For instance, membership of "exclusive clubs" is very restricted. There is a hierarchical ordering of clubs, culturally determined. The ruling class social network is the "exclusive club" *par excellence*. Everyone wants to enter this network, but most are unable to do so. The restrictive conditions of membership create exclusion.

Why do "exclusive clubs" exist? The ruling classes set restrictive conditions for membership in order to block social mobility. Their logic is to maintain the privileges of a ruling class. Rules of discrimination and segregation, based on personal characteristics, will be applied to this end. Partial social mobility may take place in the rest of the income pyramid, but it will not challenge the privileges of the ruling class.

5. *Mechanics of social inequality*

The mechanics of social inequality can be viewed as a process. Initially individuals are endowed with social assets in different amounts. Initial social inequality is a result of the concentration in the initial distribution of these assets. Changes in the distribution of social assets through time will imply changes in social inequality. An increase in the amount of social assets of individuals depends upon the way national income (flows) are distributed, which in turn depends, among other things, upon social exclusions. The exogenous variables of this dynamic system include: State policies, the market structure (Walrasian and non-Walrasian mix), the political system, and cultural values.

Within this framework, social exclusion is a category of analysis. It is not a description of an *outcome* of a social process; it is rather a theory that explains that outcome. It is hypothesized that social exclusion is one of the basic mechanisms through which the exogenous variables generate social inequality.

It is this perspective which leads to the specification of those exclusions which are important. Exclusion from basic markets (labour, credit, insurance) is a cause of poverty; but exclusion from other markets, such as markets for consumption goods (cars, telephones, durables, tourism), is predominantly an effect.

III. Empirical evidence for Peru

Peru is a multi-cultural and multi-racial country. At least six ethnic groups may be distinguished: Indians from the Andes, Indians from the Amazonian region, blacks, whites, Asians and persons of mixed race. In addition to Spanish, several native languages are still spoken: *Quechua* and *Aymara* in the Andes, *Ashahinka* in the Amazonian region.

The national economy grew rapidly during the 1950s, 1960s and the first half of the 1970s and by 1975 per capita income was almost double the 1950 value. Since 1975, however, Peru has experienced a continuous decline in average income. In 1992, per capita income was only two-thirds of the 1975 value.[1]

The national population has continued to grow, but average annual rates of increase have been decreasing — from 2.9 per cent in the 1950s to 2 per cent in the 1980s. At the same time a major transformation has occurred in the urban-rural composition of the population. The proportion of the population living in urban areas increased from 35 per cent in 1940 to 70 per cent in 1993.

1. Distribution of social assets

The distribution of *economic assets* is highly concentrated in Peru. Several studies showed that Peru was an oligarchy in the 1950s and 1960s. For the 1980s, the concentration of property was still significant: large firms were mostly in the hands of only 330 families, of which 80 constituted the major economic groups. The concentration of economic assets may also be approximated by the distribution of national income. In 1961,

---

[1] INEI, *Compendio estadístico 1992-93*, Tomo II.

the top 1 per cent of the population received 31 per cent of national income, whereas the bottom 30 per cent received 5 per cent. Although this concentration of income was already very marked, the degree of inequality has increased even more since. In 1989, for instance, 13 per cent of GDP was generated by 13 economic groups, composed of 11 families.

At the top of Peru's income pyramid are the capitalist class and "middle class" — professionals and business people. Measured by the number of households that own a private car and hire a domestic servant, this group represents 5 per cent of the population. The poorest groups in Peru's income pyramid are the indigenous populations of the Andes and the jungle areas, the so-called Andean peasant communities and the Amazonian native communities. This latter group is, however, very small.

The distribution of *political assets* has been measured in the case of the following categories:

(a) Political participation. The right to political participation is very old in Peru but it has become universal only recently. The right to vote was extended to women in 1955, and to illiterates and to people in the 18-21 age bracket in 1979. Peru has had several periods of dictatorships in which these rights could not be exercised.

(b) Property rights. Exclusion from property rights is more severe in the poorest groups of Peru. In rural areas, 37 per cent of the peasant families had no legal titles on their land in 1984; in urban areas, 43 per cent of the families living in shanty towns lacked land titling.

(c) Social protection. These rights are very limited in Peru. People under public programmes of social security also represent a small fraction of the total population of Peru. In 1986, only 42 per cent of the labour force, which represents 51 per cent of the wage-earners, were members of the Social Security System (*Instituto Peruano de Seguridad Social*). Urban-rural differences are very wide. Whereas 72 per cent of the labour force in rural areas is excluded from the system, around 60 per cent is excluded in urban areas. The fact that only half of the wage-earners are included in the Social Security System is a clear indication that wage employment is precarious in Peru. The coverage of the Social Security System in terms of pension for retirement is also very low. In 1990, two-thirds of the population above 65 years of age had no access to this right. Moreover, the amount of the pension per person is now ridiculously low. In Peru, there is no unemployment insurance.

(d) Social services. Public expenditure on basic social services (education, health, housing, and employment programmes) has fallen in

relative terms. As a proportion of the GDP, the expenditure on social services has also declined. While this proportion was 4.6 per cent at the beginning of the 1970s, it was 3.4 per cent at the beginning of the 1990s. As a proportion of the total government expenditure, the relative fall has been less marked. While 25 per cent of the government budget was allocated to social expenditures at the beginning of the 1970s, this proportion fell to 19 per cent in the first half of the 1980s, and then recuperated somewhat to reach 23 per cent at the beginning of the 1990s. But, the fall in public social expenditure has been more substantial in absolute terms. Since 1980, the level of real expenditures has continuously declined. As a result, the 1992 level represented only 49 per cent of the 1980 value. In per capita terms, the fall is even more substantial: the 1992 value is barely 30 per cent of that in 1980.[2] "Targeting the poor" was initiated in August 1990, as a means to compensate the negative effects of the adjustment programme on poverty. These resources amounted to around 1 per cent of GDP in 1991-1992. "Targeting the poor" is now the current government's main objective in the allocation of public social expenditures. This means that fewer resources will be allocated to the granting of universal rights. But "targeting" is consistent with the political logic of a clientelistic government.

In terms of *cultural assets*, we have measured those personal characteristics that clearly block individuals from participating in the process of modernization in Peru. Because modernization leads people to the aspiration for western values and culture, those with the lowest assets are the indigenous populations of the Andean and the Amazonian areas. They are mostly illiterates and non-Spanish-speaking groups. The most extreme cases of illiteracy among these populations are found among the women and the elderly.

According to census data, the rate of illiteracy in Peru was 27 per cent in 1972, 18 per cent in 1981, and 13 per cent in 1993; non-Spanish-speaking rates were lower, 12 per cent, 9 per cent, and 5 per cent, respectively. However, if we use less restrictive definitions, such as considering as illiterate anyone with less than three years of primary school, and defining non-Spanish-speaking by the language of communication within the family, the rates would be significantly higher. We estimate that illiterates and non-Spanish-speaking groups represent around 20 per cent of Peru's population today. In 1961, this figure was around 40 per cent. Migration

---

[2] Banco Central del Reserva del Perú, *Compensio Estadistico del Sector Publico Financiero* (Lima, 1989); and INEI, *Compendio Estadistico* (various years).

to the cities has reduced the size of these groups and has been a means to reduce their cultural exclusion.

2. *Social exclusion and the mechanics of social inequality*

Peru's data seem to confirm the hypotheses put forward in this study. In fact, the structure of the economy shows a significant exclusion of the labour force from wage employment. Census data of 1972, 1981 and 1993 allow us to show the increase of the rate of exclusion from wage employment, measured as a percentage of the total labour force. For Peru, these rates were 54 per cent, 55 per cent and 57 per cent for the respective years; for Lima, they were: 35 per cent, 35 per cent and 44 per cent.[3] The urban unemployment rate was near 10 per cent in Lima (the largest city in Peru) in 1993.

The size of the self-employed has therefore been stable at around 50 per cent of the labour force. With the process of internal migration, the proportion of the self-employed in urban areas has increased. The peasantry represented around 40 per cent of the labour force in 1972 and today this proportion is around 25 per cent.

Most of the surplus workers are in practice excluded from the credit and insurance markets. The incidence of poverty is very high among the self-employed and unemployed. Hence, the poor in Peru are those that are excluded from basic markets. The indigenous populations living in the Andean and Amazonian regions are the poorest and they are subject to the highest degree of exclusion from basic markets.

Surplus workers are also subject to the highest degree of political and cultural exclusion. This conclusion is derived from the data shown above on the distribution of assets. Thus, the hypothesis that the exclusion from labour markets operates as a primary mechanism of social exclusion seems consistent with the data in Peru. For the working class, as Joan Robinson said, it seems that not to be exploited is worse than to be exploited.

In Peru's multi-cultural and multi-ethnic society, the role of cultural assets is also significant. The indigenous populations are poorly endowed with economic and cultural assets and they are the group subject to the highest degree of exclusion. A significant proportion of the Indian peasantry in the Andes and in the Amazonian areas do not speak Spanish and are illiterates. They also live in remote areas with poor communication systems. In terms of rights, the peasant communities of the Andes received legal recognition in 1923, whilst the communities of the Amazonian region

---

[3] These figures were taken from national census official publications.

did so in 1969. Before these years they were not considered citizens of Peru. They had no property rights.

Most of the indigenous populations may be considered as labour which is superfluous for the functioning of the capitalist system. The fact that the subversive groups (*Sendero-Luminoso* and *Movimiento Revolucionario Tupac Amaru*) have developed most of their war operations in the regions populated by the indigenous populations seems to indicate that there is a link between severe exclusions and political violence.

3. Trends

Poverty levels have increased since the mid-1970s. In 1970, it was estimated that 50 per cent of the population were below the poverty line. For the same definition of poverty line, these proportions increased to 57 per cent in 1985 and 60 per cent in 1991.[4] Although overall income distribution estimates are not available for the last decades, it is clear from the available data that inequality between workers and property owners has also increased. The ratio of income per capita to real wages in the private sector, which in 1975 was equal to 100, increased to 258 in 1985, and further up to 278 in 1992.

How much of the observed increase in poverty and inequality in Peru in the last two decades can be explained by market exclusion? With regard to the labour market, as shown above, exclusion of workers from wage employment has increased, but the magnitude of this change is *not* very marked. What is really significant in Peru is the high level of exclusion of workers from wage employment, rather than the change. Hence, the rise in poverty can be explained only in part by changes in the exclusion rates in labour markets. The increase in poverty in Peru may be explained basically by the fall in real wages. During the period of economic regress in Peru, the major adjustment in the labour market has occurred in terms of drastic changes in relative prices and less in quantities.

Some evidence shows that the decline in the quality of wage employment has been another adjustment mechanism. For instance, the proportion of wage-earners with long-term contracts declined from 59 per cent in 1990 to 51 per cent in 1992.[5] Wage employment tends to be more precarious.

---

[4] The figure for 1970 was estimated by ECLAC and the other figures are estimated using two national surveys that are more or less comparable.

[5] Data from Ministry of Labour, *Encuesta de Hogares*.

In sum, there is a relationship between poverty and exclusion: social groups with the highest degree of exclusion are the poorest. Poverty and social inequality are a result of both some exclusions *and* particular forms of social integration. In a dynamic view, however, the Peruvian society is tending to become more homogenous in terms of political and cultural assets. This is due to the expansion of citizenship rights and to the process of internal migration. The relative size of the indigenous populations has declined. What is becoming more significant now is the degree of economic inequality, which has even increased in the last decades.

IV. Conclusions and policy implications

Social exclusion is a mechanism built into the workings of capitalist democracy. The market system generates mechanisms of exclusion as a result of the logic of the owners of capital: to maximize profits and maintain privileges. The political system also generates mechanisms of exclusion as a result of the logic of the political class: to have clientelistic relations, instead of securing universal rights. These ruling classes (joined by the middle class) also generate mechanisms of exclusion through ideology, creating hierarchies in social values, which then become cultural values. The logic is to have higher social assets. The excluders are, in this theory, the ruling classes.

Exclusion theory is a theory about processes. The effect of exogenous variables upon social inequality operates through the mechanisms of the market, the political system and the cultural values. The exogenous variables include the initial distribution of assets among individuals and the set of State policies. As structurally given factors, we include the market structure, the political system and cultural values.

The theory of exclusion predicts that social inequality is not only generated through exploitation, surplus extraction, unequal distribution of initial endowments and a regressive tax system. All these factors count. But, exclusion from markets, from rights, and from social networks are also important mechanisms to generate social inequality. Social inequality is a result of both social integration *and* social exclusion.

With the framework of the theory of exclusion, we have been able to make a reinterpretation of the causes of social inequality in Peru. The empirical evidence seems consistent with the predictions of the theory. In fact, we have found that the poor are excluded from the basic markets (labour, credit, insurance), from rights, and from the cultural process associated with modernization. These exclusions are most severe for the indigenous populations living in the Andean and Amazonian areas, which are Peru's poorest groups. In the last decade, some urban groups have also become part of this group for whom exclusion is "hard", such as recent migrants and those displaced by political violence. These social groups facing "hard exclusion" use their particular social assets to adapt themselves to this situation, mostly through collective action, using their culture of solidarity and reciprocity.

The approach developed here not only offers a re-interpretation of the causes of social inequality, but also leads to new policy recommendations. Policies must be addressed to change the market structure and the initial distribution of assets, which are the factors at the base of the exclusion mechanisms. If the significance of market exclusion is to be reduced, the policy prescription seems clear: the basic markets (labour, credit and insurance) should be *created* or expanded in the entire economy, particularly in rural areas.

In the case of exclusion from labour markets, the basic problem is how to substitute, or supplement, the logic of excess labour — as a worker discipline device — for another which could maintain some form of social integration. One possibility is to raise the degree of partnership between the employer and the worker. New forms of industrial organization need to be created and promoted.

In an overpopulated economy, the excess of labour supply will continue to take the form of self-employment. Here the challenge is how to increase productivity in this sector. But, as we have shown in this study, small producers are excluded from the formal credit market. The peasant family and the urban small producers have a demand for credit, but the formal financial system has no incentives to supply this credit. The reason is that transaction and information costs are too high for the formal financial system to lend money to small producers. The risks of activities are also high. Small producers would not be able to pay these costs. In order to reduce this exclusion, policies directed to reduce these costs need to be implemented.

How can these costs be reduced? Transaction and information costs depend upon some institutional factors, like legal property rights, the existence of small financial intermediaries, the existence of organizations of lenders, and so on. The development of these institutions depends, in turn, upon the supply of public goods, like communication systems.

In order to reduce the cost of risks, small producers should be able to shift their risks, either to other firms or, if this is not viable, to the rest of the society. As a consequence, they would have higher and more secure incomes. Today, small-scale producers self-insure. Insurance markets should be developed. Non-measurable risks (weather and market contingencies) need to be transformed into measurable risks, so that the risk can be subject to actuarial calculations. Institutional innovations are needed to do this. In sum, the exclusion of the poor from basic markets can be reduced by institutional innovations and by the supply of more public goods. The role of the State is fundamental in these tasks.

Market creation policies should not be confused with market liberalization policies. The latter assumes that the market is already there. This confusion is precisely what has happened in Peru. Under the doctrine that State banks have had a "crowding out" effect on commercial banks, the Government closed the Agrarian Bank in 1991 and expected that commercial banks would take over. This has not happened so far. This result is consistent with our theory, which states that what is needed in rural Peru is the creation and development of credit and financial markets.

In order to reduce the role of the initial distribution of assets on social inequality, new economic assets must be redistributed, universal rights and duties must be effectively secured, and cultural values must be changed. As to the first component, education seems the best candidate. In terms of political assets, rights should play the role of setting a limit to social inequality. But rights are not costless. Therefore, rights should be established and guaranteed according to a well-defined hierarchy of social needs. Maslow's pyramid of human needs could serve as a criterion. In any case, the distance between "formal rights" and "effective rights" should be reduced.

As to the question of cultural values, change is a long-term process. The school system is here the best channel. However, some actions can be taken now. Two areas that appear promising in this respect are: the use of the mass media to change the values that lie behind the present culture of inequality; and the use of "ethnic commodities" to integrate non-Western cultures with Western culture. In any case, the distance between "ideal values" and "real values" should be reduced.

Economic and cultural assets can be redistributed through the promotion of rights. Rights that help to increase other assets should have priority. This is the case of economic rights (education, health), which can increase both the human capital and social prestige of individuals. But the realization of some rights may be endogenous, that is to say, it may depend upon the individual's income. For instance, the right to justice is usually violated by the power of money; corruption in judiciary systems plays against the poor. In this case, new institutional forms of collective organizations, that could secure access to rights through the free play of democratic forces, should be promoted.

13 *Economic restructuring and social exclusion in Mexico*

Sara Gordon Rapoport, Rosario Cobo, Lorena Paz Paredes, Carlos Salas, Enrique Dusell

This paper examines the relationships between economic restructuring and social exclusion in Mexico. Its general argument is that current exclusion processes are related to the breakdown of the inclusive development model, based on a corporatist social covenant, which prevailed in the country from the 1940s to the early 1980s, and its replacement with a neo-liberal project which is being implemented through structural adjustment programmes. At present the Mexican economy is undergoing fundamental changes in its productive structure and its relationships with the rest of the world. With these changes, both the mechanisms and forms of the regime's socio-political integrating processes are being transformed. The inclusive development model was imperfect in that it was unsustainable and, ironically, its social aims of integrating the mass of the people into the benefits of development were induced by political tendencies which actually gave the model characteristics which meant that it excluded certain sections of the population. But the strategy of economic liberalization which the government is now using to regain post-war dynamism is leading to a growing social exclusion. These trends may be explained by mistakes in the design of adjustment programmes, but more fundamentally they appear to be built into the nature of the new development model.

The paper develops this argument by focusing on the relationship between economic restructuring and employment trends. This poses some problems because various sources of employment data are not completely compatible. However, this focus is necessary because in capitalist economies where wealth is concentrated, the vast majority of people have to find employment in order to get an income, and thus social exclusion is linked to access to employment and levels of income derived from work.

I. The inclusive development model and its breakdown

From the early 1940s to the late 1970s, the Mexican government launched a project whose main goal was to promote development, to provide health and education services, and to generate employment for all inhabitants of rural as well as of urban areas. Up to the late 1970s, the socio-political regime of integration aimed to include various sectors and social groups into official organizations. Sectoral groupings — workers, farmers, bureaucrats, etc. — were linked to the official party (Revolutionary Institutional Party, PRI) and to the government, and by this means the State played the role of mediator of the demands of members of these groups and, at the same time, exerted a strong hold upon them. The State established strong commitments with sectoral interests, but these commitments were based on the demands formulated within the framework of great official organisms (the Mexican Workers' Confederation, the National Farmers' Confederation, the State Workers' Union Confederation). As some analysts have suggested, the regime was the outcome of a covenant agreed upon by various social forces and superintended by the State.

This model, whose main goal was to establish relationships that could effectively integrate the population into the social and economic benefits, was based upon a State mainly concerned with its protector role. That is to say, it gave a great relevance to the collective interest and declared itself the main promoter of economic development. Also, there was established a strong relationship between economic and the social policies. Social expenditure was conceived as a part of the development project, since under the import substitution model, consumption was supposed to be promoted in order to expand the domestic market. At the same time, a protectionist policy guarded industry against the pressures of international competition. This allowed the government to foster social cohesion and to assert the State's legitimacy.

The social policy had as its main purpose to give welfare benefits to as many people as possible, but no attempt was made to set up a fully established and comprehensive welfare state apparatus as this would have involved a wide taxation programme in order to finance the provision of services. In spite of its comprehensive aims, its stratified implementation (according to the membership of certain organizations) produced an outcome in which there was increased inequality and access to certain benefits was a privilege rather than a right. This form of social organization was a selective and vertical way of promoting social integration in which the inclusion patterns actually meant segregation and discrimination.

As a consequence, the State's goal of providing collective benefits and its inclusive development model did not manage to put an end to poverty. But even so, up until the late 1970s, the model increasingly included certain population nuclei.

The unsustainability of this imperfectly inclusive development model first became apparent in the 1960s. From 1940 to 1965, the industrialization of the country was based on agriculture, which financed capital goods imports (through meeting domestic demand for foodstuffs and exporting surpluses), supplied cheap raw materials to industry, and reduced the reproduction costs of the part of the labour force required by industrial and farm capital. These functions were successfully achieved until the mid-1960s. But the agricultural sector was strongly polarized between: *(a)* capitalists businessmen (who owned most of the irrigated land, used modern technology and hired seasonal and cheap labour from peasant communities), together with agro-businesses and agro-industrialists who controlled the financing, marketing, and processing of the marketed output of small and middle farmers; and *(b)* a mass of small and middle farmers (who owned little land, had limited productive resources and cultivated crops seasonally for their own consumption and sale), together with day-workers hired seasonally in capitalist projects. In the 1960s growth of agricultural output slowed down and by 1974 the country had switched from being a net exporter to a net importer of agricultural goods. The demand of the industrial sector for imports could only be met by growing foreign debt.

In the 1970s, the agricultural crisis became a political and social one as peasants demanded that the government would keep on giving them lands to work, better prices and labour conditions, and democracy. The State responded by increasing its participation in financing, marketing and processing (to counteract the role of "middlemen"), and through fostering new organizational forms amongst peasant farmers based upon the collective working of the communal property (*ejido*). These measures brought about a greater involvement of the State in the economic activity, by means of regulating institutions like the National Institute for Coffee (INMECAFE) which took over the credit, collection and exports. They also made the peasantry even more dependent on the State, a situation which, in turn, became even more serious when the latter withdrew from certain forms of involvement. Whilst these measures contained the peasant struggles by incorporating them in "officialist" or in State-recognized associations, they did not promote agricultural growth and exacerbated the fiscal crisis of the State.

In the 1980s, the imperfectly inclusive development model based on a corporatist social covenant, which had been the mechanism of social integration in Mexico since the 1940s, was abandoned and a neo-liberal project initiated. This shift occurred at a moment when most of the world was in recession and Latin America as a whole was facing its biggest economic crisis since the 1929, the debt crisis. For Mexico, the stabilization and adjustment programmes which were launched by the government were the immediate result of the need to redesign the terms of the foreign debt with the World Bank and Inter-American Development Bank in order to get more credits. But the impetus for change was also associated with emerging global economic trends, in which competition for markets increasingly transcends national frontiers, financial and productive capital are increasingly mobile, the diffusion of technical progress is accelerating, and new organizational forms, notably flexible specialization, are being adopted.

The neo-liberal project initiated in 1982 is an export-oriented industrialization strategy based on market mechanisms and private sector activity. Policies adopted include: the reduction of public spending and the fiscal deficit; the elimination of trade protection which, after the unilateral trade liberalization carried out in 1985-87 has been carried out within the framework of the North American Free Trade Agreement (NAFTA), thus combining the opening of domestic markets to increased international competition with guaranteed access to external markets to the north; massive privatization of State-owned enterprises; the facilitation of foreign direct investment; and the downward adjustment of real wages and devaluation of the exchange rate. Within the agricultural sector, parastatals have been dismantled or transformed; subsidies have been phased out (although, at the end of 1993, measures were introduced to compensate producers for the loss of income due to the equalization of domestic and international prices); and public expenditure has been reduced (by 51 per cent from 1980-90). No selective industrial policy has been implemented, but from 1985 a number of instruments have been introduced specifically to promote exports.

Implementing this new model involved a transformation in the regime of socio-political integration in Mexico. The involvement of the State in the economy and society has been reduced, and its role has changed from protector to regulator. The expansion of the domestic market, and thus domestic consumption, is no longer integral to the growth model. Instead, the guarantee of cheap labour constitutes a crucial element of the strategy. Finally, the agricultural sector has been exposed to international competition and is expected to re-orientate production according to the dictates of comparative advantage.

II. Economic performance under structural adjustment

The World Bank, the IMF and the Mexican government claim that Mexico's performance in implementing structural adjustment policies make it a model to be followed. But on balance, after more than ten years of structural change, adjustment in Mexico has not achieved the two objectives which were claimed to be its principal aims: sustained economic growth and better living standards.

The adjustment policy has been successful in restraining inflation, which decreased from 159 per cent in 1987 to about 10 per cent in 1993.[1] It also succeeded in attracting foreign investment and increasing the exports of a few manufactured products in 1987-91, notably beer, glass, petrochemicals and automobiles.

However, economic growth was not consistently reactivated. While the average annual growth in the economy was 4.9 per cent in 1970-81, between 1982 and 1992 it was only of 0.7 per cent. From 1987 to 1991, the GDP growth rate has increased to an annual average of 2.8 per cent [ibid.]. But, the economy still fails to generate sufficient jobs for the increasing population. Most recent estimates suggest that the economically active population increased by 1.2 million people annually during 1990-92, but only 28 per cent could find formal wage employment.

Over the period of adjustment policies, the number of poor people has continued to rise and income distribution has worsened. As measured by the Gini coefficient, income inequality grew between 1984 and 1992, from 0.450 to 0.475. From 1984 to 1989, the highest income decile increased its share from 32.7 per cent to 37.9 per cent.[2] According to the latest figures for the period from 1989 to 1992, the mean income of families within the lowest levels of income fell by almost 7 per cent, whilst the income of the families at the top of the income pyramid grew by 11.3 per cent. Only 21 per cent of Mexican families have a mean income above three minimum wages per month (about US$ 405), whilst 54 per cent of

---

[1] P. Aspe: *El camino mexicano hacia la transformación económica* (Mexico, Fondo de Cultura Económica, 1993).

[2] Grupo Financiero BANAMEX-ACCIVAL: *México social 1992-93* (Mexico, División de Estudios Econ ómicos y Sociales, 1993).

families have monthly incomes below one minimum wage (about US$ 135). Research studies carried out in Mexico City, Monterrey and Guadalajara show that the percentage of the labour force with these very low incomes is lower in major urban centres. The working population earning less than the minimum wage was 31 per cent in Mexico City, 29.3 per cent in Guadalajara and 20.5 per cent in Monterrey. But for the illiterate population, the proportion of workers earning less than one minimum wage is higher. They numbered about 50 per cent in Monterrey and Guadalajara; and 60 per cent in Mexico City.[3]

Real wages began falling in 1976, but steeper declines have occurred since 1982, with only the section of the population in formal employment in large industrial enterprises experiencing a recovery in their wages. Persons in formal employment in trade and services receive on average wages that are lower than those in manufacturing; wages in *maquiladoras* are lower than those paid in the rest of the manufacturing sector; and those who work in small establishments earn less than those who are contracted in larger establishments. About 50 per cent of formal sector workers receive incomes below two minimum wages, and this is the situation of those employed in *maquiladora* activities and of the average contractual wage. To put this figure in perspective, in 1988 it took 4.78 minimum wages to cover the cost of the standard basket of basic needs, while in 1994 it took the equivalent of six minimum wages.

Within the agricultural sector, which directly provides a livelihood for around 20 million people, the polarized bimodal production structure has been reinforced. The contribution of agriculture to the GDP decreased from 8.1 per cent in 1981 to 7.5 per cent in 1989. Moreover, with the exception of corn (for which guaranteed prices were maintained) both the output and the cultivated area of domestic crops decreased between 1990 and 1993. Rural wages (in real terms) fell by 38 per cent from 1982 to 1987, and even the optimistic estimates of the Economic Commission for Latin America and the Caribbean (ECLAC) and the *Instituto Nacional de Estadística, Geografía e Informatica* (INEGI) suggest that there was a more than 50 per cent fall in the purchasing power of rural incomes in the 1980s. Unemployment and migration has increased and plots of land abandoned. Particularly affected groups have been indigenous peoples, women, children and day labourers. The last group numbered 3.6 million in 1993, and amongst them 1.7 million lived exclusively from wage labour

---

[3] G. H. Muñoz and H. Suárez Sozaya: *Educación y empleo: Ciudad de México, Guadalajara y Monterry* (Centro Regional de Investigaciones Multidiciplinarias (CRIM), UNAM, 1990).

whilst 1.9 million sought a livelihood combining wage labour and subsistence cultivation.

The reduction in public expenditure in the 1980s has had a severe and negative impact on the delivery of social services. Federal spending on social development (which includes health care, eduction and the social investment fund, *Solidaridad*) fell sharply between 1982 and 1988. In the education sector, for example, public expenditure (both federal and State) decreased by 35 per cent (at 1982 prices) from 1982-88, a period in which the children registered in educational establishments increased by almost two million pupils, with 91 per cent of these being absorbed by public sector institutions. Public expenditure on social development has increased since 1988, but it is still under 1982 levels.[4]

III. Employment trends and economic restructuring

Mexico is now in transition towards a new form of capital accumulation which, in contrast with the past, cannot be sustained exclusively through the domestic market. The development path is not yet fully defined, but some of its features are beginning to appear.

1. General employment trends

The principal observed changes in employment in Mexico since 1980 are:

(a) a decline in the relative capacity of the manufacturing sector to create new jobs;

(b) a constant share of wage-paying jobs in total employment;

(c) an increase in small-scale economic activities;

(d) an accelerated growth of service and retail employment;

(e) an accentuated feminization of the labour force;

(f) major changes in the regional distribution of economic activities.

---

[4] See Centro de Estudios Educativos A. C.: *Educación y pobreza* (Mexico, Consejo Consultivo del Programa Nacional de Solidaridad–El Nacional, 1993); and E. Hernández Laos: *Crecimiento económico y pobreza en México* (Centro de Investigaciones Interdisciplinarias en Humanidades, UNAM, 1992).

Best estimates from various data sources suggest that, during the 1980s for the national economy as a whole, paid employment (including both wage-earning and self-employment) increased by around 400,000 jobs each year. New jobs were generated, in particular, in the trade and services sector. Mexican agriculture exhausted its capacity to create new jobs more than two decades ago, and between 1979 and 1990 its share in wages paid was reduced from 25 per cent to 21 per cent.[5] About 70 per cent of the paid labour force were wage-earners and, during the 1980s there was a slight change in overall composition of the labour force towards wage-earning work. But in non-farming activities, the growth of wage employment slowed down in the late 1980s whilst the growth rate of non-wage employment increased.

Data from economic censuses of the labour force employed in fixed establishments in manufacturing, commerce and services for 1981, 1986 and 1989 (compiled by INEGI) suggests that in these sectors the net increase in employment between 1980 and 1988 was 1.7 million. But the relative contribution of the manufacturing sector to the growth of total employment has declined with the acceleration of trade liberalization since 1985, and with it there has been a fall in the rate of growth of total employment. Between 1980 and 1985, more than one-third of the growth in total employment (370,000 out of 1,077,135 new jobs net) can be attributed to manufacturing activity, but from 1985 to 1988 this sector was responsible for less than 15 per cent of net job growth (90,000 jobs net). In contrast, services and commerce were responsible for over 550,000 out of 640,834 jobs net created in the period 1985 to 1988. Almost 60 per cent of the jobs created in services and commerce were wage earning.

Within the manufacturing sector, the employment trends reflect the net balance between growth of *maquiladora* (in-bond) economic activities, mostly located along the Mexican border with the United States of America and based on foreign direct investment, and the decline associated with the losses and closures in numerous sectors of the economy oriented to the domestic market. During the 1980s, job losses in the manufacturing sector alone were around 500,000. Job losses occurred in almost all areas of manufacturing outside the *maquiladoras*, including those with modern and backward technology. The most affected sectors were the basic metals industry, the textiles, apparel and leather industry, and the metal products and equipment industry. The *maquiladora* industries, which acted to offset this decline, were export-oriented and strongly dependent on processing

[5] This estimate does not include peasant's earnings which often are in kind.

imported inputs. Imported inputs contributed about 98 per cent of all inputs to these industries in 1981 and the same proportion prevailed in 1993.

During the period 1980-90, almost 75 per cent of the jobs created in manufacturing were in *maquiladora* firms, and employment in these activities increased 2.7 times from 1980 to 1991. In 1991, the *maquiladora* activities employed more than 460,00 workers, almost 20 per cent of the labour force employed in manufacturing. The persons employed in *maquiladora* industries tend to be young and female. One survey of *maquiladora* plants carried out in three northern cities revealed average ages of between 22 and 24.2 years. In 1981, 77 out of every 100 workers were women. But in 1992, this had fallen to 59 out of 100 workers. This shift was associated with diversification of *maquiladora* industry, and especially the greater importance assumed by the construction, repair, and assembly of transport equipment, a branch traditionally associated with male labour.

The economic censuses of manufacturing, services and commerce indicate the extent of the feminization of the labour force. Between 1981 and 1985, 70 per cent of the net new jobs in these sectors were occupied by men, but between 1985 and 1988, they occupied only 46 per cent. Within the manufacturing sector, the average growth rate for numbers of female workers increased between these two intercensal periods, whilst the growth rate for numbers of male workers fell from 2.24 per cent in the period 1980-85 to 0.01 per cent from 1985-88. Greater participation of women in wage-earning employment reflected the combined effect of the *maquiladorization* of industry and the tertiarization of the economy, and occurred in spite of a trend towards defeminization in the *maquiladora* sector.

The growth in the labour force participation of women could have some positive features. However, it should be noted that the feminization of the labour force is the result of a worsening of labour conditions for men and not because women are becoming better off. Women have to enter the labour market to sustain household incomes in the face of declining real wages. Moreover, although a measure of occupational segregation by gender suggests that such segregation is declining, women are still poorly represented in professional, managerial and supervisory positions. Even if not all women hold low pay or bad quality jobs, greater participation of women in the labour force has happened in precarious, part-time activities.

The accelerated growth of employment in services and commerce has the concomitant that more and more people are finding employment in small-scale activities.[6] In 1988, the average number of persons employed per establishment was 2.8 persons per establishment in commerce; 4.9 persons per establishment in services; and 18 persons per establishment in manufacturing. Defining "small establishments" as those that have five or less employed persons for units in commerce and services, and 15 or less employed persons for manufacturing units, it is apparent that in 1988, 90 per cent of the establishments in services and 94 per cent of the establishments in commerce were in small units (accounting for 41 per cent and 56 per cent of sectoral employment, respectively). For manufacturing, small establishments represented 84 per cent of establishments, but only contributed 14.7 per cent of employed persons.

The greatest proportion of non-wage-earning work exists in small enterprises. Some of these enterprise combine wage-earning and non-wage-earning work, whilst others have no wage-earning work. The National Survey of Very Small Businesses (ENAMIN) carried out in early 1992 and using a sample which was representative of all urban areas with over 100,000 people, found that the labour force in very small economic units (defined as establishments in manufacturing, commerce and services with fewer than seven people employed) was 4.8 million persons, of whom 2.3 million were owners without help (one man/woman units) or with non-paid help, and 857,000 were unpaid subordinate workers.

Small establishments are found in activities where big capital, national and transnational, has a small presence. Production is usually not tradeable at the international level and therefore these activities appear to be secure from trade liberalization. But this type of employment can be precarious. The expansion of employment in small-scale activities reflects the increase in the gap between the expansion of wage employment and of the economically active population and the fact that more and more people are ending up in small-scale activities as a means of survival.

One puzzling feature of the employment trends in the 1980s is that official unemployment rates have been very low, falling during the deep recession of 1986 and the subsequent three years, and then rising to 4 per cent by 1993. These figures have not been "massaged" to understate the economic crisis, but they underestimate the numbers of the involuntarily unemployed. As there is no unemployment insurance, to be unemployed is, to use a phrase of Gunnar Myrdal, a luxury which few can afford. This is one of the reasons for the upsurge of very small economic units,

[6] The economic censuses provide information on the size of establishments in the manufacturing, commerce and services sectors.

including one-person units. The published unemployment statistics reflect, in part, the levels of "frictional" unemployment, that is the relative number of unemployed people who know for sure — or firmly believe — they will get a job in the short run.

2. *Sectoral shifts in formal employment*

Statistical analysis was undertaken to construct a more disaggregated view of trends in formal employment using data from the National Accounting System of INEGI which divides Mexico's economy into nine sub-sectors (*divisiones*) and 73 branches (*ramas*). All 73 branches were classified into three groups according to their average annual growth rate of wage employment during the period 1987-92. Group I consisted of branches in which the employment growth rate exceeded 5 per cent per annum, that is the rate required to absorb all new entrants to the economically active population. Group II consisted of branches in which the employment growth rate was between 1.18 per cent per annum (the average for the economy as a whole) and 5 per cent. Group III consisted of branches with an employment growth rate below the national average.

A first significant feature of this classification is the relative importance of the different Groups. The dynamic Group I consists of three branches — automobiles, other manufacturing, and construction — which together consisted of only 10.5 per cent of total formal employment during 1987-92. At the other extreme, Group III consisted of 41 sluggish or declining branches. They accounted for 50.4 per cent of formal employment during 1987-92, and employment growth was on average −0.4 per cent per annum. The most important branches in this group are agriculture (22.5 per cent of total formal employment), other services (10.8 per cent) and public administration and defence (4.7 per cent). Group II, consisting of branches which experienced employment growth above the national average but below 5 per cent, consisted of 29 branches, including notably trade, education services and transportation. These branches had 39 per cent of total formal employment during 1987-92 and grew on average by 2 per cent per annum.

There are also significant associations between employment growth patterns by Group and other economic variables. Notable associations are:

(a) Output growth is greatest in Group I, though these branches only contributed 6.8 per cent of total GDP in 1987-92.

(b) Real wages per worker fell on average by 2.0 per cent per annum during the period 1982-92, but a recovery occurred after a drastic fall

during 1982-86. However, the most dynamic branches regarding employment and GDP growth had the least recovery in real wages. In 1992, real wages in Group I branches were only 63.8 per cent of 1980, whilst in Group II they were 77.1 per cent and in Group III, 91.4 per cent.

(c) Only Group I shows a significant increase in capital productivity, the other two Groups exhibiting an increase in capital productivity through falling capital stocks. All Groups experience a fall in labour productivity during 1982-86 and a recovery in 1987-92, but for Groups II and III the improvement in labour productivity is "perverse" in the sense that it is caused by a slight increase or fall in GDP accompanied by a lower rate of employment change.

(d) Group I branches have exhibited the most dynamic performance regarding exports, with exports growing at 45.7 per cent per annum during 1982-86 and 25.4 per cent per annum during 1987-92. But this Group contributed only 5.7 per cent of total exports during 1987-92, and high export growth rates were associated with high import growth rates.

Simple econometric models were constructed to estimate the elasticity of employment-GDP, employment-real wages, and employment-exports. The results suggest that output growth is important for the generation of employment except in Group III branches, and agriculture and mining in particular, which contain the branches with the highest propensity to expel labour. They also indicate that in the manufacturing sector, which has the highest elasticity for employment-GDP, an increase in real wages is associated with a decline in employment. Finally, export growth is not related with a significant expansion of employment.

The models underline the importance of economic growth for employment generation. They suggest that, given the current development pattern, a GDP growth rate of over 10 per cent per annum is necessary to generate sufficient formal employment to absorb all new entrants to the labour market.

IV. Conclusion

Mexico has made a transition from an inclusive development model to a development model which is causing greater levels of social exclusion. These exclusionary effects arise because the neo-liberal project has failed thus far: to create new jobs at the rate required to absorb new entrants to the economically active population; to offset job losses associated with the continued expulsion of labour from agriculture and the contraction of manufacturing activities established under the old development model; and to prevent real wages from falling. The old inclusive development model was imperfect, and characterized by various inequalities and discrimination. But with the adoption of structural adjustment programmes, new patterns of exclusion are being added to the old inequality and discrimination. Middle-aged men (25-55 years), as well as older men, have suffered the impact of economic restructuring, whilst labour force participation rates have grown substantially for women and young men.

The low generation of employment since 1982 is directly related to the weakness of the economic growth process under structural adjustment. The increasing employment crisis reflects the failure of the government to address the employment dimension of the adjustment process, and the failure to coordinate macro-economic policy with sectoral policies and micro-economic restructuring policies. Some new industrial, labour, agricultural and other policies have been initiated in the 1990s after the recognition of some of the negative impacts of liberalization. But the time-lag between trade liberalization and these policies has already had dramatic social and economic effects.

The exclusionary nature of the new development path can be attributed to poor policy design. But more fundamentally, exclusionary effects may be built into its nature. The guarantee of cheap labour constitutes a crucial element in the new strategy, and there has been a high degree of State intervention to keep real wages low. Institutional mechanisms include several *Pactos Economicos* since 1987 and the recent *Pacto para la Estabilidad, la Competividad y el Empleo* (PECE), which establishes nominal wage growth ceilings in order to maintain low inflation rates. The growing importance of small-scale activities and *maquiladora* industries is strengthening the segmentation and heterogenization of industrial structure and employment structure. Moreover, industrial restructuring has been associated with a radical transformation of traditional corporatism. The increasing informalization of labour, which is occurring in *maquiladoras* and in key sectors of the Mexican industry such as TELMEX, PELMEX, Ford/Volkswagen, has depended on the (sometimes violent) dissolution of collective contracts, and the break-up of regional and national trade unions and their replacement with firm-level unions.

Respective administrations since 1982 have reinforced the authoritarian character of Mexico's government, assuming that economic freedom will probably lead later to political freedom. This has led to the exclusion of vast segments of Mexico's population from participating in and debating the adjustment process itself, as well as other issues that will change Mexico substantially, such as NAFTA. However, recent events, particularly the uprising in Chiapas, have shown the limitations of this policy and might indicate profound political changes that will also affect the current adjustment process and its exclusionary effects.

14 *Ethnic solidarity and social exclusion in Cameroon*

Samuel Inack Inack, Joseph Edou Mbida and Paulette Bea

This paper examines the way in which group solidarity, which is a basis of integration and inclusion, can lead, at the same time, to social exclusion. It focuses in particular on the micro-dynamics which relate ethnic solidarity to lucrative employment opportunities. This focus is selected because ethnicity is one of the key bases for both social integration and exclusionary practices in Cameroon.

I. Conceptualizing the relationship between social exclusion and ethnic identity

An ethnic group may be defined as a group of people speaking the same language and living in (or saying that they are from) a common area, who believe themselves to be descendants from the same ancestors, with whom they have either a real or mythical relationship. Within the national territory of Cameroon there are over 200 ethnic groups, some of which existed prior to the colonial period, and some of which were reinforced through colonial rule. Their ethnic identity is the product of a social memory, customs, attitudes and cultural behaviour held in common. The members of each ethnic group differentiate themselves from the members of other groups by: their spatial localization (in several towns there are Hausa quarters and Bamileke quarters, for example, and the latter are even subdivided by village of origin); the language they speak; their physical traits; their values and ideologies; and the rules regulating their relationships with other groups. Ethnic membership dictates, through the process of child socialization, the rights and obligations of an individual throughout their lives.

When individuals meet for the first time they tend to make a mental identification of the other's ethnicity, and individuals from the same ethnic group (sharing so many cultural elements in common) tend to develop a sentiment of "Us". This sentiment is held reciprocally by members of other ethnic groups, and it translates into a tendency to accord priority to members of one's own ethnic group in the relationships which bring advantage.

This "original" form of exclusion, based on the culture of each ethnic group in its relationships with other ethnic groups, has been reinforced by changes during the colonial period and after independence. Responses and reactions to the sentiment of division between "Us" and "Them", and the perception that advantages are being distributed according to ethnic membership, have led to reactions and responses. Those excluded adopt strategies of adaptation which create inclusion, but the formation of new groups, at the same time, excludes others. Thus, on top of the "original" form of exclusion, there develops a second form, which is brought about by integration strategies which have been deployed to deal with the "original" exclusion. In some cases, this exclusion is deliberate; in others, it arises in a spontaneous, involuntary manner.

Exclusion on an ethnic basis arises in diverse ways and it occurs as an outcome of the reinforcement of group solidarity, as the product of evolving specialization and the development of an ethnic division of labour, *and* through deliberate monopolistic practices.

A whole set of structures and institutions has developed to support and develop group solidarity, including: village associations, reunions, credit associations, and the collective promotion of infrastructure and support in case of sickness. The *tontines* are particularly important in enabling their members to acquire different goods, rights and services which they could not normally acquire. Through them, the ethnic group finances, or grants loans at a favourable interest, to individual members of the ethnic group who want to invest or to consume.

Ethnic specialization is encouraged through the process of acquisition of professional skills, and particularly a system of apprenticeship within family structures. Bamileke traders teach their sons and cousins how to trade; *peuhl* shepherds teach them how to tend sheep; and, with formal education, parental and ethnic affinities are promoting ethnic specialization even among salaried workers. Different jobs have different ideological values attached to them, and this valorization is also part of the way in which groups mutually exclude each other through specialization.

Finally, access to certain very privileged positions is protected through monopolistic behaviour. This is apparent, for example, in certain trading activities. The process of exclusion in such cases is analogous in its operation to that of a monopolistic enterprise which erects entry barriers to maintain control of acquired positions and acts to prevent other enterprises usurping its position.

The relationship between social exclusion and ethnic identity is thus very complex. Mechanisms include the formation of voluntary associations, the establishment of clientelistic networks of relations, and the everyday functioning of social norms, taboos and customs held in common.

II. Historical and macro-economic context of social exclusion

The colonial period is extremely important for understanding present patterns of social exclusion on ethnic lines. Colonial authorities not only reinforced some latent tribal identities, but also mapped out the localization of ethnic groups. With the development of an economy based on the export of raw materials and import of consumer goods, ethnic specializations began to emerge, creating a spontaneous form of exclusion. In the southern forest areas, land was rarely passed to an individual outside the clan or ethnic group, but particular areas were most suitable for the cultivation of export crops. Certain ethnic groups were also the early beneficiaries of a school education. They soon formed an elite who became clerks and employees of the colonial administration or colonial institutions, and at independence they constituted the Government and administration.

The Bamileke were in a position in which they were poorly represented in salaried employment in the administration on account of late education, and initially they were excluded from this sphere of activity as senior administrators preferred to associate themselves with persons of the same ethnic group. But, on the other hand, they increasingly monopolized trading activities, a process which was reinforced by the apprenticeship system and the associational tradition of the Bamilekes, which has been particularly important for informal financial arrangements.

In the economy which developed up to the 1980s, approximately 80 per cent of the population continued to earn their livelihood from the land. But the two most lucrative activities were import-export trading and employment in the civil service. In the 1960s and 1970s, commercial activities accounted for about 40 per cent of the GDP, and 55 per cent of the wage bill of the country consisted of civil service salaries. Private trading houses and public marketing boards were central to the process of the division of the social product in the country.

Employment and livelihood opportunities are closely linked to ethnic identity. Access to agricultural land is particularly difficult for "strangers' to an area, who are not part of the indigenous community of that locality. It is possible to buy and sell land, but a rural survey showed that the Betis had a higher propensity to buy and sell land than the Bamilekes and Bamouns.

Bamileke predominate in commerce. Recent statistics (1994) also show that Bamilekes and Betis together occupy 56 per cent of the posts of responsibility in the Cameroon civil service, a significantly greater proportion than one would expect given their numbers (38 per cent of the total population in 1987).

With the implementation of structural adjustment programmes, the GNP has fallen and it is estimated that there have been 24,000 job losses. Civil servants and other State agents, who were hitherto protected social classes, have experienced the most serious deterioration in living standards, following redundancies and also dramatic declines in real wages after the devaluation of the currency (CFA). Surveys show that civil servants have reduced their expenditure on health care by 20 per cent and on children's education by 33 per cent. However, some have responded to the situation by engaging in private trade of public goods, to the detriment of the majority.

The adjustment programmes have raised prices for farmers producing export crops. But a rural survey showed that, with regard to basic needs, many of the rural population are still very poor. The rural households in the sample purchased secondhand clothing one-and-one-half times per year on average; 82 per cent had no electricity; 30 per cent did not have rough-cast housing; their revenues were sufficient to cover 50 per cent of their education needs; and 82 per cent of health cases were handled by traditional healers. Many farmers cannot gain productive inputs, and illiteracy rates are high.

III. Ethnic solidarity and the micro-dynamics of exclusion: Findings from surveys

In order to clarify the micro-dynamics of social exclusion in relation to ethnic identity in the current economic situation, various small surveys were conducted in the frame of the IILS/UNDP social exclusion project. They included: (i) 102 households heads in Yaoundé, including 40 which had been surveyed in 1990-91 as "vulnerable"; (ii) 52 traders in markets in Yaoundé; (iii) 62 heads of voluntary associations; and (iv) 104 households heads selected from 3 rural zones (two in the West, one in the Centre). The present section summarizes the findings of the first three surveys, which illustrate particularly well the relationship between ethnic solidarity and social exclusion.

1. Urban households

The survey of urban households indicated the very difficult living conditions facing many people at the present time. Ninety-five per cent of household heads who were working did so without contracts or institutional social protection. Twenty-eight per cent were unemployed, and for these, only one-third had been unemployed for less than 10 months. Households were large (eight members on average), reflecting a strategy of household grouping to ensure that at least one person is still economically active. But household income permitted only 2 per cent of the households to satisfy all their basic needs.

Twenty-one per cent of households were identified as poor, defined as eating meat less than twice per week, having fewer than two meals per day, and not having water installed. In these poor households, the majority of children were not sent to school on financial grounds. The poor households also tend to have precarious lodging arrangements. Significantly, poor households are also much more likely not to participate in voluntary associations. Over one-third of poor households do not participate in such associations, whereas for non-poor households the proportion is only 11 per cent.

Various correlations are found between ethnic identity and living conditions. But it is notable that, amongst the household heads, the majority of the unemployed (65 per cent) are Betis, and that one Beti household head in two is unemployed. Similarly, the majority of the poor and the very poor are Betis or other ethnic groups. The relative advantage of the Bamilekes reflects the emphasis on private sector activity in the current reform programme and the dominant position which the Bamilekes have in trading, the reasons for which become clearer in the trader survey.

2. Traders

The survey of traders sought to understand the reasons why Bamileke are predominant in commercial activities, and to do this it focused on the ways in which traders financed their business and gained access to merchandise. Only nine persons in the sample were non-Bamileke, but some significant ethnic differences emerged.

With regard to initial finance capital, all groups tended to rely in the first instance on their own savings. But for the financing of on-going activities, 63 per cent of the Bamileke had recourse to finance from a credit union (*tontine*) as against only 11 per cent of the non-Bamileke. Only two traders in the whole sample sought finance from the formal banking system. For the Bamileke, this reflects a preference for informal finance, as access is simple for credit union members, even though loan terms may be more onerous than in the banks. The *tontines* are organized for the most part on the basis of kinship and ethnic identity, however, and work by excluding non-members.

Most traders have regular suppliers of merchandise. But there is a much greater tendency for these relationships to be based on ethnic affinities and common membership of a voluntary association amongst the Bamileke than amongst the non-Bamileke. Also, the practice of taking merchandise on credit, which allows engagement in commercial activity without much capital, is much more common amongst the Bamileke. It is through such preferential commercial relationships that non-Bamileke come to be excluded from spheres of trading, particularly wholesale trade.

The associational life of the Bamileke traders is more well developed than that of the non-Bamileke; the associations in which the Bamileke participate tend to be associations in which ethnic identity is a condition of membership; and whereas two-thirds of the Bamileke traders saved in associations in order to expand their commercial activities, only one-third of the non-Bamileke traders do so.

The size of the sample means that the patterns identified should be seen as tendencies. But it appears that the quasi-exclusion of non-Bamileke from commercial activity is founded on the superior ability of the Bamileke to mobilize savings through informal associations and the superior development of practices of ethnic solidarity in support of business expansion. Social exclusion is entrained in an indirect way owing to the inability of members of other ethnic groups to use or to master these procedures.

3. Associations

These findings were confirmed in the surveys of the 62 associations. The associations covered included ethnic associations, which were most numerous in the sample; professional associations; and religious and other associations (such as former pupils from the same school). About half the associations operate only at the regional level, and the majority of those with national representation tend to be ethnic associations. Three-quarters of the associations have savings as their main objective. For the Bamileke associations, these savings are oriented to commercial purposes, whilst for non-Bamileke associations, these savings are oriented towards educational expenses. The professional associations aim to promote their profession and protect members, whilst religious associations are often interested in the instruction of their members. Solidarity is shown and enacted by almost all associations at times of funerals.

Ethnic associations have ethnic identity as a condition of membership, and sponsorship is also often necessary, acting as a guarantee that loans will be reimbursed. Professional associations are naturally open to those who practise the same profession. An important condition of membership of all associations, except the professional and religious ones, is participation in the assistance funds to which members have access in case of sickness and death.

From these facts it is apparent that the associations act as a kind of informal social security system for persons excluded from official networks and rights, and as a kind of parallel finance system to the official banks and post offices, which are unattractive to the majority and which have exclusionary administrative practices. In short, many associations support individuals excluded from several economic resources and certain social rights. These associations are the most effective system of social integration in the country. But, in regrouping the excluded, the associations also exclude. This exclusion is not always organized. Often, for example, associations were started in a particular locality and, as they grow, their solidaristic practices take on a more exclusionary character. However, it is significant that as they work on the one side to promote social integration they create, at the same time, on the other side, other categories of excluded persons.

IV. Conclusion

From the analysis it is apparent that the relationship between ethnic identity and social exclusion is very complex, with group solidarities both integrating individuals positively at the same time as they exclude them. The task of drawing policy conclusions from this evaluation remains to be made. But a significant feature which this study highlights is the importance of the capacity and the skills for creating and developing associations as a major asset to escape poverty, an asset which could, through supportive programmes, be more widely applied.

15 Social exclusion in respect of basic needs in India

Paul Appasamy, S. Guhan, R. Hema, Manabi Majumdar and A. Vaidyanathan

I. Introduction

Social exclusion is a process which restricts the access of certain social groups to valued resources and entitlements, relegating them to the status of social outsiders. It is a multi-dimensional concept, conceived to capture different forms of social disadvantage — economic, social, political and cultural — that persist, in multiple variants and with different intensity, across nations. Consequently, in its widest connotation, the concept encompasses theories of poverty, inequality, racial/ethnic cleavages, long-term unemployment and citizenship.

Every difference or distinction does not, however, imply exclusion. The extent to which differences produce exclusion depends on the permeability of social boundaries. Exclusion presupposes an active process of social distancing — covert or overt; it attributes agency to groups that closely guard their domain of privilege and profit from exclusion. Thus, social exclusion is a condition/outcome as well as a dynamic process. And the mechanisms of social discrimination vary from nation to nation, and over time. Moreover, the concept seeks to explain the condition of the social outsiders not in terms of their personal characteristics, but in relation to the prevalent economic, social and political conditions. In other words, they are not excluded because of their cumulative individual failings. There are no flatly incompetent people in all spheres. Rather, structural factors cause the reiterated losses whose sum is exclusion itself.

The concept needs to be contextually embedded. In the West, for example, the focus is on the inadequacies of the current welfare state in post-industrial societies and the corresponding changing nature of social disadvantage. Accordingly, the relevant focus groups are the "new social groups", including the "new industrious poor", "immigrants", "ethnic groups", and "single parents", among others. By contrast, in the Indian context and in most developing poor nations, the problem is one of the persistent, chronic and multiple disadvantages of certain social groups in their inability to satisfy basic needs resulting in basic capability failures.

Consequently, the scope of the present study is confined to the extent and nature of exclusion from the satisfaction of basic needs and, more specifically, patterns of deprivation with regard to elementary education; health; water supply and sanitation; and social security. The motivation for focusing on basic needs arises from *(a)* the general acceptance of the notion that a civilized society in modern times has the obligation to ensure fulfilment of these needs for all segments of the population; and *(b)* the recognition that basic needs, even modestly conceived, are still not satisfied for an unconscionably large number of the people in the country.

Besides reviewing the policies designed to address exclusion in each of the selected basic needs areas, we present a brief overview of the general factors affecting access to basic entitlements and a critical assessment of India's socio-economic policies aimed at promoting inclusion in respect of these needs.

II. The approach of Indian plans to basic needs provision

That the removal of poverty, illiteracy and disease, and discrimination based on caste and community, must be among the central concerns of society, was widely accepted within and outside the Indian National Congress, even in the pre-independence days. These concerns were subsequently written into the Constitution of the Indian Republic as Directive Principles of State Policy. These Directive Principles enjoined the State to promote distribution and control of material resources to subserve the common good; to prevent concentration of wealth and the means of production which would be detrimental to popular welfare; to ensure a decent standard of living and, within the limits of economic capacity and development, to make effective provisions for the right to work, to education and public assistance in the case of unemployment, old age, sickness, disablement and in other cases of undeserved want; and to protect the interests of "backward classes". Whilst the Directive Principles, being non-justiciable, are not legally binding (as the Provisions on Fundamental rights are), they have shaped successive governments' development policy and the allocation of resources during the last five decades.

Broadly speaking, Indian plans have followed a four-pronged strategy in pursuit of the above broad aims. First, they have consistently seen sustained rapid growth and diversification of economic activity as a fundamental prerequisite to eliminate malnutrition, illiteracy, poor health and poor housing. Rapid growth increases employment and incomes all round, thereby progressively augmenting the ability of all classes to secure their basic needs.

Second, while rising incomes resulting from the growth process are expected to make the mass of the people better able to afford education, health care and a better physical living environment, the State was seen to have the primary responsibility for providing universal elementary education, basic health services and protected water supply for all sections of the population. Accordingly, the government has invested substantial resources in creating the necessary physical infrastructure and in providing these services free of charge in many cases (and at highly subsidized rates in others) to all segments of the population.

Third, overall growth, while necessary to increase the ability of people to meet their basic needs, may not be sufficient in so far as it is not fast enough relative to population growth, nor sufficiently diffused in space and across social groups to ensure that all classes and regions automatically benefit more or less proportionately from the rising employment and incomes. Therefore, state intervention aimed specifically at stimulating development of relatively backward regions and segments of the population, and providing wage employment, has become an integral and increasingly important part of the plans.

Finally, there are interventions designed to tackle "exclusion" reflecting systematic differences between social groups in the opportunity to satisfy basic needs due to social and cultural factors. In the Indian context such differences exist on account of the institution of social hierarchy based on caste. Recognizing that certain castes, especially the "untouchables" and indigenous people (referred to in India as Scheduled Castes and Scheduled Tribes), suffer from the cumulative effects of systematic exclusion from land ownership, education, access to common sources of water, and various types of work, the Constitution mandated positive discrimination in their favour. This has resulted in reservation of specified proportions of membership in legislatures, public sector jobs and higher education for these groups, as well as development programmes and assistance meant specifically for their benefit. Though not mandatory, the scope of positive discrimination in public jobs and education have been extended to cover the "Other Backward Castes".

More generally, compulsions of electoral politics in a system based on an universal adult franchise, have gradually led to a situation in which all political parties find it necessary actively to woo the votes of the poor by promising to address their needs. This has increased the awareness among the Scheduled Castes, Scheduled Tribes, and "Other Backward Castes" of the potentials of the political process to secure benefits from the State. Political articulation of their concerns and interests, and their fight against discrimination, has therefore become progressively stronger. The resulting sharpening of conflicts in society does increase pressures for reform to address the problem of social exclusion.

III. General achievements

These policies have yielded mixed results. In terms of overall growth, between 1950 and 1990 India's GDP has nearly quadrupled and per capita income has risen by about 70-75 per cent. The overall growth rate quickened appreciably during the mid-1970s and 1980s. Since this was also a period when the rate of population growth slowed down somewhat, per capita income growth also recorded a significant improvement. Nevertheless the fact remains that the pace of growth — in both aggregate and per capita terms — is low compared to the attainment of many other developing countries, especially in east and south-east Asia. Also, in absolute terms, India's per capita income remains low.

Evidence on distribution of income and inequality in living standards is patchy and somewhat contradictory. There is evidence of a trend towards greater concentration of land and other productive assets in agriculture and growing informalization of the economy — all of which suggest increased inequality. Inter-regional disparities in per capita output have also increased. However, the extent of inequality in consumption does not show any sustained or significant trend. Since per capita real consumption has risen, the proportion of the population below the generally-accepted poverty line has declined, especially in the last two decades. The extent of reduction in poverty incidence across different regions has, however, been quite uneven. Moreover, the fact remains that a sizeable portion of the population (some 40 per cent) still cannot afford the rather modestly-defined level of the minimum living standard.

We do not have data for assessing trends by socio-economic groups. But there are indications that, while the process of growth along with state intervention (especially affirmative action) has widened the access of disadvantaged groups to assets, public sector jobs and higher education, the extent of disparities between these and the rest of the community remains unacceptably large.

IV. Nutritional status

The improvement in per capita real consumption has led to little improvement in the overall intake of staple food grains or of calories and protein. Moreover, despite the reduction in overall incidence of poverty, the proportion of people with less than the prescribed norm in 1987-88 is reported by the National Sample Survey to be higher than in 1977-78. In rural areas, the proportion of the population below the poverty line is estimated to have dropped from 58 per cent to 32 per cent between 1977-78 and 1987-88, whilst the proportion below the prescribed calorie norm rose from 58 per cent to 66 per cent. In urban areas, a similar pattern is found. The proportion living below the poverty line fell from 51 per cent to 21 per cent over the same ten-year period, whilst the proportion below the prescribed calorie norm rose from 49 per cent to 57 per cent.

Improvement in average calorie intake is much less than one might expect even with the modest increases in per capita real income during the past 20 years. In large part this seems to reflect shifts in consumption patterns from food to non-food items, from staple grains to subsidiary foods (like fruits and vegetables, oils and fat, milk, etc.), and from coarser grains (which have been and remain one of the cheapest sources of calories) to finer grains (which cost more per unit of calorie). The shift seems to be occurring in all classes, including the poor groups. Increases in income alone may not therefore automatically lead to the eradication of deficiencies in the consumption of basic food and perhaps other basic needs. The public distribution system, meant to provide basic needs at subsidized prices, has only a limited coverage and fails to ensure that the benefits accrue mainly to the poor, especially in rural areas.

Given that food intake of those on average income is well below the nutritionally satisfactory level, one would not expect significant improvements in nutritional status, especially among the poor. Better control of communicable disease, improvements in curative health services, availability of antibiotics and water supply may have contributed to more efficient use of food consumed. But their overall impact is rather modest and the impact on the poor even more so. Unfortunately, data necessary to assess the various manifestations of nutritional status (such as nature and intensity of activities, body weight and morbidity) for different socio-economic groups are either not available or inadequate.

V. Elementary education

Nearly half the Indian population is illiterate; about 45 per cent of the children in the age group 5-14 are not currently attending school; and nearly 44 per cent of rural children in the age group 6-11 have never enrolled in schools. These simple but starkly disconcerting statistics expose, perhaps only partly, the magnitude of persistent educational deprivation in the country. Indeed, the constitutional imperative of universal elementary education notwithstanding, elementary schooling, in theory open to all, in practice remains inaccessible to a large section of disadvantaged social groups. This has long-term consequences. Children who are "drop-outs" from the educational system in the early years of their lives eventually grow up to become "social drop-outs", unable to enter the mainstream of society and enjoy the status of full citizenship, and children of these families in turn tend to be educationally deprived.

There are systematic differences between socio-economic groups both in overall literacy and enrolment of children in elementary education, and multiple socio-economic handicaps converge to find cumulative expression in educational impoverishment. Females are in general more disadvantaged than males. Rural literacy and enrolment rates are everywhere lower than in urban areas; this disparity compounds the gender disparity. In 1986-87 nearly 55 per cent of the female children in the 6-11 age group in rural areas were reported to have never enrolled in schools, as against 23 per cent in urban areas. The comparable proportions for males were 35 per cent and 16 per cent, respectively. Disadvantaged social groups, especially Scheduled Castes and Scheduled Tribes (SCs/STs), are also educationally more deprived. Scheduled Caste literacy in 1981 was about half the level attained by non-SC/STs, and that of Scheduled Tribes was even lower. There is also a systematic relation between per capita income and educational participation. In 1986-87, for example, the poorest quintile households in rural India in terms of total monthly expenditure accounted for a third of non-enrolment in the 6-11 age group in school compared to a mere 5 per cent in the richest quintile. In sum, multiple forms of inequality — market inequality (poverty), status inequality (membership of a "backward" caste), gender, and spatial disparity — render certain social groups incapable of achieving freedom from illiteracy and innumeracy.

Policies aimed at limiting exclusionary outcomes in the field of education have effected some positive changes. Over the years, literacy rates have shown a rise for all categories of people. More encouraging still, relevant statistics point not only to a considerable improvement in the general situation of literacy and education, but also to a narrowing of disparities between rural and urban areas, between males and females, and between SCs/STs and other, "forward" communities. All this suggests that inter-group differences in the degree of educational disadvantage are diminishing. Alternatively, the incidence of disproportionate exclusion of vulnerable communities from educational assets is becoming less severe.

This modest progress notwithstanding, educational accomplishments of marginalized social groups in the country remain far from satisfactory. The forces that have worked to depress the pace of progress in combating exclusion from basic education are complex and defy easy description. They range from strong social and economic disincentives to feeble political commitments and to wasteful use of already limited resources. In broad outline, three issues are relevant here: *(a) the timidity of effort* on the part of the state; *(b) the so-called lack of demand* for education among the excluded; and *(c) the political economy of public spending* on education.

While the Indian Constitution calls for compulsory elementary education, the State has not taken any legislative action to make elementary schooling compulsory. On the contrary, *persuasion* and not *compulsion* has been the primary policy strategy, relegating to the parents the ultimate right to either sell the labour of their children or to forgo such earning through children's schooling. Since the State has not been bold enough to impose a *duty* on parents, irrespective of their economic circumstances, to send their children to school, the already vulnerable social groups have been neither prodded, nor aided by legal instruments, to overcome the barriers to educational participation. It is hardly surprising that, in the absence of any legal compulsion, economic disincentives for children's schooling (which also involves substantial private expenditure) appear formidable to poor parents in perpetual need for extra income. Simply put, the State's failure to generate demand for education through legislative means has worked to reinforce, and not to weaken, the other formidable constraints yielding exclusionary outcomes.

One popular thesis about the "perception" of the excluded groups themselves needs mention in this respect. It is often argued that the educationally deprived groups do not strongly react to their exclusion and that it indicates their satisfaction with their current educational status. What this desire-based approach unfortunately ignores is the fact that the deprived frequently adjust their aspirations to the low level of life they have known. The absence of any information or idea of an alternative way of life, compounded by cultural disincentives, prevents formation of the desire for education.

Finally, the pattern of public spending on education has further worked to limit the scope of educational participation for the poorer sections. On the whole, inter-ectoral allocation of the educational budget has been disproportionately favourable to higher education at the expense of elementary education. Given that the beneficiaries of higher education are primarily upper-income families, more investment in higher education at the cost of elementary education has had regressive redistributive effects, which in turn have further jeopardized the chances of excluded groups to enter the world of education. Only recently are possibilities being explored to expand the level of expenditure on elementary education by economizing on wasteful investments in some branches of higher education. Policies designed to promote vigorous expansion of elementary education will undoubtedly make a significant contribution by quickening the pace of inclusion of the social outsiders.

VI. Basic health care

The overall health policy has focused on eradicating communicable diseases, improving water supply and sanitation, and providing a network of health centres easily accessible to the people, especially in rural areas. There has been an impressive growth and coverage of health-care facilities. But rural locations remain much poorer compared to the urban locations. This is evident from the fact that about 30 per cent of the registered doctors, 42 per cent of the hospitals and dispensaries and 18 per cent of hospital and dispensary beds in the country serve about 75 per cent of its population that lives in rural areas. The overall indicators of health status are still low, and there are wide disparities between classes and regions. There is still a long way to go in providing adequate basic health care for all.

Mortality rates (infant and crude death rates) are higher in rural areas than in towns. While females have a higher life expectancy at birth, rural infant and child mortality rates are much higher for females than for males. Inadequate allocations for nutritional and medical care for female offspring, and social factors leading to female infanticide may be responsible for this.

We have little data on mortality levels by income or social group and nothing on trends. It is, however, reasonable to suppose that the reduction in mortality due to control of communicable diseases has benefited all classes, including the poor and disadvantaged social groups like the Scheduled Castes and Scheduled Tribes.

Estimates from the National Sample Survey (NSS) indicate that the incidence of morbidity is higher in rural than urban areas, but a smaller proportion of ailments result in treatment and hospitalization. About 82 per cent of all reported ailments in rural areas and 89 per cent in urban areas are treated (without hospitalization); at the same time, one in every 29 ailments in rural areas and one in 24 in urban centres receives in-patient treatment.

The poor, which includes the socially disadvantaged, less educated groups, resort to government rather than non-government hospitals much more than others. Poverty prevents people from attending to their ailments as fully as the well-to-do and (where hospitalization is involved) makes them use relatively less expensive sources of care. And yet, relative to their resources, the burden of health care is higher for the poorest quintile compared to the richest quintile. Rural groups spend a higher proportion of their monthly per capita income on treatment of illnesses compared to urban groups, and this burden of expenditure is higher for lower-income groups in both rural and urban India. The per capita financial expenditure on medical treatment in a year (for both hospitalized and non-hospitalized cases) in rural areas is on average about one-and-a-half times the urban, and as a proportion of total annual per capita expenditure, the rural figure (5.96) is two-and-a-half times the urban (2.29).

In sum, the rural Indian population in general and the low-income (expenditure) groups are at a definite disadvantage regarding access to curative health care facilities. This differential access to health care and the attendant economic burden has to be viewed in conjunction with the fact that the economically and socially disadvantaged groups are also poorly placed in terms of food intake, access to safe drinking water and sanitation, all of which have a bearing on health status. The marked preference for non-governmental sources of outpatient treatment and the relatively high economic burden of health care in rural areas and for the poor suggest that government policies in respect of health care have not quite accomplished their goals.

Improvement in the efficacy of basic health care must necessarily be the responsibility of the State. Inadequacies are only partly the result of shortage of funds. A great deal can and should be done to ensure that staff are in position to attend to their duties. There is also considerable room for better targeting of subsidies to the really disadvantaged sections; better financing of health care delivery mechanisms that would bring down "transaction" costs for users; and reallocation of budget provisions so as to remove subsidies from medical education, high cost tertiary care and so on to provide more resources for cost-effective basic health care.

VII. Access to housing, water supply and sanitation

Exclusion of disadvantaged groups from the Indian mainstream is most apparent in respect of housing. The proliferation of squatter settlements and slums in all the major urban centres of India and the segregated settlements of the Scheduled Caste/Scheduled Tribe populations of rural India are a visible reminder of their physical exclusion. Ironically, government policies and programmes have accepted the status-quo, namely, physical exclusion or clustering of the poor in separate settlements both in urban and rural areas. Since housing is largely a private sector activity, government policies have been restricted to a large extent to providing tenure, services, etc. Despite vigorous efforts by the National

Campaign for Housing Rights, de facto government policies have not been able to guarantee decent housing as a "social right". Data collected by the National Sample Survey and others only serve to confirm the depressing state of affairs in this sector. Thirty-nine per cent of rural households and 11 per cent of urban households live in temporary structures — much of it in poor condition and unsuitable protection against rain, wind, etc., and 89 per cent of rural households and 31 per cent of urban households lack latrine facilities. Inadequate waste disposal facilities contribute to communicable diseases. Seventy-two per cent of households in urban areas supposedly have access to safe drinking water, but in rural areas the proportion is less than half.

The recent outbreak of plague in the city of Surat, and the numerous epidemics of water-borne diseases such as cholera, gastro-enteritis, malaria, in the major metropolitan centres of India soon after the monsoon, clearly indicate the unsatisfactory state of affairs with regard to urban water supply and sanitation. The largest casualties are those who live in the shanty towns and squatter settlements. The poor are also the most vulnerable to industrial accidents, as was evident in the Bhopal gas disaster.

Why does such exclusion take place? In rural areas, caste-based *discrimination* is an explanatory variable. There is not only segregation in housing, but also in terms of access to water supply. In many villages, the Scheduled Castes have separate water supply sources; while in villages where water is shared, they must either have the water poured out for them or draw water at different times of the day. Despite various attempts to end the sickening practice of "scavenging", it is carried on in many villages and towns because those involved in this occupation have no other means of livelihood.

In urban areas, the poor are priced out of the land and housing markets. Since the settlements are often "illegal", they are not provided with services such as water supply, sanitation and garbage disposal. Urban development programmes, such as slum upgrading, accept the physical clustering (except in hazardous areas), but seek to provide better services.

Despite all these shortcomings, these excluded groups have used various survival strategies. The Indian political system confers one major benefit to all, namely, the right to vote. The urban poor in particular have used this right to extract some benefits for themselves — land tenure, food, and some urban services. The Scheduled Caste population of rural areas has tended to migrate to urban areas not only in search of employment, but because they can merge into the urban "melting pot" and thereby avoid overt exclusion. But their poor economic status may still exclude them from full participation in the benefits that urban areas provide.

VIII. Social security

India has built up a formal social security system in a series of phases. The earliest legislation was the Fatal Accidents Act of 1885 which, having proved ineffective, was replaced in 1923 by the Workmens' Compensation Act. A Maternity Benefit Act was pioneered by the State of Bombay in 1929 and was followed by similar legislation in a number of major states in the 1930s and 1940s. It was only in 1961, however, that a Central Maternity Benefit Act was enacted. Health insurance was introduced in 1948 through the Employees State Insurance (ESI) Act. Along with institutionalized medical care, the ESI provides sickness, maternity, disability and employment injury benefits. The Employers Provident Fund Act was passed in 1952 and was supplemented in 1978 with a family pension scheme and in 1976 with insurance linked to deposits in the Fund. The Payment of Gratuity Act 1972 provided supplementary retirement benefits.

These schemes have been legislated in accordance with ILO recommendations and are confined to the "organized sector", that is, public services (in government, public enterprise, local authorities and quasi-government bodies) and non-agricultural establishments in the private sector employing 10 or more persons. Employees in this sector comprise not even 10 per cent of the total labour force and, even within the organized sector, public employees are much better placed in access to social security and levels of benefits than workers in the private sector. However, there has been no serious policy approach for social security provision to the unorganized sector of the workforce, the unemployed and the unemployable (such as the old and the handicapped). The size of the excluded population (well over 90 per cent of the population) makes this inexcusable while the daunting magnitude and complexity of the problem also in part explain the policy blindness. While there has been no nationwide approach in terms of policy or programmes for extending social security to unorganized workers, or more widely to poor households, in practice a patchwork of schemes which provide different types of social security entitlements to the poor have come into being at the national and state levels. They can be grouped into: *(a)* insurance schemes; *(b)* promotional schemes which seek to prevent or ameliorate contingencies requiring relief; and *(c)* specific protective schemes.

The most direct form of social security available to the poor consists of social assistance schemes implemented by state governments. The most important of them are old-age pensions for the "destitute" poor. In addition to general old age pension schemes, many states have more liberal schemes for agricultural labourers who are likely to be the poorest among the elderly. Pensions have also been provided to widows and to the physically handicapped constituting forms of survivor and disability benefits. Some states provide survivor, disability and employment injury benefits to families or victims involved in specified high-hazard occupations. There is wide variation in the coverage, benefits and eligibility conditions among the States and also in implementation efficiency, take-up, and levels of budgetary expenditures.

Table 1 (p. 250) summarizes the gross availability of standard social security entitlements to various segments of the population in India. It clearly brings out that a very large proportion of the population is excluded from most benefits and that social security provision is extremely skewed towards a small class of the workforce, with public employees being the most advantaged. As far as social security is concerned, exclusion thus is the rule rather than an exception.

At a second and further level, exclusion arises from several other factors, administrative and otherwise. While the actual degree or magnitude of such exclusion in effective access is difficult to quantify, available evidence from scattered studies indicates that it can be quite serious.

To sum up, a very large proportion of the Indian population consisting of workers in the unorganized sector, the unemployed and the unemployable is excluded from social security. The characteristics of the Indian labourmarket and financial and administrative constraints would make it unfeasible for the formal social security model to be extended to them. However, a sizeable dent on exclusion can be made through a combination of promotional measures, the insurance market and social assistance. The financial cost of a reasonable social assistance package is entirely affordable and sustainable in budgetary terms. Since the excluded are politically powerless and the establishment is elite-oriented, sustained and reasoned advocacy at the national and international levels will be important in breaking the barriers to exclusion.

IX. Conclusion

To sum up, despite progress over the past five decades, a sizeable segment of the Indian population continues to be experience basic needs deprivation. Some segments of the population are more deprived than others. The factors contributing to exclusion from basic needs range from inadequate private incomes on the one hand, to socially constructed barriers on the other. Among others, income level and caste status appear to be the two most important factors in determining the ability of social groups to achieve a certain basic standard of living. What is more, the caste factor and income factor are correlated to a considerable extent: groups with low caste status typically belong to low-income groups and, on that account, become doubly excluded from social rights of citizens. While the relationship between private income or caste position and the quality of life is quite strong, it is not immutable. For example, the nutritional or educational status of a child is not just a question of household income, but also one of consumption patterns, intra-family distribution of resources and parental education.

The State has played on active role in ensuring wider basic needs satisfaction and mitigating exclusions by measures to promote general development, taking responsibility for providing basic social services, and trying to correct social and political discrimination in access to such services. These policies have undoubtedly contributed to making basic needs more easily accessible to the disadvantaged groups. But significant disparities remain.

The current policy reforms of the Indian government are aimed at unshackling the economy's growth potential. More rapid growth, it is claimed, will make it easier to provide basic needs to everyone. But there are legitimate fears that public provisioning of basic social services, affirmative action and targeted poverty alleviation programmes will bear the brunt of the squeeze on public expenditure. There are, of course, possibilities for getting more from current spending by enforcing greater accountability in the working of public agencies, by reallocation of resources in favour of basic needs programmes, and by rationalizing the disposition and use of poverty alleviation programmes. But even though these aspects should receive much greater attention than at present, the disparities in coverage and quality are so large that the level of allocations for basic services and a minimal social security to the vulnerable poor will need to be increased. Ensuring this should be a matter of high priority in the reform process.

Table 1: Gross availability of social security in India

Contingency	Public employees	Workers in private sector to whom social security legislation is applicable	The general poor
1. Medical care	Free treatment in government hospitals; reimbursement of treatment costs and drug costs	Treatment costs and drugs costs under ESI	Treatment in public hospitals
2. Sickness benefit	Medical leave on full pay	Sickness leave under ESI	Nil
3. Maternity benefit	Maternity leave on full pay	Maternity benefits under ESI or under Maternity Benefits Act	Social assistance schemes for maternity assistance in certain states
4. Unemployment benefit	Retrenchment benefits under National Renewal Fund for employees of public sector enterprises	Retrenchment benefits under Industrial Disputes Act	Public employment generation schemes limited schemes in certain states for educated unemployed
5. Employment injury	Ex-gratia relief	Benefits under ESI or under Workmen's Compensation Act	Social assistance from welfare funds for those engaged in hazardous occupations in certain states
6. Invalidity benefit	Ex-gratia relief	Benefits under ESI or under Workmen's Compensation Act	Pensions for physically handicapped in certain states
7. Old-age benefit	Pension and gratuity or contributory provident fund and gratuity	Payments under EPF and under Payment of Gratuity Act	Old-age pensions provided by state governments for the destitute poor
8. Survivor benefit	Subsidized group insurance for death while in service: family pensions in the case of death after retirement	Deposit-linked insurance and family pensions under EPF	Subsidized life insurance and accident insurance to the extent available; survivor benefit and accident relief schemes in certain states; pensions for widows in the states; compensation under the Motor Vehicles Act

Part III:
Policy issues

16 The design of policy against exclusion

Gerry Rodgers[1]

Policies intended to prevent, reduce or eliminate social exclusion cover a lot of ground, because of the different conditions under which exclusion occurs, because of the variety of sources and patterns of exclusion, and because of the diverse ways in which the problem can be approached. However, as noted above, the concept of social exclusion has been relatively little used in low-income settings and, as a result, this terminology is rarely found in policy debates. Instead, the main relevant policy issues come up in the context of strategies against poverty, affirmative action for vulnerable groups, provision of public goods, employment creation programmes, social security and the like. Most of these would have a place in a comprehensive strategy against social exclusion. But because they are not explicitly designed to overcome social exclusion, such policy measures are rarely integrated into a coherent framework. Moreover, they generally fail to address the specificities of the issue of exclusion, particularly its multidisciplinarity, and its focus on agency and process.

In order to reflect on the design of policy against exclusion, then, it is preferable to start not from conventional policies against poverty in low-income settings, but by examining some of the experiences in industrialized countries where eliminating or preventing exclusion has been an explicit objective. While such policies have been implemented in many settings, it is in France that the vocabulary of exclusion has been used the longest in the design of policy; the ideas have now spread more widely in the European Community. Below we summarize some of the more prominent policies of this type and discuss the role of different social actors in their implementation, before returning to the issue of similar policies in low-income settings.

---

[1] This paper regroups parts of a paper prepared by Gerry Rodgers [1994], including contributions by José B. de Figueiredo, Charles Gore, Frédéric Lapeyre and Hilary Silver. But many other project participants, who are undertaking empirical studies in countries around the world, have contributed directly or indirectly to this work.

Throughout the discussion reference will be made to different ways of understanding exclusion, which in turn lead action against exclusion in quite different directions. These approaches are founded, as Silver (Ch. 2) argues, on different ways of thinking about the structure of society and the relationship between citizens and the State. The most important ways may be labelled "solidarity", "specialization", "monopoly" (the three mainstream paradigms according to Silver), and "organic". A *solidarity* model sees society as a "moral community" with a core of shared values and rights and interprets exclusion as a breaking of the social tie, a failure of the relationship between the society and the individual. The *specialization* model sees exclusion as resulting from individual behaviours and exchanges. Individuals may exclude themselves by their choices, may be excluded because of patterns of interests or contractual relationships among other actors, or their exclusion may occur as a result of discrimination, of market failures or of unenforced rights. The *monopoly* model views society as hierarchical, with different groups controlling resources. Insiders protect their domains from outsiders, constructing barriers and restricting access to occupations, to cultural resources, to goods and services. *Organic* notions of society, which take a variety of forms, see society as composed of groups, which may be functional, regional or ethnic in character. Exclusion in such systems arises where not all groups are players in the game, where political or economic power becomes concentrated, and when individuals are not well integrated into the mainstream groups around which society is constructed.

I. Policy experiences in Europe: The interventions

1. Labour market interventions

Long-term unemployment is at the centre of the debate over exclusion in Europe. The expression *chômage d'exclusion* captures this well. The problem is the risk that those who lose their jobs enter a spiral of cumulative exclusion. The labour market provides not only income but also the social and symbolic values which tie the individual to society. The longer unemployment persists, the more these values are put at risk.

As a result, much of the action against exclusion has been specifically aimed at the unemployed. The most obvious way to reintegrate the unemployed, of course, is to create jobs, but European economies have been increasingly unable to do this. Moreover, the variety of State job-creating programmes that have been put into effect, for instance of the public works variety, have either *(a)* created new forms of precarious labour market insertion, because they do not offer long-term employment possibilities, or *(b)* as a French report puts it, "experience shows that all the specific measures for employment created in recent years for the most disadvantaged population groups have tended to mainly benefit the less poor among the poor, or even the non-poor" [DRTE, 1993]. However, there are important and successful experiences in this domain. A recent report by the *Centre d'Etudes de l'Emploi* in France, discussing a form of job creation for the unemployed called *contrats emploi-solidarité*, concluded that a million people had benefited over three years, and that while the jobs created were temporary they helped many people back into the labour market.

If the total number of jobs in the economy is not increased, then for every unemployed person who finds a job another person loses one. This is clearly a severe constraint on policies aimed at "integrating" the unemployed without a corresponding macro-economic policy. Nevertheless, several approaches to overcoming labour market exclusion have developed in recent years, with mixed success.

First, there are policies which increase the capacity of the unemployed to organize and to participate in society. An example is the proposal from the *French Commissariat au Plan* to offer a *chèque associatif ou syndical* to the unemployed [de Foucauld, 1992] — a sum of money which they spend on membership in the organization of their choice. Another is the "Unemployed Centres" which have been created by the Trade Union Congress in the United Kingdom. These centres provide advice, legal aid and information to the unemployed and access to the trade union movement, and they constitute an active political lobby. A "European Network of the Unemployed" has been formed in order to distribute information and lobby on behalf of the unemployed. Note the difference in approach — the *chèque syndical* linking the unemployed to mainstream organizations in a republican fashion, the unemployed centres helping the unemployed to defend their interests with an underlying monopoly paradigm.

Second, there are broader State policies aimed at labour market insertion. Of course, employment exchanges play this role. In the specialization paradigm this is sufficient, but it is generally agreed that more active programmes are required. Many such programmes can be enumerated. They include the development of new types of service enterprises, financial incentives to enterprises to recruit among the long-term unemployed, improvement of the management of the low-skill labour market where many of the excluded can hope to find work (this is often regarded as a low-skill job in national employment services), *stages d'insertion* (which includes temporary employment intended to generate contact between the unemployed and potential employers), and other such detailed policies. Labour market policies dealing with the particular needs of women — child care, maternity leave, return to the labour market after child-bearing — are also important in preventing exclusion. There are also policies aimed at promoting self-employment, through the development of appropriate skills and access to credit, information and markets (e.g. the *Association pour le droit à l'initiative économique*) [Yépez, 1994]. A detailed analysis of labour market integration policies by the French *Commissariat général au Plan* concluded that on the whole the results were disappointing [CGP, 1993]. The main problem with most of these programmes is not their content or their intentions, but the fact that they create labour market opportunities in the thousands or tens of thousands, when the problems are in the millions.

Third, many other labour market interventions may be designed to prevent unemployment and exclusion, by discouraging lay-offs, supporting labour-intensive forms of production, developing work-sharing and other new work formulae, developing coordination between employers and employees.

But the problem of unemployment is not the only facet of labour market exclusion. Exclusion within the labour market arises out of the dualization or segmentation of the market, the growth of a range of precarious or unprotected jobs. There is a distinct risk that policies to reintegrate the unemployed aggravate this phenomenon, overcoming exclusion from the labour market by increasing exclusion within it (a problem highlighted by the French *Commissariat au Plan*). Diametrically opposed policies are suggested by the different paradigms of exclusion: the monopoly paradigm suggests a need for the effective extension of regulation, the specialization paradigm the abandonment of regulation, the solidarity and organicist paradigms the building up of institutions to establish partnership and concertation.

2. Raising capabilities

Among labour market interventions against exclusion, those designed to increase capabilities are sufficiently important to be treated separately.

Training programmes invariably form part of policies against exclusion. They may be simply part of the regular programme of support for the unemployed, or may be specifically designed to overcome exclusion, as in the experimental programme in France, *Contre l'exclusion, une qualification*. The latter attempted to deal with the tendency for the excluded to participate less in training programmes, and benefit less from them when they participate. This involved the development of particular institutional mechanisms (especially the active support of a range of social actors), attention to the design of courses (and their alternation with work), career advisory services and, above all, an active involvement of representatives of excluded groups in the overall design of the programme. Although small, this programme has shown considerable promise. But it required much time and intensive efforts.

The general problem with using training against exclusion lies in demonstrating that these programmes do actually lead to labour market reinsertion when there are no jobs to be had. In the United Kingdom, the phenomenon of permanent training, simply to keep the unemployed out of the statistics, has been widely noted. The excluded drop out of such schemes when they realize that they lead nowhere. In France, there is a long experience in State support to training within enterprises in internships of one sort or another. The danger here is that such schemes end up merely providing enterprises with cheap labour in precarious jobs.

It can be argued that the basic problem is less one of training than one of education. Exclusion often has its roots in the educational system, and behind this in the problems faced by some households (single parent households with poor resources, households with strong conflicts between members, households with members subject to ill-health or to drug or alcohol abuse, etc.) which affect school attendance and learning ability. A strong case can be made that action against exclusion needs to be concentrated here, with direct attention to the situations which exclude from schooling. Where unemployment is high and expectations of income earning at the end of regular schooling limited, attention to the groups concerned — youths in their teens — is particularly important. These situations, neglected in the specialization paradigm, would be interpreted in terms of mobilization and the building of social relationships and networks in the monopoly and solidarity paradigms.

3. *Social security, social assistance and social integration*

Traditional social assistance is aimed at providing a safety net for those unable to obtain a decent income through the labour market, while social security covers health risks and old age and provides for particular vulnerabilities (including, of course, unemployment). On the whole, such policies have been regarded as a complement to or a substitute for social integration policies, and attempts to promote the extension of social security systems to provide a "citizenship" or "basic" income to all are based on the same logic. There is, however, at least one exception — a programme in France aimed specifically at linking the provision of basic income support to a more systematic mechanism for social and economic integration. This is the *revenu minimum d'insertion* (minimum income for integration – RMI), which merits some discussion.

The adoption of the RMI in December 1988 was a very important step in the design of policies to promote social integration. The fundamental goal of the law was to link the right to the satisfaction of basic needs with the aspiration for social and professional insertion. The RMI in part responded to the growth of "new" poverty, and in particular to the perception that groups were emerging which were not covered by existing social services and thus were excluded from the social security net. While the population benefiting from the RMI is very heterogeneous, it is generally an underprivileged population which is characterized by low income, low educational level and unemployment. However, if the decision-makers were aiming at a target group consisting of the marginalized population living in the "fourth world", it appears that most of the RMI recipients do not belong to this group; they are mostly young and isolated individuals, who have suffered schooling failures and who are looking for a job.

The RMI combines an income allowance with an "insertion contract". While the income provided is low (an average of FF 1,800 per month per individual), it allows recipients to satisfy some basic needs. Moreover, the regularity and the stability of this income permits longer-term planning by recipients and so gives them a chance of social insertion. Through the RMI, individuals regain their dignity and are stimulated to undertake actions aimed at their social insertion. Several means for insertion are proposed: (i) actions aimed to help recipients to develop their social autonomy — shelter, health, education, culture; (ii) training oriented to professional insertion; (iii) a period of instruction in enterprises through, for example, *emploi-solidarité* contracts; and (iv) collective interest activities in public administration or NGOs. The "insertion contract" is the main innovation; signed by the individual and the administration, it is, from an individual point of view, the formalized means to guarantee the link between income allocation and the actions for integration to be undertaken by the individual and the State. Without this fundamental goal of integration, the RMI would just be a new mechanism leading to a classic assistance relationship between the recipients and the State. But by establishing a linkage between the rights to basic needs satisfaction and to social insertion, the RMI is a revolution with regard to social aid which opens up a new route to fight exclusion.

The RMI has clearly played a major role in French social policy. In recent years, between 500,000 and 1 million persons were receiving this allocation at any point in time, and while there is of course a stigma attached to the RMI its income support role has been undeniable. The "integration" aspect has been somewhat less convincing. While substantial numbers of RMI receivers have found their way into the regular labour market, success is biased towards the young and the better educated. Many RMI receivers do not have a meaningful "integration" contract, especially those over 40. The RMI has a tendency to create a limbo between inclusion and exclusion, but cannot overcome the fundamentally poor labour market prospects in the present-day French economy.

4. Territorial approaches

Given the wide-ranging nature of social exclusion, cross-sectoral and interdisciplinary approaches appear to be important. One route is the RMI. Another is to use the geographical zone as the basis for action against exclusion, trying to build up coherent strategies at the level of the locality or the community. The idea is that particular urban slum areas, or deprived regions, require broad-based action on economic, social and infrastructural fronts. This is, of course, a very solidaristic notion.

Yépez [1994] reviews a number of experiences of policy against exclusion which are based upon deprived areas and zones. She argues that such policies are more readily cross-sectoral, make it easier to take account of infrastructural needs (e.g. educational facilities), and can more readily stimulate collective initiatives. The components of such initiatives include local labour market policies of they type discussed above, the provision of public infrastructure (schools, roads) and community services, the development of community activities, the development of incentives for enterprises, shops and agencies to start activities in the zone, improvements in housing and the like. What is important is the institutional base of such initiatives, involving partnership and cooperation between the central government and local administrations, local associations, trade unions, enterprises and various other non-government bodies. The local nature of the initiative makes it easier to build the networks of personal relationships between the actors which such coordination requires.

Yépez reports on an experience in Charleroi in Belgium. The main source of exclusion was the decline in the heavy industries on which local economic activity was based. Some 60 local associations developed a range of projects for housing, occupational reinsertion, cultural development, and other domains with national State funding support. These programmes appear to have some impact, but in the job market the effects were estimated at 100 to 120 jobs per year, while local unemployment stood at 62,000. It also has to be pointed out that, if local areas compete with each other to attract enterprises, the net job creation in the economy as a whole is overestimated by local estimates.

5. The legislative route

Whatever the paradigm, the legislative route is valid. Even in the specialization paradigm, equal opportunities legislation controls any tendency for discrimination to emerge. Indeed, in the specialization paradigm, legislation to control the excesses of individual behaviour (when they threaten the rights of others) is the only accepted form of intervention. However, in practice, legislation alone is rarely enough; social legislation is difficult to implement and enforce, and affirmative action in favour of vulnerable groups is invariably needed to counter the effects of past discrimination. The French Commission on Social Cohesion noted the limits to the possibility of action through legislation alone, and argued strongly in favour of forms of partnership.

But the reference point provided by legislation offers essential support for more direct forms of action. This is as true for legislation aimed at protecting workers, of the type discussed below in relation to ILO action, as it is of more general legislation designed to prevent racial or gender discrimination. The need for such legislation is generally accepted, and has not emerged as a result of a growing perception of economic exclusion. But the design of legislation to provide social rights and, above all, the strategy for giving effect to such legislation, fits logically into more general strategies against exclusion.

II. Policy experiences in Europe: The actors

Policy analysis is not merely a question of the State intervening in the public interest, but involves a wide range of social actors.

1. Trade unions

Trade unions are widely concerned about exclusion. Much exclusion is in direct contradiction with the rights of workers, and the fight against unemployment is, of course, central to trade union action. There is therefore little need to convince trade unionists of the importance of the question. The problem, however, is that the excluded are often excluded from the labour market and from effective representation in the trade union movement. It is often argued that for this reason trade unions cannot fully defend the rights of the excluded. They tend to focus on the needs of their members, who on the whole are in work. This leads to a stress on defending the rights and preventing the exclusion of those in work, rather than on finding new routes into the labour market for those who are excluded.

This being said, in Europe a very wide range of actions against exclusion has been undertaken by unions, on their own or in co-operation with others. The *Confédération française démocratique du travail* (CFDT) in France, for instance, has been active in local level policies of the type discussed under the territorial heading above, both within and beyond the labour market. Yépez [1994] describes several actions of this type. The European Trade Union Confederation has reported diverse trade union actions in the countries of the European Community, involving demands for minority rights and campaigns against racism, development of capabilities (training gets high priority), institutional development, development of "insertion enterprises" which help the excluded back into the labour force, and participation in local development. They also aim at a wide range of target groups, including women workers, youth, and a variety of specific vulnerable groups ranging from seasonal workers to drug abusers. Trade union action often falls within a monopoly paradigm, but there is a strong current aiming at solidarity with the State and other social actors, and corporatist mechanisms involving trade union participation are widespread.

The advantage of trade unions would appear to be that they are solidly implanted at the local level but, through their federations, they also have a powerful influence at the national level although this is, of course, contested in countries where the specialization model dominates such as the United States and the United Kingdom. Their main disadvantage would appear to lie in situations where the interests of those in regular work are at variance with those of the excluded.

2. *Enterprises*

The employment and income aspects of social integration necessarily involve enterprises. In discussing the role of enterprises in exclusion policy, the French Commission on Social Cohesion and the Prevention of Exclusion highlighted two views: one in which firms will necessarily try to "export" the social costs of their activities — virtuous behaviour by firms then requires external compulsion; and a second (supported by a majority of the Commission) in which firms can be mobilized because participation in policies against exclusion is in their own self-interest, provided the appropriate institutional framework can be provided. We can recognize "monopoly" in the first of these and "solidarity" in the second. In fact, casual observation strongly suggests that both types of behaviour are very widespread, and that this depends on a range of factors: the intensity of competition, the moral values of the owners or managers of the firm, the nature of the labour force, the degree of local integration, no doubt the type of production process as well since some forms of production require workplace consensus and concertation whereas others appear to function efficiently with intense labour coercion.

Although some enterprises have been specifically created to provide a mechanism for labour market access for the excluded, the more typical and more important issue concerns how normal enterprises behave, faced with choices in terms of who to employ, and what options to provide them at the workplace. Within a solidarity model, it seems normal that enterprises should participate in a partnership between different actors, and should have a direct and active role in social policy. In 1992, in France a manifesto was prepared, entitled "enterprises against exclusion". This manifesto, initially signed by some 30 employers from large French firms,[2] identified a number of actions that enterprises could undertake: avoid unstable and precarious employment; take social criteria into account in recruitment (bias recruitment towards groups at risk of exclusion); if necessary undertake complementary training; ensure that unskilled workers can participate fully in the life of the enterprise; contribute to the social insertion of employees; contribute to community development activities in the areas where the firm is implanted. The European Commission has documented many cases where firms have successfully undertaken actions of this sort.

There are also many actions which the State and other actors can undertake to promote such attitudes among employers. A wide range of incentives in tax and social security payments can be devised; rules for collective bargaining may be relevant; human resource development activities may be particularly important, because of the direct interest of firms in the skills of their workforce. Agreed standards, along the lines of those governing conditions of work, may also be applied to actions and orientations aimed at social integration.

A particularly difficult area involves small and medium enterprises. Many such enterprises operate on the basis of local or family solidarity, but building their actions into wider coalitions seems difficult. At the other extreme, international firms with mobile capital may have little interest in local development, and merely wish to exploit local resources, including human resources. And in countries where there is less of a tradition of the

[2] Apparently other firms joined this movement subsequently. No details are available at the time of writing.

socially conscious enterprise, such as the United Kingdom, a considerable educational effort may be required. But the situation does not seem hopeless.

3. Associations, interest groups and other non-governmental organizations

Beyond the ILO's traditional partners there is a wide range of associations and organizations active in the fight against poverty and exclusion. These include broad-based groups such as *ATD Quart Monde*, Emmaüs International or the European Anti-poverty Network; focused groups such as Shelter acting against homelessness; bodies whose existence has another purpose but which undertake important social activities — particularly religious and political groups; and many local associations and community groups. Often such groups are much more effective actors at the local level than are official national organizations or State bodies, because they are built up from the local community, which is better represented and participates directly in the actions concerned. This is, for instance, the logic behind the action of *ATD Quart Monde*. One finds similar notions behind popular economic organizations in Chile [Quiñones Escobar, 1993] and elsewhere. Such groups are also prominent in debates and in the raising of public consciousness. On the other hand, they rarely have the resources needed for a major impact at the national level, and their action can rarely be carried out directly contrary to major economic interests, nor is it easy for them to construct sustainable institutional structures to maintain any social gains after a particular action is completed.

Despite their weaknesses, it seems to be vital for groups of this sort to be at the core of action against exclusion, for it is through this type of structure that the excluded can most effectively organize and present their demands. After all, virtually by definition, the excluded do not participate effectively in the mainstream organizations of society.

4. The State

Despite the pressure to roll back the frontiers of the State, it is obvious that the State has to play a major role in actions against exclusion. The various policy options outlined above often involve other social actors as well, but few are likely to go very far without the commitment and participation of the State.

A first point, however, is to assess the extent to which the State is responsible for exclusion, notably in its own employment policies. A recent tendency in many industrialized countries has been for the State to collaborate in the creation of precarious employment conditions in privatized services linked to State activity (cleaning is the classic example). More fundamentally, State actions may tend to create sheltered groups among the population, contributing to the dualization of society. Unless the State has the capability to regulate the society as a whole, it becomes the instrument of a part of society which is able to ensure that the rules are enforced in their interest, but possibly against the interest of others.

Governments are heavy, fragmented and bureaucratic. The French Commission on Social Cohesion devotes a great deal of attention to the restructuring of the State with a view to making it a more effective actor against exclusion. In particular, effective action against exclusion requires coordinated cross-sectoral interventions. In most countries, this is difficult to achieve because of the territorial claims of different ministries. Often training, social security, macro-economic policy, education, labour market interventions and urban infrastructure, all important elements in the design of policy against exclusion, will be spread across four or five ministries. And the financial decisions are taken elsewhere. So the institutional structure of the State has to be reconsidered, innovations are required in the way in which domains of activity are defined and in the ways in which partnerships are created between different State agencies. This also applies to the division of labour within the State between centre and local activities, and to the rules governing contractual relationships between the State and other actors at the local level. The vision which the Commission proposes is one in which the State is active in implementing policy but also acts as the guarantor of social cohesion, the referee of the game in which other actors also participate.

5. *The institutions for dialogue and action*

Implicit in much of the foregoing is the idea that coalitions of social actors are likely to be much more effective than individual interests operating alone. This is clearly a corporatist vision, based on the idea that the interests of different social groups are different and potentially in conflict, but that accommodation can be reached. But, even in the specialization model, one important means of overcoming exclusion clearly lies in the institutional mechanisms by which societies control the adverse side-effects of the pursuit of self-interest. Regardless of the paradigm of social integration, the institutional structures within which actors operate are central to the effective implementation of policy against exclusion.

The European Commission's Poverty 3 Programme, involving pilot actions at local level in different countries of the European Community, is an example of an attempt to systematically build up programmes involving the cooperation of several actors, bringing in partners from both public and private sectors [EC, 1991]. This sort of approach is easiest in a "territorial" framework, where enterprises, unions, State bodies and local associations and solidarity associations can work on different aspects of exclusion in a coordinated framework, e.g. in deprived urban zones. But the European Commission's programme also illustrates the political difficulties of working with local actors, for the follow-up programme (Poverty 4) now appears to be seriously threatened by a refusal to make the necessary financial allocations.

This point apart, often the institutions, and especially the rules governing State action, are inconsistent with partnerships in which the excluded themselves can participate effectively. New rules may be needed, and this in turn may involve the creation of new and autonomous entities within the public sector. In this the notion of a social contract seems useful — an institutional mechanism which spells out the terms of intervention of different actors, and which can make clear the rights, obligations and benefits of each. Making commitment public and mutually interdependent seems likely to reinforce action.

It is not only at the local level that institutional innovation is likely to be useful. In many countries, institutions for dialogue between different actors are sadly lacking at national level, too. If institutions are built at several levels, they can reinforce each other.

III. Policy against exclusion in low-income settings: The relevance of the European experience

This brief review of policy against exclusion in industrialized countries suggests that success has been uneven, to say the least. Many interesting routes have been explored, but a range of institutional obstacles remain to be overcome, and it seems to be difficult to move from experimental policy to full-scale intervention without diluting the impact. Nevertheless, a great deal of experience has been acquired. Is this relevant and helpful in low-income settings? The answer depends on whether the patterns of exclusion in developing countries are similar to those in industrialized countries, for it is this which sets the policy agenda.

What is the significance of low income as such? It is mainly that the issues of exclusion and poverty are more closely intertwined, since low incomes imply that the absolute subsistence threshold is that much closer. As a result, exclusion is more likely to result in poverty. There is clearly a difference in kind between situations where a majority of the population are excluded from adequate livelihood, as in much of Africa, and industrialized country situations where exclusion concerns perhaps 10 or 20 per cent of the population. And the nature of exclusion, as country studies show, also varies greatly from one low-income country to another.

Nevertheless, most of the policy issues discussed above are also important in low-income settings. Unemployment, for instance, and especially unemployment leading to social exclusion, is of growing importance in many cities of Latin America, Africa, and West and South Asia. Labour market measures aimed at the integration of the unemployed are a constant concern of policy-makers. The problem is that, while labour market intervention in industrialized countries is generally small in scale in relation to the problem, this discrepancy is still greater in most low-income situations. Policies aimed at organization of the unemployed and labour market insertion are also highly relevant, but they require formal mechanisms and institutions which are often lacking in low-income settings, making them difficult to implement. On the other hand, capability building is crucial at any level of income or industrial development. As far as social security and social assistance is concerned, few low-income countries have universal income support mechanisms, although policies such as the RMI might be relevant in some higher-income countries in Latin America and East Asia, where meaningful "integration" contracts might be designed. The territorial approach is highly relevant, and indeed already forms the basis for much State action against poverty. Finally, the legislative route is also valid regardless of income level, although the resources for effective inspection and enforcement may be lacking in many low-income situations.

So some of the items on the industrialized country policy agenda are relevant, but not all. What is more, there are many additional policy issues which come up in thinking about social exclusion in developing countries, including:

(a) land reform, and access to credit and productive assets in general;

(b) adult literacy programmes;

(c) legislation and/or action against child labour;

(d) provision of basic social infrastructure (drinking water, sanitation, primary schooling, basic health care);

(e) the social integration of the informal sector;

(f) exclusion from modern consumption goods;

(g) exclusion from international markets.

These differences in policy priorities are reinforced by differences in the roles and importance of the various actors concerned: States which are often highly visible in the economy but which lack an adequate resource base or sufficient autonomy to implement redistributive policy or enforce legislation; trade union movements which can organize only relatively small groups of workers; relatively weak intermediary institutions.

So the industrialized country experience has to be used with care. Nevertheless, it is important not to become locked into an opposition between industrialized and developing countries. Low-income settings are themselves highly diverse. In much of South America, broad-based industrial systems and powerful formal institutions comparable with those in Europe coexist with extensive poverty. In Africa, rural institutions which are entirely different in nature dominate. There will be situations in which the design of policy against exclusion can profit extensively from European experiences, and others where this approach would be quite inappropriate. And underlying the issue of exclusion at the national level are international exclusions which provide a linkage between experiences and policies in different parts of the world. In the next section we offer a framework which tries to take this into account.

IV. A framework for developing policy against exclusion

In order to discuss policy it is convenient to distinguish four levels at which intervention against exclusion may occur: the global or international; the national; the local or regional; and the social group. At each of these levels, a variety of types of exclusion can be identified. We give priority to two broad categories: exclusion from livelihood, and exclusion from basic rights. It is important to differentiate, within these categories, between what might be regarded as transient or conjunctural, and structural and inter-generational aspects of exclusion or, more generally, the pattern of exclusion over time, itself linked to the notion of exclusion as a process. Finally, a wide range of agents need to be considered at each level, agents who act as excluders and need to be controlled, or who may contribute to a strategy to overcome exclusion and need to be mobilized. Each of the spaces defined by positions within this framework gives rise to specific policy issues, and particular possibilities or demands for intervention.

1. The international and global level

The increasing internationalization of economic and social relationships is responsible for both inclusions and exclusions. Important exclusions include those from international commodity markets on acceptable terms; from high-wage labour markets; from the benefits of transnational company operations; from security; from global resources. These affect entire nations and so contribute in important ways to global inequality. But they also affect the structure of exclusion within nations, as when the demands of the international trading system lead investment, employment and wealth to be concentrated in small parts of the economy, or when elites participate in an international consumer society from which the bulk of the population is excluded. Capital may also be difficult to attract to countries where social policy objectives are imposed, forcing a trade-off between exclusion within countries, and exclusion between them. Both structural and conjunctural effects are present — conjunctural in so far as burdens of economic adjustment are shifted onto particular countries, and within those countries onto particular groups. Structural effects include inter-generational transmission of exclusion linked to the unsustainability of global consumption style and resource use.

The agents of exclusion and inclusion at this level include intergovernmental organizations; transnational companies; the media; international coalitions (of unions, of NGOs, of academics); powerful States. At the international level, agreements on universal rights and global social policy objectives exist, but the institutions for enforcement are weak and effective mechanisms to provide accountability are rare. Redistributive goals are notably weak in the use of international resources. There are fundamental difficulties in promoting effective policies at this level, and this is a major challenge for the international community.

Examples of policy issues and interventions:

(a) International migration. Countries may export exclusion by closing off opportunities for migration, or migration on unfavourable terms may lead to exclusion in the countries of destination. Restrictions on labour mobility contrast sharply with the free flow of capital. Large-scale forced migration movements lead to particular vulnerabilities. Exclusion of labour from high-income labour markets needs to be combatted by insisting on the moral responsibility of high-income states and consumers to help raise the livelihoods and extend the rights of the workers concerned. Simultaneously, transnational coalitions of unions and NGOs should press for the improvement of

wages and conditions in less developed countries.

(b) Increasing international competitiveness discourages employers from internalizing social costs. There is a need for international codes in order to control the tendency for this to lead to exclusions of workers from social protection, or of rural populations from land. Many ILO standards are relevant here.

(c) Globalization generates both opportunity and exclusion. Global agreements and charters, e.g. guaranteeing livelihood and basic rights, need to be linked to appropriate international policies in the areas of official development assistance, trade and finance to promote equality of access to global markets. Such agreements need a resource base and enforcement mechanisms. They need the active participation not only of States but also of other powerful actors.

2. *The national level*

The exclusions at this level include exclusion from the labour market; from land; from decent wages and safe jobs; from public services (health, education, public safety, justice); from social protection; and from basic rights (such as equality before the law, freedom of association, freedom from discrimination, right to livelihood). The dominant problem is one of the structural exclusion of many from livelihood, because their rights are not recognized or their economic and social assets are insufficient. In addition, individuals become trapped in downward spirals, moving from vulnerability to dependency to disaffiliation or marginalization. Intergenerational transmission occurs through insufficient education, poor health or child labour. National development patterns create exclusions either by creating new inequalities, or by actively excluding groups from livelihood in order to integrate them in the dominant mode of development.

There are many national agents of both exclusion and inclusion, some of which were discussed above in the review of industrialized country experiences. They include:

(a) different components of the State: central and local government, public enterprises, parliaments, the courts and the judiciary;

(b) political organizations;

(c) the military;

(d) private enterprises, industrial groups and associations of enterprises or employers;

(e) trade unions and other associations of workers;

(f) community or ethnic associations;

(g) action groups, rights movements;

(h) philanthropic groups;

(i) religious bodies;

(j) the media;

(k) "think tanks'";

(l) educational bodies.

The State is important both as excluder and includer; excluder because it operates in the interest of dominant groups, because it may promote an economic policy which fails to integrate particular groups, or integrates them against their will, or distributes public goods and services unequally; includer through regulation of markets and employment practices, as guarantor of civil, political and social rights, as the primary agent of redistribution. The problem is one of identifying the points of pressure which can influence the behaviour of the State in the direction of inclusion. In many circumstances, the major policy issue is the promotion of intermediary institutions which may control the State and render it accountable. These may include formal structures such as the judiciary and parliaments, but also many of the non-government organizations listed above. The roles of these different groups and their interaction with the State are at the heart of the different paradigms of social integration. Each of these different agents may either itself exclude — one ethnic or religious group may exclude another, enterprises may discriminate or may take over resources — or may act against exclusion, either directly representing the interests of the excluded, or in alliance with the State as more general agents in favour of social integration. The basic problem is one of empowerment for, by definition, the excluded have little control over resources.

Trade unions constitute a particularly important agent of inclusion or exclusion. It is widely argued that in low income settings, they tend to represent a relatively small, protected elite among workers. While this is easy to contest, it is undeniable that it is very difficult for trade unions effectively to represent excluded groups in many developing countries, because the marginal self-employed, casual workers, rural labour and other insecure and unprotected labour categories are so numerous in relation to the more readily organizable formal sector workers. This renders the need for alliances between different groups all the more pressing. By the same token, many more enterprises are small, and there is great diversity in conditions of employment. Enterprises nevertheless offer, as in industrialized countries, considerable possibilities for contributions to social policy – again, probably in alliance with other groups.

Examples of policy issues and interventions:

(a) Perhaps the most fundamental issue is the control of market mechanisms: in the Peruvian study (Ch. 12), it is argued that the State needs not only to regulate, but also to expand markets if it is to overcome market exclusions. Here, the issue is one of promoting intermediary institutions such as collective bargaining institutions or lobbies on behalf of particular excluded groups, as well as some of the active labour market policies reviewed above for industrialized countries. Key questions include the extent to which enterprises will accept to internalize social policy, and the degree to which unions representing active labour can be mobilized in favour of excluded labour.

(b) The development of coalitions between different actors with a common interest in inclusion may require institutions, legal structures and financial support. The basic question is one of the institutional framework for NGO access to resources and decision-making bodies. This applies both to demands for livelihood and to the defence of human rights, often against the State.

(c) The balance between active (participatory, bringing people in) and passive policies (safety nets, social insurance) needs reflection. The active route is intrinsically more desirable, but is unlikely to be universal.

(d) Dualistic or unbalanced growth paths are likely to cause exclusion, because they do not create enough opportunities for decent livelihood, and because inequality is endemic — growth depends on advanced technology which creates few jobs, or on growing demand for advanced consumer products which only the relatively rich can afford. Designing the institutions for inclusion in growth is an essential underpinning of any strategy against exclusion.

(e) The importance of the design of new institutions for social policy is thrown into sharpest relief when the old institutions collapse, as was the case in Siberia (Ch. 7). There the abdication of the State led to the growth of local systems of patronage aimed mainly at the personal enrichment of those who control them, rather than at regulating

general access to public resources. Aspects of social insurance formerly organized by trade unions also deteriorated sharply because of the inability of the institutions in place to deal with new situations.

3. The regional and local level

The problems and types of exclusions which appear at the regional and local level are basically an extension of those at the national level to encompass spatial exclusion. This may take the form of exclusion from public goods and services, but also exclusion from economic and social opportunities. Spatially unbalanced development policies may lead to increasing deprivation of some areas. Labour market exclusions may be regionally concentrated, as industrial decline or resource depletion occurs. It is at this level that struggles over common property resources are most likely to occur.

The shift of focus from the national to the regional or local level may not substantially change the nature of the problem, but it offers a different perspective on solutions. The relative importance of the actors is not the same, for those which are closer to the grassroots — community groups, action groups, local enterprises, decentralized administrations — can play a more effective role. Thus the advantages of the "territorial" approach discussed above are reproduced here, offering the possibility of partnership between local actors with common interests. There is clearly scope for the development of local housing, employment, infrastructural and public service delivery and other initiatives within such a decentralized framework. The danger of this approach is that problems of exclusion will then be given less priority in national policy, leaving local policies as a palliative within in an exclusionary overall model of development. There is also the considerable risk that local actors will, as in the Siberian case noted above, capture the resources concerned in their own interests. Institutions for accountability are required here, too.

Examples of policy issues and interventions:

The key policy issue which is specific to this level is the formation of alliances and coalitions between different groups, including State agencies, in order to construct non-marginal interventions at the territorial level, or in order to establish a position of strength vis-à-vis other local actors. But many of the broad actions identified at the national level above, or at the group level (below), have to be put into effect at the regional or local level.

4. Groups vulnerable to exclusion

Most of the exclusions listed under the "national" heading above can also be viewed in terms of which social groups are excluded. Different situations can be distinguished: the systematic exclusion from livelihood or rights of all those with a particular characteristic or origin; a tendency for those with particular characteristics to be disadvantaged; and a process of exclusion in which the situation of exclusion defines the group — the unemployed; child workers — which then becomes a source of progressive marginalization. The nature of the exclusions vary from one group to another — an ethnic group may be excluded from public sector employment, but not from other labour market positions; another group may have access to economic opportunities, but be refused the right to cultural identity; refugees may be systematically excluded from society; women may be excluded from particular occupations or from training.

Thinking about exclusion in terms of the groups which are suffering is attractive from the point of view of policy because it makes it possible to be very direct and specific, identifying interventions which should reach particular groups and measuring their impact. It is possible to take either an active or a passive view — active, when social groups can become agents of their own inclusion, or passive, as a target group for policy. The diversity of these groups makes it difficult to talk of the issue in general. Some groups — religious or ethnic, for example — are clearly much easier to organize than are child labourers or the handicapped. In some cases the mobilization of excluded groups is aimed at influencing State actions, while in other cases the aim is to increase bargaining power vis-à-vis the agents of exclusion within society and economy, for instance by increasing the value of the group's social assets or by imposing costs on excluders. But the agents of exclusion are diverse, and not always easy to identify, as when the structuring of traditional society excludes women from economic opportunities. The danger of this approach is that it becomes a palliative. If the real problem is the segmentation of market opportunities, or the capturing of the benefits of development by small elite groups, then focusing on the groups which are excluded and attempting to improve their lot will do little to tackle the underlying mechanisms of exclusion.

Examples of policy issues and interventions:

(a) Affirmative action programmes are widespread and often effective instruments against exclusion. The most powerful example is intervention in favour of the Malays in Malaysia, covering reservations and quotas in education, labour markets, government posts

and corporate capital, but there are interesting examples from India (action in favour of Scheduled Castes; see Ch. 15), the former Peoples' Democratic Republic of Yemen (action in favour of the *akhdam*, see Ch. 10) and elsewhere. Such programmes require a powerful long-term commitment on the part of the State, and the included are likely to react if they see their interests seriously threatened. The success of the Malaysian policies was associated with the rise to political power of the excluded Malay groups (so the policy was controlled by those in whose interests it was effected). In such policies there are always losers, of course: usually relatively powerless groups (in the Malaysian case notably the Indian community).[3] Affirmative action may therefore also exclude. In addition, there is evidence that it tends to promote inequality within the groups in whose interests it is implemented.

(b) Policies to overcome the exclusion of women have probably received more attention than policies for any other group. This issue was identified as a priority in most of the case studies, especially Tunisia (see Ch. 9). Affirmative action programmes and many specific actions are widespread, though if they do not form part of a broader attack on exclusion this may limit their effectiveness.

(c) If groups which are otherwise excluded from public services are well organized, they may provide such services within the group. An interesting example is mutual credit and insurance funds, which may substitute for State-sponsored security and insurance schemes. Funds of this sort are, for instance, organized by many ethnic associations in Cameroon (see Ch. 14). This raises several issues. Do such services in fact provide adequate support to all; and can all groups organize in such a way, or only the better-off among them?

(d) An alternative to the mutual credit approach would be to build social security and social insurance in such a way as to compensate for, rather than replicate, existing patterns of exclusion. The Indian study (Ch. 15) shows how, in the past, social security policy has been "blind" to the needs of the excluded and has been concentrated on the included. By organizing insurance and assistance around the needs of different excluded groups, combining promotional and protective measures, a very considerable extension of the safety net should be

[3] For a review of the literature on the Malaysian case, see Lim Teck Ghee [forthcoming].

possible. In this, the excluded groups provide an identifiable target which can render policy design much more efficient.

(e) An important group for action against exclusion concerns child labour, because of the lifetime exclusions to which it leads. This is a case where the specific nature of exclusion demands particular policy interventions, involving labour market regulation, education, skill development and income support, and policies aimed at more effective labour market integration.

(f) The possibilities for alliance between particular excluded groups and other social actors merit reflection. Important actors include the media, political parties, particular factions within the State, workers' organizations. New institutional links are required to give voice to the excluded. In this the role of the media is particularly worth investigating.

(g) The risk should be noted that policies aimed at inclusion can become instruments of exclusion if forced upon groups that prefer to maintain a separate cultural or economic identity.

All of this offers a very wide policy agenda, and one which too easily can become fragmented, but the definition of coherent, integrated policy packages is only possible in specific contexts. However, it is worth making two points here about the design of such integrated approaches.

First, one can identify two basic strategic alternatives in the fight against exclusion, with different implications for social integration. One could be classified as "reactive" in the sense that it basically attempts to limit the adverse economic and social side-effects of economic policy. This would include, for example, interventions designed to reduce the socially negative repercussions of a particular economic growth path, or safety nets or programmes of social support for those excluded from economic benefits. The second alternative might be characterized as "proactive", in that the explicit objective is the promotion of social cohesion and the wide sharing of the benefits of development, and in which social policy is directly integrated into the design and implementation of economic strategy. The former approach attempts to limit the adverse effects of exclusion, whereas the latter attempts to prevent it from occurring. The former would tend to concentrate on the design of external interventions, the latter would try to effectively integrate the excluded not only as objects of policy, but also as actors defining the contours of their own integration.

Second, if we return to the different paradigms of exclusion discussed previously, they give rise to different policy visions. Solidarity is very much concerned with building social ties with a unitary society; specialization with legislating limits to individual behaviour; monopoly with building countervailing power; organicism with the institutions for integration and consensus-building. Designing policies against social exclusion is not just a question of reversing exclusion; it is at the same time defining the terms of inclusion.

V. Social exclusion in the work of the ILO

What particular value does the notion of social exclusion have in the ILO?

The general philosophy of the ILO has elements of each of the different paradigms of social exclusion, but the solidarity model and the more voluntaristic among the organic models are most heavily represented. The idea that there are common goals for the social partners, which can be promoted through dialogue and agreement on general principles of behaviour, is one which, even if it does not go quite as far as a solidarity vision of society, nevertheless involves a belief in a core set of social values and rights which should be extended to all. It is also broadly consistent with the "Christian democratic" model of pluralism, based on consensus-building among autonomous groups. Tripartism, then, involves an organic or solidarity perspective much more than specialization or monopoly. But the ILO's model is not monolithic and notions of both specialization and monopoly are widespread in ILO analysis. In one sense, solidaristic ideals are reflected in many labour standards, but the standards are designed to overcome the evils arising out of specialization (e.g. discrimination) or monopoly (e.g. forced labour). What is clear is that the general philosophy of the Organization is one of inclusion: that there is a general right to the sharing of benefits, to protection, to participation. In this sense, much of the work of the Organization is in practice aimed at preventing or overcoming exclusion, although this language is not generally used.

A first aspect of exclusion and inclusion which directly concerns the ILO involves the constituents of the Organization: employers, governments and workers. Each have their own pattern of inclusion and exclusion, which affects the work of the ILO. The extent to which governments represent the population at large varies greatly. Democracies are as subject to this comment as dictatorships, for minority groups are often as effectively excluded from political participation in democracies as they are in dictatorships. Trade unions can represent the relatively more stable, better protected workers more easily than they can casual and precarious workers or the marginal self-employed. The representation of employers suffers from somewhat different problems, but small-scale and informal enterprises tend again to be excluded from effective representation. In practice, action against exclusion, for instance in France, tends to involve coalitions between diverse actors, some of them active in the ILO, some not: local authorities, poverty action groups, religious groups, solidarity organizations, sometimes — but not always — acting in tandem with trade unions, enterprises and central government. Similar phenomena are often found in low-income countries too, where associations of small-scale producers, women's action groups, political organizations of rural labour, church-based solidarity groups and other national or international non-governmental organizations play an important role in action against poverty — a role which in practice is often aimed at social inclusion as an element in the fight against poverty. The ILO's success in participating in and promoting alliances with such groups has been patchy, precisely because they go beyond its traditional constituency. But this would appear to be an important future route for the Organization, and a focus on exclusion may help to promote it.

There are two rather distinct streams in the work of the ILO: one based on rights, which tends to find its expression in international labour standards; and one based on welfare, notably found in work on the promotion of employment or the reduction of poverty. In both cases, notions of exclusion can be helpful in identifying problems and target groups. There are legal instruments which are directly aimed at particular population groups: ethnic minorities, or the handicapped, for example. In addition, from a perspective which is more sociological than legal, it is useful to analyse legal instruments in terms of their effective coverage — who is included and who is excluded, both in theory and in practice. One of the basic problems of labour legislation in low-income settings is precisely the difficulty of applying it to the population as a whole. This is not only a problem of evasion by employers or slack implementation by governments, but also inability or unwillingness by workers to press for conditions which put their jobs at risk, or inconsistency between grand principles and the ways in which people actually run their lives.

The welfare and developmental side of the work of the Organization, notably with respect to work on poverty and employment, has in practice been to a large extent concerned with exclusion from livelihood and, to a lesser extent, social protection. Work on unemployment and underemployment is a case in point, and the current focus on active labour market policy, for instance, stresses heavily mechanisms for labour market access, e.g. through training. However, the exclusion from livelihood and participation in society which arises from long-term unemployment, or from a life of peripheral, casual employment interspersed with days or months of joblessness, has perhaps received less attention than it merits. With respect to poverty, various policy approaches have been adopted, and were reviewed in a symposium in 1993.[4] Among the policy concerns which can be visualized in terms of exclusion, important ones include access to land and other assets, access to skills, and access to social goods and transfers. Labour market policy against poverty is also most effective when directed towards the groups which are vulnerable to exclusion either from the labour market as a whole or from protection or decent working conditions when in the labour market.

The critique of ILO action against poverty developed in that symposium was that it lacked an integrated approach: that there were many elements which were successful in their own terms and domains, but which were not effectively linked together to form a coherent overall strategy. The design of such a strategy, however, requires a linking together of diverse ILO programmes which have traditionally operated in isolation. An example in the case of poverty is the ILO's work on social security, which has a great deal to say on the design and functioning of social security systems to provide pensions and health care, but on the whole has not integrated this with other approaches to poverty developed in other parts of the ILO, for instance through employment promotion. One problem is that poverty as such is not an economic category or an element in the analysis of economic systems — it is the result of diverse processes. An integrated approach must therefore encompass a range of different and perhaps initially unrelated elements. In this respect, an approach which starts from an understanding of exclusion may have some advantages. Not all of the processes underlying poverty involve social and economic exclusion, and so work on exclusion and work on poverty are not congruent. But there is a substantial intersection between the two domains, and it may be easier to develop an integrated approach in the case of exclusion than in the case of poverty. Different forms of exclusion are inter-related, and a focus on the mechanisms of exclusion makes it easier to identify the most useful forms of intervention, while at the same time permitting the identification of target groups for policy in terms of the groups which are most vulnerable to exclusion.

In the work of the ILO, the mechanisms of exclusion can be more clearly seen in most of the different domains of the Organization than can

---

[4] They are discussed in more detail in the ILO background paper for that symposium published in Rodgers [1995].

the causes of poverty. Among the areas of ILO work where exclusion is a major issue, we can cite:

(a) training and education (lack of access thereto);

(b) labour markets (precarious employment contracts, minimum wages;

(c) employment creation (unemployment, etc.);

(d) the informal sector (access to credit, labour protection);

(e) organization and representation (trade unions; collective bargaining);

(f) labour legislation (national and international);

(g) conditions of work (exclusion from adequate);

(h) child labour;

(i) discrimination in employment (race, gender);

(j) social security systems (coverage);

(k) disabled and handicapped workers.

For example, the issue of education and training can be expressed in terms of the factors determining exclusion from human development: discrimination against women or other groups, lack of resources, lack of facilities, lack of perceived benefits from training, etc. Labour legislation can be interpreted in terms of the extent to which it actually reaches and protects the populations concerned, so looking at the issue from the point of view of exclusion leads one to focus on the factors which render legal protection ineffective for some members of society. Social security can likewise be interpreted in terms of coverage — which groups fall outside effective provision for pensions, health care and other major aspects of social insurance and assistance. Action against child labour needs to try to reconcile the need for livelihood with the cost of exclusion (from personal development, from a decent career). Organization and representation are clearly central here: virtually by definition, the excluded are difficult to organize by traditional means — hence the various non-formal approaches to mobilization and participation noted above. In an ILO context, the problem is to properly provide for the effective representation in the ILO of groups who lie outside the economic mainstream. Much of the ILO's work still reflects a vision of the world which is, or should be, formal and regulated. As a result, the informal and unregulated tends to be under-emphasized.

This does not exhaust the dimensions of social exclusion, of course.

Other aspects, less directly linked to ILO work, include those involving housing and urban infrastructure, various public services, political representation, participation in community and cultural life, nationality and citizenship.

The important point is that there is correlation between exclusion in one dimension and exclusion in another. Sometimes, exclusion is sufficiently systematic that one can speak of marginalization. There are individuals and sometimes groups (often identified in ethnic terms, or based on particular handicaps), whose exclusion cuts across labour markets, housing, public services, social security and representation. Even in countries with formally universalistic social safety nets, such situations are present. But there is a more general and perhaps more pernicious linkage between different dimensions of exclusion, which does not necessarily totally marginalize, but which leads to deprivation and to poverty. Women may be excluded from labour markets and from effective representation, and subject to severe discrimination, without being necessarily excluded from livelihood (many are, but the point is that exclusion is important even when it does not mean poverty). Exclusion from training, from regular jobs, from effective coverage of labour legislation and social security are likely to coincide if they are due to discrimination or to poor social entitlements and assets. But those in such situations are not necessarily marginalized, indeed in some circumstances the majority of workers may be subject to such deprivations. These patterns become reflected in the structure of labour markets, which segment in such a way that different parts of the labour market offer quite different patterns of livelihood, inclusion and exclusion. Because these patterns and mechanisms cut across different technical fields within the ILO, they provide a challenge to the Organization, which has traditionally been rather compartmentalized, but also a means by which the different elements in a systematic attack on social exclusion could be developed. For, just as different aspects of exclusion reinforce each other in a negative sense, so also policies against exclusion may reinforce each other positively. This is recognized more overtly in some of the ILO's international standards, especially some of the more recent standards, than in specific programmes. For instance, Convention No. 169 on indigenous and tribal peoples, which in reality is largely concerned with the exclusion of these groups from representation and livelihood, explicitly recommends broad-based participation in decision-making, protection of land rights, equal employment opportunities, equal access to training and social security and other dimensions of social inclusion, and so recommends coordinated intervention across a range of ILO concerns. Table 1 (p. 282) provides a first, and rather incomplete, look at some other ILO standards in terms of exclusion; a more systematic analysis would probably be worthwhile. It might well lead to new ways of thinking about how standards can contribute to a linkage of different technical domains of the Organization in action against exclusion.

To effectively attain such objectives requires alliances between the ILO's traditional constituents who clearly have a key role to play, but one which does not extend to the totality of the problem, and other social actors. If we return to the alternative models of exclusion, each offers a different route. The solidarity and organic models suggest the promotion of dialogue and consensus-building around common values; the specialization model the design of legal and institutional frameworks to direct individuals away from exclusionary behaviour; and the monopoly model the identification of common interests among different excluded social groups, which may enhance the power of those concerned. Perhaps all three approaches may be required, or the balance of the three will depend on the prevailing political and cultural systems of the countries and groups concerned.

Bibliographical references

Commissariat général au Plan (CGP). 1993. *Cohésion sociale et prévention de l'exclusion.* Paris, La Documentation française.

Direction régionale du travail et de l'emploi (DRTE), Rhône-Alpes, et les délégations Rhône-Alpes du Mouvement ATD Quart Monde. 1993. *Contre l'exclusion, une qualification*, Report of activities for the year 1992. Lyon.

Foucauld, J.-B. de. 1992. "Une citoyenneté pour les chômeurs", in *Droit Social*, Nos. 7/8, July-August.

European Commission (EC). 1991. *Europe against poverty.* April. Brussels.

Lim Teck Ghee. Forthcoming. *Effectiveness of policies aimed at the social and economic integration of different ethnic groups in South-East Asia, with special reference to Malaysia*. Discussion paper Series No. 82. Geneva, IILS.

Quiñones Escobar L. 1993. "The organization and representation of the poor". IILS Symposium on Poverty, Geneva, ILO, November.

Rodgers, G. (ed.). 1995. *The poverty agenda and the ILO: Issues for research and action.* Geneva, IILS.

—. 1994. *Overcoming exclusion: Livelihood and rights in economic and social development.* Discussion Paper Series No. 72. Geneva, IILS.

Yépez, I. 1994. *Review of the French and Belgian literature on social exclusion: A Latin American perspective*. Discussion Papers Series No. 71. Geneva, IILS.

Table 1: Selected ILO Conventions and exclusion

Group-specific Conventions		
Convention No.	**Title**	**Target (excluded) group**
89	Night work of women employed in industry	Women workers
103	Maternity protection	Pregnant women workers
128	Invalidity, old-age and survivor's benefits	Invalids, retired, widows, children
159	Vocational rehabilitation and employment	Disabled
118	Equality of treatment of nat. and non-nat. in social security	Migrants
169	Indigenous and tribal peoples	Ethnic minorities
168	Employment promotion and protection against unemployment	Unemployed
138	Minimum age for admission to employment	Children

Universal Conventions		
Convention No.	**Title**	**Mechanisms of exclusion**
102	Minimum standards of social security (SS	Conditional access to and/or insufficient or deficient provision of SS
117	Basic aims and standards of social policy	Absence or prevalence of economic over social goals
122	Employment policy	Lack of access to jobs; inadequate policies for specific sectors (informal, rural...)
131	Minimum wage	Exploitation through below subsistence wages; deficient enforcement and adjustment procedures
142	Vocational guidance and vocational training	Inadequate skills; obstacles in the access to and/or inadequacy of courses
111	Discrimination in respect of employment	Gender, race and other biased selection procedures; unbalanced bargaining power or capabilities
154	Promotion of collective bargaining	Institutional obstacles to presentation of needs and demands
155	Occupational safety and health and the working environment	Undue risks in the workplace; lack of control and enforcement of regulations

17 Policies to combat social exclusion: A French-British comparison

Hilary Silver and Frank Wilkinson[1]

The multiple meanings of social exclusion give rise to different approaches to combat it. Therefore, it is not surprising to find national differences in insertion policies. This paper contrasts French and British insertion policies as exemplars of the solidarity and specialization paradigms of social exclusion.[2] It examines four types of national policy in particular: income support tied to social insertion; training programmes for unemployed adults and youth; insertion by economic means; and locality-based social integration policies.

Policies to combat social exclusion go beyond the traditional post-war social insurance and means-tested transfer programmes designed to address "poverty" and "inequality" through the passive receipt of assistance. In so far as eligibility for transfers is based on social categories or prior contributions, such policies themselves can be a source of exclusion. Since the mid-1970s, it is precisely those categories diverging from normative, standard career and family life cycles that have been growing: the long-term and intermittently unemployed, single-parent families, ethnic minorities, and the like. These populations are increasingly dependent on means-tested programmes once reserved for residual "deserving" categories of the poor, or are ineligible for assistance altogether. Such "excluded" groups are the target of new social policies introduced in France and Britain during the 1980s that require active participation in one's own insertion.

Exclusion is a multi-dimensional phenomenon and therefore, requires multi-pronged policies to combat it. The French and British governments

---

[1] This is an abbreviated, revised summary of a paper to be published by the International Institute for Labour Studies [Silver & Wilkinson, forthcoming]. The full references upon which the argument of the paper is based can be found there.

[2] For a discussion of these paradigms, see Silver, Ch. 3.

have sought to address the problem in comprehensive, global, and individualized terms, "tailoring" and "targeting" multiple types of interventions to address what are often cumulative disadvantages. For example, urban policies may simultaneously tackle economic, political, and social as well as spatial aspects of exclusion. Nevertheless, national political debates have emphasized some aspects of exclusion over others. Institutional persistence grounded in different national social policy traditions and political ideologies has produced a certain degree of continuity between earlier French and British social policies and even the most innovative insertion programmes. Pre-existing programmes and agencies create policy and institutional legacies, creating a strong tendency toward sectoral differentiation in tackling exclusion. Both countries still make institutional distinctions among income, employment, training, and urban policies, reflected in the conventional classification of programmes used here. None the less, all these programmes may target the very same people.

The multi-dimensional nature of exclusion has pressured different professions, agencies, and levels of government to cooperate in administering insertion policies. Thus, in the fight against exclusion, interministerial bodies and regional or local partnerships have proliferated in both France and Britain. Unfortunately, rather than enhancing cooperation and coordination, evaluations suggest that the existence of so many new and different agencies of this sort, varying in composition and function, has increased complexity, opacity, and duplication of effort. Indeed, some policies may work at cross-purposes. Successive reforms have tried to address these problems, but often at the price of confusion. Moreover, with so many actors in the field, it is difficult to isolate and evaluate the effects of any given policy. None the less, this paper reviews some of the early evaluations of the new insertion programmes. Aside from the problems of administration and coordination, research suggests that some policies are more effective than others. It also reveals important national differences in approach and effectiveness at combating social exclusion.

I. Exclusion in France and Britain

There is little doubt that social exclusion is increasing in both France and Britain. Conventional indicators adjusted for comparability document the trend. Income inequality and poverty rose in both countries. Standardized OECD unemployment rates show that at the end of the 1980s, the British unemployment rate was 6.9 per cent, but remained higher in France, at 8.9 per cent [OECD, 1991, p. 208]. Indeed, France is the only

OECD country to have experienced a continuous rise in unemployment from 1970 to 1993, with the brief exception of 1988-90. Who bears the brunt of unemployment also varies cross-nationally. For example, youth suffer disproportionately in France. British men have higher unemployment rates than women, but in France, where the growth in part-time work had been regulated and generous child-care provision exists, the reverse is true. In 1990, long-term unemployment of over a year constituted 36 per cent of British unemployment, and 38 per cent of French unemployment, down somewhat since the mid-1980s [OECD, 1993, p. 196]. Finally, labour force participation and the number of "discouraged workers" who drop out of the labour force entirely after very long bouts of unemployment have risen more in France than in Britain, highlighting France's greater employment problem.

Not only did the composition of excluded populations differ cross-nationally during the 1980s, but the French conceptualization of these problems and the policy approach taken to address them differed considerably from the British. In line with the Republican ideology of solidarity, problems like long-term unemployment and rising poverty were construed as manifestations of "social exclusion" or "a rupture of the social bond". Thus, even the names of new French policies reflected the goals of "insertion," "integration," "cohesion," and "solidarity". While policies to fight exclusion occupied centre stage in French social policy reforms, "there cannot in any real sense be said to have been a general debate concerned with "social exclusion" in the UK" [Room, 1992, pp. S33-S35]. Except in academic circles, British social policy discourse used the terminology of long-term "dependency," "new poverty," and the "underclass", problems to be combated with "self-reliance", "enterprise," "opportunity," "citizenship", "partnerships" and "community".

These policies are the subject of the following sections. Before they are discussed, however, one caveat is in order. It is somewhat misleading to compare social insertion policies without placing them in the context of French and British macro-economic strategies. This is because fiscal, monetary, trade, and labour market policies may counteract social initiatives. Economic policy may itself fuel social exclusion which insertion policies are then supposed to address.

Space limitations preclude a full comparison of economic policies. In general, both countries deregulated the labour market, weakened unions and promoted flexible, precarious employment, although less so in France than in Britain. While France raised its minimum wage, Britain abolished its own. There, monetary and political pressure to curtail public expenditure, privatize assets and services, and reduce the size of government had a strong influence on the funds available to combat social exclusion. Therefore, as one might expect from the predominantly liberal conception of exclusion in the UK, British policies increasingly targeted the most disadvantaged populations, relied much more heavily on the private sector, and used work incentives to promote social insertion.

II. Income support and insertion obligations

Throughout Europe, most of the expenses devoted to combating individual patterns of exclusion have in fact gone to income replacement; less money is spent on the prevention of exclusion or on insertion [Room, 1990]. In both Britain and France, as rising poverty, low wages, long-term unemployment, and precarious non-standard jobs increased the number of people whose social insurance benefits expired or who never qualified for them to begin with, many fell back on means-tested assistance. During the 1980s, both countries reformed these programmes and tied income support to the obligation to participate actively in social insertion.

However, the manner in which this was done and the interpretation of the required insertion activity differed sharply. In France, a new minimum income programme filled a gap for those excluded from existing "solidarity" allocations, eligibility for which is largely categorical. Existing transfer programmes were modified, but on the whole remained intact and were generous by British standards. Moreover, French insertion activities could take social as well as economic forms. In contrast, insertion in the UK referred largely to paid employment, mandated training, or active job-seeking, as in American "workfare" programmes. Not only were British social insurance programmes altered to shift people into less generous means-tested benefits, but the real value of those minimum benefits was decoupled from wages. Yet, two similarities between France and Britain were the rising number of people participating in the new insertion programmes and the prominent role played by new "partnerships" in executing them.

In December 1988, France belatedly introduced a minimum income, le *revenu minimum d'insertion* (RMI). RMI differs from the guaranteed incomes of many European countries in requiring the transfer recipient to sign a "contract" pledging to pursue some kind of insertion activity. In principle, the income grant is contingent upon moving toward a job or social insertion. While the RMI's income support has been effective in reducing poverty and the programme helped to extend health care and housing assistance for which recipients are eligible, its impact on the insertion of recipients has been below expectations.

In 1992, even with the extra effort of the 900,000 Programme for the long-term unemployed launched that year, only a third of all RMIists ended up in unassisted or supported work or training, and some of those continued to receive RMI [Delahaye, 1994, pp. 260]. By mid-1992, only 44 per cent of RMI recipients had even signed a contract [ibid., p. 254]. After signing a contract, recipients waited six months on average to be offered an insertion action, twice the anticipated waiting period. In general, the contracts tilted toward social insertion more than professional insertion. Some express concern that without a successful insertion component, the RMI may devolve into a form of social control or an "Anglo-Saxon vision of insertion based on levels of consumption" [ibid., p. 265].

While the State pays RMI transfer benefits, insertion activities are a joint responsibility of the State and department, to which the department must devote a sum of at least 20 per cent of State RMI funds. The programme is administratively decentralized. Departmental and local insertion commissions are comprised of local politicians, representatives of relevant agencies, social workers, associations and the like. However, there is little coordination with education, urban, and other agencies charged with serving the same population as RMI. In some places, there was even local hostility to the RMI insertion mandate. These insertion commissions also faced political and technical problems: over-expansion, lack of consensus, absenteeism, declining participation, infrequent meetings, and the overwhelming number of cases to review. A subsequent *Commissariat général au Plan* (CGP) report by Fragonard proposed creating a Secretary General for insertion in each prefecture to better coordinate local insertion agencies. In response to a 1992 national commission evaluation of the RMI, a July 1992 law detailed and expanded the roles and practices of the departmental and local insertion commissions and Social Action. It also extended the types of insertion expected of recipients to include involvement in city or neighbourhood life, leisure, culture, and sport as well as work or job training.

By early 1994, there were 765,000 RMI recipients in France. Most RMI recipients are socially isolated: 77 per cent lack jobs and 76 per cent lack a spouse [Castel, 1991]. The largest group are single men. About a fifth of RMI recipients are single mothers and another fifth are married couples, but most live alone, are unemployed and live in cities. Indeed, there is a strong correlation between local unemployment and RMI rates. In line with their elevated unemployment rates, foreigners in a stable, regular status account for 13 per cent of the recipients. RMI recipients also tend to have multiple disabilities [Delahaye, 1994].

Moreover, access to the RMI remains selective. It is only for those ineligible for some other programme: unemployment insurance, API, pensions, or old age minimums. Some groups — about 10 per cent of those financially eligible — are excluded from the RMI: those under 25 with no children, students, trainees, older detainees, and conscientious objectors. Foreigners can qualify only if their official status is in order. Some eligible groups, like independent workers and farmers, remain under-represented. It has been estimated that about half the homeless do not receive RMI because they lack papers, addresses, access, or patience with the system [André, 1994].

Unlike the French minimum income, Britain's national minimum dates from the Second World War. It is conceived more as an absolute level of subsistence than as a minimum right of citizenship [Walker, 1993]. That minimum has always been set at a very low level and excluded the cost of meeting social obligations or exceptional expenses. Recipients of British national insurance often had to seek supplementary benefits, rental assistance or discretionary allocations to address special needs, all distributed on a means-tested basis. By 1990, social assistance supported one out of every seven Britons.

Recent attempts to reduce public expenditure and work disincentives have caused British benefit levels to diverge increasingly from minimum subsistence levels. It is estimated that by the late 1980s "benefits were worth only about one-eighth of the average male earnings for a single person" [Glennerster, 1991, p. 54]. Moreover, since earnings rose faster than inflation during the 1980s, the income gap between the employed and those out of work increased. Also, "The national insurance system has been unable to offer security to new and growing groups of people who are unable to build up a sufficient insurance record" [Walker, 1993, p. 27] — the disabled, lone parents, unemployed youth, in brief, the excluded.

As unemployment and single parenthood climbed, the number of Supplementary Benefit recipients rose and changed the composition of the programme. The proportion of Supplementary Benefit recipients who were unemployed rose, as did the percentage of lone parents receiving Supplementary Benefit. However, in 1984-85, it was estimated that 840,000 families of the 5.25 million entitled to Supplementary Benefit did not claim it [ibid., p.152; Fry & StarK, 1989]. Although lack of information, complex rules, and eligibility for very low benefits may have deterred some, the low take-up rate may also reflect the stigmatization of means-tested benefits. Thus, with respect to the lack of universal coverage by the national minimum, Supplementary Benefit resembles RMI.

During the 1980s, British social security and income maintenance policies underwent considerable change. A 1985 Green Paper proposed major reforms to address the rising share of the poor comprised by families with children, compared to pensioners; rising public social security expenditure; lack of choice; and administrative complexity responsible for the poverty and unemployment "traps", reducing the incentives to work. Many have noted that the reform proposals embraced contradictory goals. Freezing public expenditure levels while increasing "self-reliance", "independence" and work incentives required targeting benefits at families, in this case at the expense of pensioners. However, more reliance on means-testing would increase, rather than reduce, adminstrative complexity. While the reform would eliminate the "poverty trap" that made people on benefit worse off if they worked (unless child care and work expenses are included), it also shifted more people into means-tested programmes where they would be at risk of the slightly reduced work disincentives.

Despite much opposition, the 1986 Social Security Act, implemented in 1988, coordinated existing means-tested programmes. Income Support replaced Supplementary Benefit, Family Credit replaced Family Income Supplement, and Housing Benefit was consolidated into the system to eliminate the "poverty trap". Income Support replaced the distinctions between short- and long-term rates, between householders and non-householders, and between base premiums and special needs allocations with personal allowances based on marital status, number and ages of children, disability, and age. Family Credit supplements the incomes of low-income families working full-time, reducing the difference in benefits between working and unemployed families, seen as a cause of the "unemployment trap." The new Social Fund became responsible for special single payments, but recipients lost their rights to them. These discretionary payments are now provided primarily as loans instead of grants. Finally, the entitlement of 16- and 17-year-old school-leavers to Supplementary Benefit was withdrawn in order to shift young school-leavers into new employment and training programmes.

As in France, British long-term unemployed were less likely than the short-term unemployed to regain a job. In 1990, over a third of men and a quarter of women receiving Unemployment Benefit were out of work for over a year and, by 1987, 74 per cent of the unemployed relied on Supplementary Benefit [Atkinson & Micklewright, 1989]. Yet British unemployment benefit levels have always been relatively low. There is little evidence that generous payments created work disincentives or seriously contributed to rising unemployment rates. British Unemployment Benefit, regardless of how long contributions are made, has a maximum duration, recently reduced from one year to 6 months. This measure also shifted more of the long-term unemployed onto Supplementary Benefit. In contrast, French unemployment benefits can be continually renewed, and some insertion programmes requalify those whose eligibility previously expired.

Despite these considerations, concern about the work disincentives and inefficiencies of the programme dominated Conservative policy in Britain throughout the 1980s. Between 1979 and 1988, Unemployment Benefit was changed at least 17 times, abolishing some benefits, taxing or reducing the value of others, expanding grounds for disqualification and tightening eligibility. Administrators were added to expose fraud, goad the "work-shy" into employment, and intensify the supervision of the long-term unemployed. The "Restart" programme of counselling and interviews monitors a claimant's availability for work on a regular basis. Since 1988, this interview is supposed to result in a "personal action plan," similar to the RMI "contract". However, failure to attend it or a week-long Restart course can lead to a loss of benefits. The requirement to be "available for work" at Restart interviews was reinterpreted as being "actively seeking work", i.e. proving to a State official that one sought a job or entered Employment Training (ET). After unemployed 16-17-year-olds were disqualified from Income Support in 1988, they were expected to join the Youth Training Scheme to receive any benefits. American "workfare" policies have made British benefits more punitive; refusal to work results in a loss of support. As the following discussion of training will also show, the British policy preoccupation with work incentives and low-wage re-employment differs greatly from the *social* insertion mandate of the French RMI.

III. Training policies for adults and youth

Job training policies are a second way to combat exclusion. If properly integrated with other economic policies and adjusted to labour demand of enterprises, raising skill levels can not only increase hiring of disadvantaged groups but also raise labour productivity. However, in the absence of economic growth, training alone has not been very effective in promoting permanent insertion in the labour market, especially of those with multiple disadvantages.

After initially concentrating on youth and women who have never worked, French training policies were targeted at the long-term unemployed in general. That these people were called long-term job seekers (*demandeurs d'emploi de longue durée*), rather than unemployed (*chômeurs*), again contrasts with British discourse about "malingerers on the dole." In December 1989, existing French policies were consolidated into three main instruments: namely, the CES (*contrat emploi-solidarité*); AIF (*actions d'insertion et de formation*); and CRE (*contrat de retour à l'emploi*). The names of these policies were not the only indicator of the shift from an employment to an insertion policy. To qualify, one no longer had to have been on the ANPE unemployment rolls so that "excluded" groups qualified. CREs and CESs give additional subsidies and priority to the most disadvantaged people in difficulty: the unemployed over 50 years old, those out of work for at least three years, RMI recipients unemployed for over a year, and the handicapped. These groups constituted 37 per cent of CRE, and 23 per cent of CES, recipients in 1992.

The CES offers a contract of 20 hours a month for 3 to 36 months working for a locality, association or public enterprise at the minimum wage. They receive some subsidized training and a partial subsidy of their wage, while employers receive tax exemptions and sometimes compensation for costs. CESs are more likely to result in successful insertion when applied in the framework of an *association intermédiaire* (see below) rather than in a regular part-time job where the "social framework" is insufficient [Delahaye, 1994]. AIF provides personalized training by the public employment service that can include an on-the-job training component in an enterprise. The CRE provides direct access to an ordinary job, whether permanent or temporary, for 24-39 hours a week in a private firm. Workers should receive even more subsidized training and a salary for up to 39 hours of work, while their employers again receive exemptions from social charges. Yet the CRE rarely led to on-the-job training. Rather, smaller enterprises in weaker industries that had always made intensive use of unskilled labour simply used the subsidies for unemployed workers to reduce their labour costs. At least one study of CRE found that, while the least advantaged integrated well into the workplace, employers selected the better elements of even this disadvantaged population [ibid.].

In 1992, as unemployment rates in France continued to soar, the public employment service made an all-out effort to offer the 900,000 long-term unemployed a job, training, or community activity of general interest. While virtually everyone's case was reviewed, the crush overloaded the system. Rather than meeting its goal of insertion tailored to the individual, people were increasingly classified into standardized profiles. As many as 290,000 or 28 per cent of the 900,000 cases never received a proposal of a job, training, or insertion activity. Most of those "excluded" were older or very long-term unemployed.

In 1982, the government declared that no youth under 18 should lack vocational qualifications. The major training approaches for unskilled 16-25-year-olds were State-remunerated training courses and partially subsidized, on-the-job training. The September 1989 introduction of *crédit de formation individualisé* (CFI) consolidated and rationalized youth training and occupational insertion policies. It organized a wide variety of programmes into logical sequences ending in a job. They include the *contrat local d'orientation* (CLO) which gives 16- and 17-year-olds without a diploma a three to six month full-time job with some collective utility under CES; apprenticeships; *actions de formation alternée*; *ateliers pédagogiques personnalisés*; *contrats de qualification*; *contrats d'orientation*; *contrats d'adaptation*; and *préparation active à la qualification et à l'emploi* (PAQUE). The latter is the first stage under CFI for the most disadvantaged youth, providing basic knowledge and active discovery of a range of jobs prior to holding one. Then training is to be partly provided on the job through limited-duration *contrats de qualification* (six months to two years for the least schooled) or *contrats d'adaptation* (for those who already had some recognized skill but not adapted to the job). In principle, the youth insertion programmes were supposed to provide individualized, global treatment through local employment and training committees.

Yet, during the 900,000 Programme interviews in 1992, youth in disfavoured urban settings complained of long delays in obtaining a slot in CFI or PAQUE. They resented being subjected to being "parked" in a series of training courses. Indeed, these various training courses rarely led to permanent employment and quickly lost legitimacy. Evaluations found that CFI *formation professionnelle alternée* had limited effectiveness because it was too detached from enterprises and did not address the special needs of certain youth. They recommended focusing more on social problems and reorienting CFI towards *contrats en alternance* providing access to real, if short-term, jobs. The CFI reforms also did not go far enough in consolidating youth insertion programmes. In 1994, student demonstrations against the *contrat d'insertion professionnelle* (*SMIC-jeunes*) again revealed discontent over the government's ineffective youth insertion policies.

The British training system resembles the French in several respects. The programmes target youth and the unemployed, try to integrate classroom and on-the-job training and rely on partnerships with employers. They have also helped reduce official unemployment rates. During the 1980s, Britain, like France, instituted reforms of unemployment benefits and training programmes that require recipients to develop a "personal action plan" in which the unemployed exchange a commitment to train or seek work "actively" in return for income support. However, a closer look reveals some important differences in perspective. Although contractual language was also used to justify British insertion requirements, as in the RMI, it reflected Lockian ideas more than Rousseau's solidary conception of the social contract. As King [1992, pp. 238-239] notes, British politicians "adopted the language of contract and duty familiar from the United States and promoted by the New Right".

As unemployment soared in the early 1980s, the Manpower Services Commission (MSC) became "the central institution in the government's attack on unemployment". In 1982, the MSC introduced the Community Programme which provided the long-term unemployed with temporary employment on "projects of benefit to the community". Of the 250,000 places in 1985, half were sponsored by local authorities and the others by voluntary associations [OECD, 1988]. However, these "social" insertion programmes were increasingly disfavoured. In 1983, expenditure rose for the Youth Training Scheme (YTS) and other technical and vocational youth training, but cuts in job creation programmes for the older long-term unemployed increasingly compelled them to participate in a "'socially useful activity' in return for a 'wage' which was little more than benefit levels" [Atkinson & Lupton, 1990, p. 54].

In 1988, two White Papers, *Employment for the 1990s* and *Training for employment*, spelled out Britain's "new training and enterprise policy". First, it made administrative changes. Nationally, the Department of Employment absorbed the Training Commission (the MSC's successor) and renamed it the Training Agency. Regionally, it established Training and Enterprise Councils (TECs) in 82 travel-to-work areas. Modelled on the American Private Industry Councils introduced under President Reagan, TECs are independent companies "born of the enterprise culture" with a two-thirds majority of business executives and a one-third minority of local authority, education, union, and non-profit representatives. Because they by-passed local authorities, TECs have been criticized as unaccountable and politically exclusionary, and since TECs cannot levy fees on local employers as could the earlier Industrial Training Boards, they tend to be underfunded.

In 1988, TECs were made responsible for Employment Training (ET) which consolidated all existing adult vocation training programmes. They contract for training services from local providers in order to adjust skills flexibly and rapidly to local demand. Trainees are paid a benefit-related "allowance" but, for the adult unemployed, receipt of social security benefits while undergoing training operates as a cap to wages. Training became increasingly compulsory. Since 1990, those unemployed for over two years who reject help at their Restart interview must take a training course. Although the government promised up to 600,000 ET places for an average of six months, ET for the long-term unemployed has had a high drop-out rate, and its replacement, Employment Action, has an insufficient number of places although, like the Community Programme it replaced, it is a temporary work programme without mandatory training. After an initial expansion, expenditure on employment and training programmes, like the number of places, were cut back. The public-private partnership approach to training has not lived up to its promise.

TECs were also given control over training credits (vouchers for private training), the TA's small business promotion schemes, Careers Service, and school-industry Compacts, another American import. The latter, introduced first in London and adopted by Action for Cities, bear a certain resemblance to French RMI contracts. Students set goals like school attendance which, if met, give them work experience or jobs guaranteed by local employers. However, "their impact is relatively marginal to the wider unemployment problems of 16-17 year olds" [Hill, 1994, p. 178]. In 1988, as youth under 18 lost their rights to social security, the TECs also took over Youth Training Scheme, renamed Youth Training (YT) in 1990. By requiring 16- and 17-year-old school leavers either to work or train, the government eliminated official youth unemployment in Britain by *fiat*. The reform disqualified those who dropped out, were expelled, or declined a place in YTS without "good cause." Indeed, in areas of the country where few jobs were available, YTS became a cheap labour scheme with a variable training content (*Financial Times*, 20 January 1989). Like the CFI in France, YT has been unable to live up to its guarantee of a training position for every under-18 unemployed school leaver [Hill, 1994]. None the less, with a few exceptions, unemployed French youth do not qualify for "benefits" at all.

While more YTS graduates obtain full-time work and fewer become unemployed than in earlier years, a rising proportion enter another YTS scheme, a trend reminiscent of the French trend of parking people in training courses. Some areas with high youth unemployment were locally dubbed "scheme-lands" in which early adulthood "consisted of a seemingly endless round of government schemes and dead-end jobs punctuated by often lengthy periods of unemployment" [MacDonald & Coffield, 1991, p. 230].

One of the major insertion goals of the new training scheme was to socialize the new generation in the "enterprise culture". "Regular diatribes against scroungers" [King, 1992, p. 225], coupled with threatened loss of benefits for those not in work or training, were designed to stigmatize "dependency" and inculcate a new morality of "enterprise." Business penetrated the British school and university systems. Beginning in 1985, with the Mini-Enterprise in Schools Project, enterprise training was incorporated into higher education, YTS and other training programmes. These initiatives fall under the rubric of Britain's version of insertion by economic means.

IV. Insertion by economic means

The liberal approach to job creation has traditionally used supply-side policies to reduce the cost of labour. Both Britain and France relaxed employment regulations and offered private enterprises a variety of tax exemptions to promote job creation and the hiring of new labour market entrants, re-entrants, the unskilled and the long-term unemployed. In contrast to profit-enhancing incentives for employers, the idea of insertion by economic means (*l'insertion par l'activité économique*) is to integrate the economic goal of job and business creation with social purposes in the effort to combat social exclusion. Such policies can be found in both France and Britain, but their underlying conceptions of insertion profoundly differ.

Insertion by economic means in France explicitly combines economic and social purposes: the offer of a real job or other insertion trajectory tied to personalized social services. The ideology underlying this approach is to respect market competition as well as pursue solidarity. *Entreprises d'insertion (EIs), associations intermédiaires (AIs),* and *régies des quartiers* conceive of the work group as a "community" with social as well as economic benefits. Like many small enterprises, they draw upon a tradition of companionship and evoke the moral or civic duty of patrons toward their employees. Insertion goes beyond the cash nexus; a job should integrate all the cultural, educational, health, familial and other aspects of an excluded person's life.

In contrast, the British approach is to encourage "enterprise" by the excluded themselves to fight a "dependency culture." The business community and voluntary associations as well as central government are involved in promoting entrepreneurship and small business development by local communities and the unemployed. Given the diverse activities and actors involved, it should not be surprising that "enterprise" has multiple meanings, "sometimes referring to an individual ability considered amenable to improvement and at other times to a form of economic activity, usually in small businesses" [MacDonald & Coffield, 1991, p. 29]. However, compared to France, the assistance and training provided is more narrowly economic or commercial than social, and focuses more on changing individual behaviour than insertion into a work group or community.

In 1979, France officially recognized insertion by economic means by creating a formal status distinct from legally-protected employment for work organizations serving the disadvantaged, especially those who have trouble holding a traditional job and who are unassisted by more conventional insertion programmes. Although often compared to American policies of the New Deal and War on Poverty, EIs, AIs, and *régies des quartiers* originated not in the public sector but in the efforts of ordinary citizens, social workers and social action groups. Often headed by strong, even charismatic leaders, they none the less require active participation of volunteers and the beneficiaries of their services. Most serve a population of long-term unemployed, ex-convicts, substance-abusers, homeless persons and others with multiple difficulties and a history of defeats in the labour market. Many are referred by *Action sociale*, and health, criminal justice, and training agencies. But others are walk-ins, taking advantage of the organizations' open-door policies. This has made it possible to reach isolated persons who have no other contact with State insertion institutions.

Enterprises d'insertion (EIs) seek to function like ordinary enterprises. They produce goods and services for the market, must become economically viable and, though recruiting workers from the most disadvantaged elements, offer at least the minimum wage and expect real productivity and conventional workplace behaviour. While the failure rate of EIs is below that of small businesses generally they tend to operate in less-profitable sectors — construction and local services — served by neither the market nor the State. These activities regularize what was often undertaken in the underground economy. Such labour-intensive activities also make it possible to take on predominantly unskilled workers in need of employment. EIs provide a personal project or job for an average length of nine months, during which workers adhere to ordinary work rules and enjoy the same rights as they would in the regular labour market.

In general, the *associations intermédiaires* (AIs) are more flexible than EIs in their expectations for participants. While EIs stress the economic aspects of punctuality, reliability and work quality, AIs emphasize the social aspects of insertion, such as daily schedules, regular attendance, and the nature of the tasks accomplished in predominantly part-time jobs. These differences are also reflected in the gender composition of the clientele: 87 per cent of EI workers are male, while 52 per cent of AI workers are female. Yet both institutions demand that participants follow conventional workplace norms, like refraining from alcohol or drugs.

By offering interim employment, AIs were initially conceived as a form of work-sharing. Created under a January 1987 law to prepare the most disadvantaged job-seekers for work and to follow up their progress, AIs deal with very few RMI recipients, but do hire the most disadvantaged for non-market activities and "odd jobs" exempt from business taxes and normal labour regulations governing temporary work. By 1991, over a third of their employees were permanent. Over time, they have launched local partnerships to establish work sites (*chantiers d'insertion* and *chantiers-écoles*), which do not have official status, and have encouraged new economic activities like family and environmental businesses.

Economic insertion activities are decentralized efforts adapted to local conditions. Therefore, they combine economic and urban dimensions of insertion. For example, the *régies des quartiers* are local partnerships of inhabitants, elected officials, and landlords that establish a neighbourhood structure for insertion by economic means. They operate in markets that serve the locality — building maintenance, gardening, and other neighbourhood services — but also seek to increase access to the rest of the city. The *régies* give the most disadvantaged local residents priority in hiring, couple employment with training and social services, and provide opportunities for residents to participate in all stages of a project, most aimed at developing the social life of disadvantaged neighbourhoods. Although their activities are local, EIs, AIs, and régies have national confederations to serve as government interlocuters, information networks, and technical assistance providers.

Increasingly, these essentially private enterprises and associations have received public subsidies. One important funding source are the *plans locaux d'insertion économique (PLIE)*. Like the English Partnerships and TECs, the PLIE are designed to coordinate and rationalize the actions and funding of the many different partners in the local insertion effort. Every PLIE organizes a local partnership, assesses local conditions of deprivation, agency capacity and employment opportunities, and lays out individualized trajectories for the insertion process. Under contracts, the PLIE disburse the *Fonds social européen (FSE)* under Objective 3 and State funds from the Labour, Social Affairs, and Urban Ministries. On average, subsidies cover 20 per cent of EI budgets, but EIs may also receive tax exemptions and subsidies to compensate for low worker productivity. It is unclear whether the subsidies per job exceed the worker's value-added, but they are probably about double those used to finance a CRE or CES.

Evaluations of insertion by economic means tend to be favourable [Hatzfeld, 1993]. They effectively reorient for work those who have not held a job in years, transforming those deemed unemployable due to a lack of motivation or respect for basic social norms or an inability to learn or negotiate the social organization of time and space. The *esprit de corps* in these community associations helps to integrate the least advantaged citizens into the world of work and provides the foundation for a revitalized local democracy.

However, these economic associations are still few in number and have limited capacity in relation to the enormity of the problems they seek to address. There are no more than a few thousand such initiatives (500 EIs, 960 AIs), and their geographical distribution is uneven. All told, they have created about 22,000 full-time equivalent jobs. National subsidies and rules are designed to increase their size and number. Despite national-level consolidation and widespread popularity, their short life-span and diverse forms and activities mean that assessments are most often based on anecdotal evidence. Their social and economic goals also may conflict. They have low productivity, often lack professional management, use very traditional labour processes, rather than innovating the production process, and contribute to the precariousness of work. While the EI ideology is to provide the excluded with a "real" socially-recognized job, the limited duration of employment increases turnover, discourages the development of a trained workforce and lowers productivity. Finally, the employment prospects of former participants were not much enhanced by their experience. Associations do little to place departing workers in jobs. Family or other forms of social insertion are deemed as important as the economic.

Insertion by economic means has its British counterparts. For example, the growing voluntary sector has supplemented central government initiatives to fight social exclusion in British localities. Religious initiatives include the Church of England's Faith in the City project, established in 1985 and now the tenth largest charity in Britain, and Evangelical Enterprise, a partnership between black churches and Inner Cities Task Forces to organize constructive projects for the unemployed.

Corporate initiatives also exist. Business in the Community, a privately-funded association of UK corporations, created in 1981, works with local councils, local enterprise agencies, and neighbourhood partnerships through ten regional offices. Its Centre for Corporate Responsibility encourages targeting investment, selective local hiring and training, and participation in partnerships and charitable activities. Local enterprise agencies operating in over 400 localities are private-sector led counselling services for unemployed people considering self-employment. Enterprise Trusts assist small firms through advice, training and support services.

Most similar to the French EIs and AIs are Community Enterprises: development trusts, community companies, cooperatives and other voluntary associations. They comprise a grass-roots approach to "sustainable, people-centred development" in partnership with local business and government. Established in the 1960s and 1970s, local non-profit community development trusts now number in the hundreds, some funded through Task Forces, City Grant, or City Challenge. Despite successful examples, community enterprises in some places consisted of "short-term, disorganized activities" that contributed to the confidence and skills of the unemployed but did not realize their grander aims. Communities have also engaged in real planning exercises to influence local economic development. None the less, community-led development remains small-scale, under-funded, and marginalized in a national context favouring insertion in new or existing for-profit businesses.

As mentioned, Britain developed an extensive set of training policies during the 1980s to promote an "enterprise culture." To assist would-be entrepreneurs outside the YTS, schools, and universities, the Training for Enterprise Programme (TFE) expanded rapidly over the decade. TFE includes such programmes as the Business Enterprise programme (week-long training in skills to establish and run a small business); Private Enterprise Programme (day-long training modules for existing businesses); Management Extension Programme (for unemployed managers to move into small businesses); and Graduate Gateway Programme (to encourage graduates to enter business). The most important programme to combat exclusion is the Enterprise Allowance Scheme, which expanded to over 300,000 places since its introduction in 1983. For up to a year, it provides a £40 weekly supplement to the profits of any new business established by the previously unemployed on unemployment benefit or income support, provided they invest at least £1,000 and work full-time in a government-approved business. Enterprise Allowance did not require a business to be profitable. Thus, while enterprise schemes often provided jobs for bureaucrats and enterprise trainers, many of the new enterprises — most sole traderships rather than cooperative or community ventures — were marginally viable or failed.

Self-employment did rise spectacularly in the UK during the 1980s, from 6.6 per cent of non-agricultural employment in 1979 to 11.6 per cent in 1990. Although the UK figures do include some owner-managers of incorporated businesses, the self-employed proportion of nonagricultural employment in France fell continuously during this period from 11.4 per cent in 1973 to 10.3 per cent in 1990. This is just another indicator of the lack of French employment growth.

France and the United Kingdom justfied rising government incentives to self-employment as a way to reduce unemployment. However, there does not appear to be any systematic variation between unemployment rates and self-employment trends over time or cross-nationally. Some of the unemployed do use self-employment as a stepping stone into other jobs, but not all the unemployed are likely to do well in self-employment. Although UK self-employment rose 57 per cent between 1981 and 1989, accounting for over 75 per cent of the new job growth during the decade, another 20 per cent of new jobs were in fact in government training schemes, suggesting that the new entrepreneurs hired few people. Also, self-employment rose primarily in the prosperous South-east. Since the self-employed are not entitled to unemployment, injury and other benefits, the trend may actually reflect rising demand for independent contractors to avoid job security legislation and social security contributions. Rising self-employment may also reflect changing production processes, aided with new technologies and the rise of segmented markets served by small specialized firms.

Finally, even among the economically inactive, access to "social capital" coupled with free time may enlarge one's social world through participation in the "household economy" and local voluntary activities. Thus, aside from self-employment, advanced industrial countries have also experienced a renaissance in self-help activities and household economies among the poor, a phenomenon once confined to developing countries. Although such "concealed employment" is notoriously difficult to measure, most indicators suggest it is rising [OECD, 1986]. However, rising unemployment does not appear to be related to informal economic activities for several reasons. "Social capital" is more plentiful in some economic enclaves, groups and communities than others. Informal economies are less likely to work among the socially disaffilated, and the unemployed are less like to engage in informal economic activity. The State may be their only recourse.

Policies to promote insertion by economic means are designed to provide an organized social framework of activities to prevent the long-term unemployed from becoming isolated, losing the discipline of daily routines and social practices, and falling into illegal activities. EIs and small business programmes can help regularize informal enterprises or effectively compete with them. However, the small economic scale of such insertion efforts is insufficient to cope with the enormity of the unemployment problems in Britain and France.

V. Urban insertion

The application of urban policy to address social exclusion is relatively recent, especially in France. Urban policy in both Britain and France grew out of post-war land-use planning, infrastructural development, slum clearance, and related subsidized housing construction. The wedding of urban to social policy received a major impetus in both countries from ethnic disorders in subsidized housing estates.

France did not develop a specifically "urban" policy until the 1981 riot at Les Minguettes which led to the creation of the National Commission for the Social Development of Neighbourhoods (DSQ). In late 1988, urban policy was further oriented towards insertion with the creation of the *Conseil national des villes (CNV)*, *Comité interministériel des villes (CIV)*, and the *Délégation interministérielle à la ville (DIV)*. Their goal was to fuse infrastructure, public works, housing and local citizenship policies (like anti-delinquency and social development efforts) in order to address problems globally and on a decentralized, experimental basis. Yet, in May of the following year, a moratorium on urban policy was declared.

It took the violent incidents in Vaulx-en-Velin, Sartrouville, and Mantes-la-Jolie during 1990 and early 1991 to prompt a rethinking of State policy towards the city and especially, the peripheral *banlieues* (outer estates). To deconcentrate the poor in the name of solidarity, the Loi Besson passed in May 1991 declared a right to housing.[3] To reduce police provocation of local conflagrations, DSQ and delinquency prevention policy incorporated the police. Immigrant integration policy was also formulated. The *Ministère des Affaires sociales et de l'integration* has since pursued social policies that bestow legitimacy upon ethnic associations and immigrant cultural life [Barou, 1993]. A new French urban policy at last emerged in July 1991 with the *Loi d'orientation pour la ville (LOV)*. New financial arrangements redistributed resources from richer to poorer areas under the principle of solidarity. In addition, the LOV and the *protocoles d'occupation du patrimoine social (POPS)* revamped low-income housing policy. A full-fledged Urban Ministry was also established in 1991.

In contrast, the origins of the British Urban Programme in 1968 can be traced to the rediscovery of poverty, itself stimulated by the Great Society programmes and race riots in the United States. Initially focused on the personal and family problems of inner-city residents, the Urban Programme provided grants to local authorities to meet special social needs

---

[3] The *fonds de solidarité logement* and *prêts locatifs aidés d'insertion* were created.

through social and community programmes. The Community Development Project established 12 Inner Area Projects. A shift from social to economic concerns, and from public to private provision was signalled by the Labour government's 1977 White Paper, *Policy for the inner cities*. The Inner Urban Areas Act of 1978 enhanced the Urban Programme by incorporating economic and environmental as well as social programmes. The CDP was phased out, and resources were redirected at seven "inner city partnerships" (ICPs) of private sector interests, the police, voluntary groups, the Department of Environment, and local authorities and made responsible for 25 per cent of the cost of "regeneration" in the most deprived "programme areas". The ICPs, however, remained fragmented.

As in France, British urban policy received new impetus with the urban riots of 1981. The events added violence and delinquency to the connotations of race and poverty already implicit in the notion of "inner-cities." While some local authorities reacted with policies on racial discrimination, the solution of the Conservative government was to encourage "enterprise and the means to participate in mainstream economic life — while exercising firm control over crime and disorder, and discouraging dependency" [Hill, 1994, p. 169]. Thus, to existing programmes, like the 150 Urban Programme projects, were added policies to leverage private investment and relax regulations in selected areas of deprivation. The most important of these were Enterprise Zones (EZs) and Urban Development Corporations (UDCs), both of which gave a prominent role to business leaders and reduced local authority discretion in redeveloping derelict land in spatially targeted areas. Indeed, during the 1980s, just as France was decentralizing power to the departements and communes, British central government was reasserting control over local authorities. New decentralized, unelected, quasi-governmental administrations executed centrally-determined policies.

Despite the impetus of social unrest, the legacy of physical redevelopment activities left an enduring imprint on French and British urban policy. In both countries, evaluations have been highly critical of this emphasis. French critics urged urban policy to concentrate on economic and social development activities that would fight exclusion in the areas where it is most crystallized. British evaluations, like the French, called for a "better mix of social and economic objectives" [Hill, 1994, p. 195] and spatially targeted interventions in deprived areas.

Nevertheless, there are national differences in the conception of urban insertion, with discourse in France again stressing "solidarity" and in Britain, "community" and "citizenship". Underlying French urban insertion policies is an assumption that one's proximate neighbourhood (*cité*) is a legitimate source of attachment or identity, deriving from a specific history and cultural accretion. The demand for new forms of production and social organization evokes the French 1848 revolutionary tradition of fraternity and solidarity in Hatzfeld [1993, p. 91]. Yet the term *banlieue* also came to connote a "ghetto", much as the English term "inner-city" became a metaphor for poverty, crime, and race; indeed, in both countries, some of the worst urban conditions were found on "outer estates". British discourse of urban policy also featured the term "community" as an assumption of shared interests among business, local government and institutions; "regeneration" as a biological reference imported from the US that, by analogy, cures "pathology"; and "enterprise" or "self-reliance" as the antithesis of "underclass' dependency."

While French urban policy increasingly aspires to couple social concerns to economic integration, British urban policy decidedly shifted from social interventions towards market-led economic solutions. British "inner-city" programmes, as in other areas of social policy, moved increasingly in the direction of American urban initiatives and came to share that country's liberal conception of social exclusion. Over time, Britain relaxed planning regulations, used public funds to leverage private investment, created competition among localities, and largely relied upon real-estate development to create jobs. Social problems remained the responsibility of local authorities, while urban subsidies went to other public and quasi-governmental agencies for physical and economic development.

French and British urban policies have not been very successful at alleviating the social problems they were supposed to address. French evaluations found the LOV policy deficient in several respects [Geindre, 1993; Herrou, 1993]. They proposed that French urban policy should concentrate even more on fighting exclusion and increasing local democracy in the most disadvantaged neighbourhoods, coordinating economic and social interventions, and incorporating urban policy into physical planning of metropolitan infrastructure. In Britain, too, the emphasis on property development did little for deprived populations . The assumption behind EZs and UDCs was that concentrated social exclusion could be tackled with "trickle-down" economics, when no arrangements guaranteed that local residents would benefit. Only a minority of the new jobs, often relocated from elsewhere in the city, went to local residents. Canary Wharf in the Docklands provides the most spectacular example of failure. The Audit Commission found that new derelict spaces increased faster than their reclamation during the 1980s. In 1992, the Policy Studies Institute's *Urban Trends 1* reported that job creation was limited, deprived areas still had high poverty rates and poor housing, and the gap between these areas and the rest of England had widened. Even violent disorders erupted in areas targeted by urban policy.

The emphasis on physical rather than social development is not the only thing French and British urban policies have in common. Both increasingly rely upon "partnerships" between government agencies and between public and private sector representatives to administer and execute urban policy. This has resulted in two problems the countries share: lack of coordination among agencies and insufficient participation by local residents.

In France, the rapid expansion of urban policy created extreme confusion. The goals of urban policy and its relationship to efforts at other levels of government remained ambiguous. Urban policy, in fact, encompassed a broad range of State, departmental, communal, and neighbourhood activities. Unlike in Britain after 1977, urban activities were poorly integrated with economic development, occupational insertion, and unemployment agencies in the target areas. The 221 local missions for the insertion of youth in difficulty were oriented more towards employment than global treatment of problems. Numerous agencies and ministries intervened in local affairs, with very uneven impact. At the same time, inter-ministerial bodies proliferated: for disadvantaged neighbourhoods; for delinquency; for *contrats de villes*; for youth insertion; for income support and insertion; and for integration. Despite inter-ministerial efforts, sectoral logics — e.g. housing, education, urban, security — prevailed. The Belorgey report endorsed the idea of sub-prefects to coordinate all these State activities at the local level and endorsed promotion incentives for police, educators and social workers who work in these zones. The Geindre report [1993, p. 237], too, condemned the "real tangle of respnsibilities", and iIt also called attention to the lack of inter-communal cooperation, with some towns refusing to accept poorer residents or social housing.

As in France, the British government tried to coordinate urban policies among government bodies. In the mid-1980s, it established 8 City Action Teams (CATs) and 16 Task Forces. CATs were regional bodies of the Departments of Environment, Employment, and Trade and Industry, while Task Forces of civil service, local government, and voluntary sector representatives dispensed loans and advice to local small enterprises. Other reforms came in 1987 and 1988. In 1989, the Department of the Environment took on more responsibility for coordinating these urban policies. Social programmes associated with "dependency" remained the council's responsibility, while new partnerships between central government agencies and business shut local authorities out of their activities to create an "enterprise culture" and promote "civic pride." The 1990 White Paper, *People in cities*, signalled a shift from physical regeneration through

Enterprise Zones and UDCs to the building of "partnerships," including local residents and councils. The approach gave priority to improved coordination, leveraging private capital, and reduced cost. Partnerships seemed more "community-oriented" and "people-friendly" than the UDCs, but business interests remained central. Including local residents led to tokenism, insufficient representativeness, or cooptation into "US-style growth coalitions" [Colenutt, 1993].

In 1991, the City Challenge programme created new local public-private partnerships which further concentrated on small areas and disadvantaged groups. Local authorities competed for City Challenge funds partly by showing in their bid that they had strong business and community involvement. However, City Challenge was quickly phased out, replaced in 1993 by the Urban Regeneration Agency which took over inner-city initiatives from the Department of the Environment. Under the control of a regional director who coordinates government departments and consolidates the budget of 20 existing programmes, the URA also created the English Partnerships between local councils, resident associations, and the private sector to acquire, plan and redevelop derelict land.

As in France, British evaluations cited the lack of coordination among urban initiatives as a major problem. In 1989, the House of Commons Public Accounts Committee and the Audit Commission (1989) severely criticized urban policy, the latter calling it a "patchwork quilt of complexity and idiosyncracy with few resources to match the scale of the attendant problems". By 1992, "there were 34 different urban policy initiatives covering five government departments" [Hill, 1994, p. 192]. Since the same areas could have more than one urban policy designation and reported to different agencies and levels of government, duplication and poor coordination arose. In this sense, the UK lacks a coherent urban policy.

Urban policy in neither country did much to increase citizen participation. In France, despite its rhetoric of local citizenship and solidarity in LOV, resident participation was limited. While associations were consulted, urban protesters demobilized and the idea of local empowerment lost legitimacy. The Belorgey report speculated on the reasons for this apathy, suggesting that associations brought into decision-making and policy execution may not be truly representative and that local politicians remain uninvolved or even hostile to neighbourhood efforts [Belorgey, 1993]. In Britain, where UDCs were composed primarily by appointed business people, there was no systematic monitoring of the corporations' proceedings, which were often secret. The Urban Development Grant, renamed Urban Regeneration Grant in 1987 and City Grant in 1988, increasingly by-passed local authorities. Thus, by neglecting local consultation, UDCs may have added to political exclusion. Critics charge that the URA has "increased central administrative powers along the lines of the French prefecture system" [Hill, 1994, p. 174]. In addition, British urban policy since 1981 has increasingly marginalized race issues.

Some observors consider the partnerships created under the enhanced Urban Programme and City Challenge to be more "integrationist" while UDCs and English Partnerships are more "exclusionary" [Burton, 1994]. Coordinated, cross-departmental initiatives involving private and voluntary sectors as well as State services can be viewed as a method to reintroduce the excluded to full participation. While the partnership approach suggests more incorporation of social and community goals in urban policy, "exclusion from political concern" and urban policy-making remains a problem in Britain, as in France.

It is worth noting that the Major government launched its own approach to the question of government responsiveness to popular concerns. Its July 1991 Citizen's Charter aimed to give "more power to the citizen" by strengthening consumer rights, improving the responsiveness of public services, fighting discrimination and providing multilingual services. In this view, "citizenship" refers to quality, choice, standards, and value for money implied by the ability to pay.

In sum, British urban policy increasingly excluded elected local representatives, deregulated the local economy and emphasized partnerships with business. French urban policy, in contrast, increased public intervention in deprived neighbourhoods and went beyond economic and physical redevelopment to incorporate more social insertion programmes. Yet both countries have problems coordinating urban agencies and programmes, encouraging resident participation, reducing unemployment and poverty, and responding to the specific needs of ethnic minorities.

VI. Conclusion

This comparison of French and British insertion policies has shown how programmes fighting exclusion differ from the income transfer programmes of post-war European welfare states. While social insurance programmes redistribute income over the life course as individuals encounter a series of relatively predictable, but temporary, risks, social insertion programmes reattach individuals facing the risk of permanent exclusion to a social fabric woven around work, training, associational and community activities. While means-tested programmes for residual categories of non-workers fight poverty through the passive receipt of social assistance, social insertion programmes condition income transfers on the active participation of the excluded in their own integration.

Not all the insertion programmes examined here have been equally successful in achieving these goals. Training and economic insertion policies need more involvement by, and better coordination with, the private sector. Some "creaming" of clients has occurred, so that the most excluded economically and socially are often excluded from insertion programmes as well. Urban policies in particular have suffered from insufficient citizen participation. Top-down policies and conflicts between central and local governments have weakened grass-roots initiatives. Most obvious were the problems of coordinating the administration of new insertion programmes.

Nothing better illustrates the novelty of the problem of exclusion than the institutional innovations made necessary to combat it. Both France and Britain have created new agencies to coordinate the work of different ministries in treating the multiple dimensions of exclusion. Both countries have also instituted programmes to coordinate public and private sector activities. The "alphabet soup" of these new insertion institutions includes, in France, CDIs, CLIs, PLIEs, *missions locales*, *régies des quartiers*, PAIO, and the DIV. Counterparts in Britain include the TECs, School-Industry Compacts, CATs, Task Forces, ICPs, URA, and English Partnerships.

Evaluations of their work demonstrate how difficult it has been to overcome the pre-existing logics of sectoral differentiation and achieve the coordination necessary to tackle exclusion. New agencies have been added on top of old ones. Different agencies have overlapping functions, and some even duplicate the work of others. Insertion agencies at different levels of government have different functions that mesh together poorly. Rather than being treated in one's totality as an individual, clients must often move between agencies for different services. Progressive administrative reforms to address these problems have still not succeeded in simplifying and coordinating the system of insertion programmes.

British and French insertion exhibit a number of similarities. Income support is increasingly tied to supported work and job training. In France, RMI recipients sign an insertion contract, while in the UK, benefit recipients develop personal action plans in Restart interviews or set personal education targets in School-Industry Compacts. Employers are also subsidized to hire the unemployed, provide on-the-job training, or create new jobs. Although youth training programmes have not been very successful in promoting employment, the British and French governments have both declared that youth has a right to a recognized qualification and have deregulated minimum wages to fight youth unemployment. France and Britain also provide subsidies and training to promote self-employment and small business formation. More socially-oriented, local productive initiatives, like *associations d'insertion* and Community Enterprises, exist in both countries. In reaction to violent disturbances, France and Britain also introduced urban policies targeted on areas with high rates of unemployment, poverty, crime, delinquency, housing dilapidation, and ethnic minorities. However, neither country has been very successful in alleviating these spatially concentrated problems, reorienting interventions from physical to social redevelopment, or increasing resident participation in community regeneration.

Nevertheless, French insertion policies have different emphases than the British. Most French programmes purportedly serve both social and economic purposes, in line with the ideology of solidarity, whereas British programmes emphasize economic "enterprise". French income support is more permissive in accepting social, as well as economic, insertion activities, whereas British benefits are accompanied by more coercive requirements to move towards economic insertion alone. Employment Training is more punitive and oriented towards the private sector than the French *contrats emploi-solidarité*, *actions d'insertion et de formation*, and *contrats de retour à l'emploi*. The French government has intervened to combat exclusion from both the demand and supply sides of the labour market, and business participation in insertion efforts is greater there than in the UK. In contrast, the key British insertion strategies have been targeting the most disadvantaged groups and areas, providing legal remedies for discrimination, insuring the quality of local public services, and reintroducing excluded groups to full participation through "coordinated, cross-departmental initiatives" [Room, 1992, p. S35].

The national contrasts are particularly striking with respect to urban policy. While French urban interventions are poorly coordinated with local economic insertion programmes, public involvement and expenditure in the ZUP have been increasing over time. Newly decentralized powers also allow French local governments to innovate in ways adapted to local conditions, if not all municipalities are willing to do so. In contrast, the British approach to urban policy has been to relax business and labour market regulation, give priority to physical and economic regeneration, and increase the power of employers and reduce the power of local authorities and citizens to determine the direction of urban redevelopment. Institutionalizing new "partnerships" has not done much to move urban policy back in the direction of social insertion.

In brief, to the extent that social exclusion is a newly-perceived social problem distinguished from poverty or inequality, it has promoted a new set of social insertion policies and new institutions to carry them out. Nevertheless, there are important cross-national differences in the social construction of the problem, its diagnosis, and the ways that welfare states are adjusting to address it.

Bibliographical references

André, C. 1994. "La France des pauvres", in *Alternatives économiques*, No. 114 (February), pp. 23-32.

Atkinson, R.; Lupton, C. 1990. "Towards an enterprise culture? Industrial and training policy under the Conservatives", in Savage, S.; Robins, L. (eds.): *Public policy under Thatcher*. London, Macmillan.

Atkinson, T.; Micklewright, J. 1989. "Turning the screw: Benefits for the unemployed 1979-1988", in Dilnot, A.; Walker, I. (eds.): *The economics of social security*. Oxford University Press.

Barou, J. 1993. "Les paradoxes de l'intégration: De l'infortune des mots à la vertu des concepts", in *Ethnologie française*, Vol. 23, No. 2 (April-June).

Belorgey, J.-M. 1993. *Evaluer les politiques de la ville*. Paris, Conseil économique et social.

Burton, P. 1994. "Integration and exclusion in urban policy", paper presented at the Conference on "Shaping the Urban Future", Bristol.

Castel, R. 1991. "De l'indigence à l'exclusion: la désaffiliation", in Donzelot, J. (ed.): *Face à l'exclusion: Le modèle français*. Paris, Esprit.

Colenutt, B. 1993. "After the Urban Development Corporations? Development elites or people-based regeneration?", in Imrie, R.; Thomas, H. (eds.): *British urban policy and the Urban Development Corporations*. London, Paul Chapman.

Delahaye, V. 1994. *Politiques de lutte contre le chômage et l'exclusion et mutation de l'action sociale*. Paris, Ecole nationale d'administration.

Fry, V.; Stark, G. S. 1989. "The take-up of supplementary benefit: Gaps in the 'safety net'?", in Dilnot, A.; Walker, I. (eds.): *The economics of social security*. Oxford University Press.

Geindre, F. 1993. *Ville, démocratie, solidarité*. Paris, La Documentation française.

Glennerster, H. 1991. "The radical Right and the welfare state in Britain: Pensions and health care", in Glennerster, H.; Midgley, J. (eds.): *The radical Right and the welfare state: An international assessment*. Hertfordshire, Harvester Wheatsheaf.

Hatzfeld, M. 1993. *L'insertion par l'activité économique: des expériences, des pratiques, des acteurs*. Paris, Ministère du travail, de l'emploi et de la formation professionnelle, Syros.

Herrou, M. 1993. *Ouvrir les quartiers: Politique de la ville et déplacements*. Paris, Délégation interministérielle à la ville.

Hill, D. M. 1994. *Citizens and cities: Urban policy in the 1990s*. New York, Harvester Wheatsheaf.

King, D. 1992. "The establishment of work-welfare programs in the United States and Britain: Politics, ideas, and institutions", in Steinmo, S. et al. (eds.): *Structuring politics: Historical institutionalism in comparative analysis*. Cambridge University Press, pp. 217-250.

MacDonald, R.; Coffield, F. 1991. *Risky business? Youth and enterprise culture*. London, Falmer Press.

OECD. 1986. "Concealed employment", in *Employment Outlook*. Paris, Organisation for Economic Co-operation and Development.

—. 1988. *Measures to assist the long-term unemployed*. Paris, OECD.

—. 1991. *Employment Outlook*. Paris, OECD.

—. 1993. *Employment Outlook*. Paris, OECD.

Room, G. 1990. *"New poverty" in the European Community*. London, St. Martin's Press.

—. 1992. *Observatory on national policies to combat social exclusion, Second Annual Report*. Brussels, EC Commission.

Silver, H.; Wilkinson, F. Forthcoming. *Policies to combat social exclusion: A French-British comparison*. Discussion Paper Series No. 83. Geneva, IILS.

Walker, C. 1993. *Managing poverty: The limits of social assistance*. London, Routledge.

List of acronyms

French

AI	Associations intermédiaires
AFI	Aide forfaitaire au poste d'insertion
AIF	Action d'insertion et de formation
CES	Contrat emploi-solidarité
CFI	Crédit de formation individualisé
CLO	Contrat local d'orientation
CGP	Commissariat général au Plan
CIV	Comité interministériel des villes
CNV	Conseil national des villes
CRE	Contrat de retour à l'emploi
DIV	Délégation interministérielle à la ville
DSQ	Développement social des quartiers
EI	Entreprise d'insertion
FSE	Fonds social européen
LOV	Loi d'orientation pour la ville
PAIO	Permanence d'accueil, d'information et d'orientation
PAQUE	Préparation active à la qualification et à l'emploi
PLIE	Plans locaux d'insertion économique
POPS	Protocoles d'occupation du patrimoine social
RMI	Revenu minimum d'insertion

British

CATs	City Action Teams
ET	Employment Training
EZ	Enterprise Zones
ICP	Inner City Partnership
MSC	Manpower Services Commission
TA	Training Agency
TECs	Training and Enterprise Councils
TFE	Training for Enterprise Programme
UDC	Urban Development Corporations
URA	Urban Regeneration Agency
YT	Youth Training
YTS	Youth Training Scheme

List of discussion papers from the IILS/UNDP social exclusion project

DP 62 (1994). *Social exclusion and Africa south of the Sahara: A review of the literature*. Charles Gore.

DP 63 (1994). *Some paradoxes of social exclusion*. Marshall Wolfe.

DP 69 (1994). *Social exclusion and social solidarity: Three paradigms*. Hilary Silver.

DP 70 (1994). *Social exclusion in Latin America: An annotated bibliography*. Vilmar E. Faria.

DP 71 (1994). *Review of the French and Belgian literature on social exclusion: A Latin American perspective*. Isabel Yépez.

DP 72 (1994). *Overcoming exclusion: Livelihood and rights in economic and social development*. Gerry Rodgers.

DP 77 (forthcoming). *Social exclusion and South Asia*. Arjan de Haan and Pulin Nayak.

DP 78 (forthcoming). *Social exclusion in relation to basic needs in India: Some preliminary findings*. Paul Appasamy, S. Guhan, R. Hema, Manabi Mjaumdar and A. Vaidyanathan.

DP 79 (forthcoming). *Social exclusion in the Philippines: A review of literature*. Institute for Labor Studies, Philippines.

DP 80 (forthcoming). *Bibliographie de l'exclusion dans les pays arabes du Maghreb et du Machreq (Afrique du Nord et Moyen-Orient)*. Mongi Bédoui.

DP 81 (forthcoming). *Review of literature on the social impacts of economic renovation in Vietnam*. Do Duc Dinh.

DP 82 (forthcoming). *Effectiveness of policies aimed at the social and economic integration of different ethnic groups in Southeast Asia, with special reference to Malaysia: Review of the literature and empirical material*. Lim Teck Ghee.

DP 83 (forthcoming). *Policies to combat social exclusion: A French-British comparison*. Hilary Silver and Frank Wilkinson.